THE TRAIN RIDE

A Story of Friendship in the Land of Division II Football

THE TRAIN RIDE

A Story of Friendship in the Land of Division II Football

JIM HALL

BOOKLOGIX®
1264 Old Alpharetta Rd.
Alpharetta, GA 30005

All rights reserved. No part of this book may be reproduced or transmitted in any form or by any means, electronic or mechanical, including photocopying, recording, or any information storage and retrieval system, without permission in writing from the publisher. For more information address Permissions Department, 1264 Old Alpharetta Rd., Alpharetta, GA 30005.

Copyright © 2011 by Jim Hall

BookLogix softcover edition September 2011

ISBN: 978-1-61005-119-4

(For information about special discounts for bulk purchases, please contact BookLogix Sales at sales@booklogix.com.)

10 9 8 7 6 5 4   1 0 21 13

Printed in the United States of America

∞This paper meets the requirements of ANSI/NISO Z39.48-1992 (Permanence of Paper)

The Author would like to thank the following people for their generosity aiding in the publishing of this book. Without the help of these people, this effort would not have been possible.

Thanks to my lovely bride of twenty-seven years and the true love of my life, Becky Jackson Hall and my grown kids, Jimmy Jr., Jessie and Jenna Kate, the greatest legacy a man could hope for.

I'd like to thank my English Composition teacher, Mrs. Linda Spriggs, the nicest teacher to ever flunk me. She told me once I might write a book someday. May you rest in peace.

Ralph North, who told me many times "Hall, who ever told you the world was fair?" and he was right. "Conduct cuts" all around for possibly believing it might have ever been true.

Cary Chandler, my friend who encouraged me to continue writing when I might have stopped. You are "proof" that a friendship can work, regardless of geography and circumstance. War Eagle!

*Scott McKown. A flipped 1970 442 led to a great friendship. May you always be "The Man." It's rare that two dudes with the same sense of humor get to ride around in a truck for fifteen years.

Ronnie, my brother-in-law, a true hero in every sense of the word. "Bravery" has your picture beside it in the dictionary, a brilliant philosopher, poet, and one hell of a helicopter pilot. It's an honor to know a true patriot.

My brother George, who brings real meaning to the term "going postal," at least while driving. No man is an island, but my brother is…The Isle of George. Being your brother is a most unique experience.

Lithia Springs Comprehensive High School class of 1978

Troy University…By the way, we are even on every level.

My Dad. Great fathers are so rare, and you are just that. I'm proud to be called your son. Your life is proof that God can take a young man forced into manhood at thirteen from the backwoods of Hanging Dog North Carolina and take him places he might have only dreamed of. Of all the accolades you have garnered in your life and career, being a terrific father has been your greatest achievement. In the same way a son can only believe he is truly a man is when his father tells him it is so, I hope that when a son tells his father what a great example of truth, fairness, kindness and love he was, his father believes it too.

To the reader of this book: You'll find a lot of words here which are traditionally Southern in nature, words like "gotta" and "shoulda" and they are here on purpose. If that *kinda* thing offends your sense of literary justice, please accept my apology...and read it anyway.

Chapter · I

NOTICE
Persons attempting to find a motive in this narrative will be prosecuted:
Persons attempting to find a moral in it will be banished:
Persons attempting to find a plot in it will be shot.

BY ORDER OF THE AUTHOR Per G.G., Chief of Ordinance

(Inside cover of The Adventures of Huckleberry Finn)

IT WAS 1984, and I was graduating into a world with no home computers, no DVD, BluRay, cell phones, surround sound, or numerous other electronic offerings, gadgets. Devices my generation mistakes for magic and this generation is fully convinced it can't live without. Jimmy Carter had been president and Ronald Reagan was still considered a former actor who went into politics. I had met who was to be my future wife, and I was stuck in Troy, Alabama for what would be the last days of my college career. I was looking forward to leaving college behind and all the things that went with it. My college football days were behind me by then, and I had joined a fraternity mostly to spite my coach, a former Marine drill instructor and psychology major.

That's the place where I met the man who would become my life-long best friend, Brian.

Brian was the closest person that I have met and could describe as being totally fearless. He was a few years behind me age wise, and I know now that I may not have been the best influence on him. We had pledged the same fraternity, Pi Kappa Phi, in the spring quarter of '82 with fall quarter 1983 being the last year of my collegiate sports endeavors. I was relieved when my football career ended and I had survived the ordeal basically intact.

I had invited hell on myself my final season as my football coach hated fraternities and all they stood for. To top it off, the football team I played on and the fraternity I had pledged constantly fought each other at every opportunity. Be it at the local bars, parties, you name it, they (we?) fought. Understand that I was not trying to extend any sort of imaginary olive branch between the "Hatfield's and McCoy's." I was just trying to piss off my coach.

It worked.

My football coach was the kind of gentleman who thought water breaks were counterproductive and sweating was a lack of discipline. This guy was a walking Pat Conroy novel. Think of Mr. Conroy's coach in *My Losing Season* and a cross between his father in *The Prince of Tides* and *The Great Santini* with the looks of Lou Holtz and the split personality of Charles Manson and a Game show host. I tell ya that dude could insult your mother (for not pinching your head off at birth—*his words*), your girlfriend (for making your legs weak—*again, his words*) and never swear once, all the while invoking the Holy Spirit to please give him "the strength of character" not to kill you dead on the spot. When I think of the key influences in my life, he is at the top of the list. In that list, I include Jesus (Yep, the Son of God Jesus himself), my dad, and Charlie Bradshaw. Oh, and Mark Twain falls in fourth. Just barely, but fourth.

I won't delve into Jesus or Religion in any detail. I have called on Him in numerous situations and survived with what I am sure was His help or mercy, even when I am sure I didn't deserve it. If you have any common sense then I am certain as you continue to read this story you'll either agree about God's saving grace or question His patience. God has proven to me that He is real on many occasions, because I made promises to Him in desperation a time or two and came out the other end unscathed. I talk to his son every day in my prayers and He reminds me I am "grafted in." I'm cool with Him and He with me. Work yours out with fear and trembling, the Bible says…I have.

And that's all I have to say about that.

My dad, who is my personal hero, came from humble beginnings in Murphy, North Carolina. He was born in the same home as his five brothers and sisters, which was built for my grandmother by my grandfather. My grandfather bought the land and milled the trees harvested from the land to build the home my dad and his siblings grew up in. My dad was the oldest and the man of the house, as his father passed when he was thirteen years old. He became the man of the house then; can you imagine the press that would garner today? To my dad, it was just the circumstances then, by golly, and he never questioned his circumstances. He just did what was required of him to aid in the survival of his family. He did all his chores in the morning, ran to school eleven miles both ways every day, and never complained…ever. He loved his family, honored his parents—especially his mother, until she passed at ninety-nine years old. He was a high school football hero and also marched in the band (at halftime with his football uniform on) just because someone pointed out to him that he shouldn't. After graduation, he joined the Marine Corps where he met my mother. He was a government employee for forty-five years, an MIT graduate and the kindest, smartest man I have ever known. Kind and very smart, but able to keep things brilliantly simple. He owns the funniest and sharpest wit of any human being I have ever known. He told me once that "a good attitude is worth faking." I have said it so much that I have been credited for it. I know so many grown men raised by crappy fathers and the profound sadness that goes with that most unfortunate legacy. I am truly blessed to say I am not one of those guys. My dad was the mold and model for a great father, and I am a better man because of his influence.

Oh, and Mark Twain, just for writing *The Adventures of Huckleberry Finn.* The first book I ever read as a very young boy and the most influential book in life and literature for me. I have read it every two years for the past forty-four and I still love it. The political ramification of its writing in the time it was written was astronomical. As a boy, I loved the adventure and the loyalty that Huck had towards Jim. It taught me about friendship, loyalty, and adventure and should be required reading for every young man in the USA, both white and black. He wrote a bunch of other great books too, but Huckleberry Finn is mine.

Twain is also credited with saying that "Golf was a nice nature walk shot all to Hell"…and I agree. Mr. Twain and I are kindred. If I ever want to be that pissed off again, I'll take up tiddley winks or anything cat related. Golf is definitely not for me.

I tell you my influences so you'll have a better understanding of this writer. I loved sports of all kinds, but I did not want to be considered an athlete as the primary thing that defined me as a human being. I was well read when most of my peers were not (not to say I was a lick better than anyone), and that was a good thing for me. It happened when my father came home one day from a long day at work to find us (my brother, sister and me) in front of a television. TV in the 60s consisted of three network channels and that's it. No cable, no satellite channels. Other than "Telstar," the United States' answer to Sputnik, satellites of any sort was limited to the two contained in this sentence. Back then, Telstar and Sputnik were just fancy flying "beepers," mostly proof that man could put something into orbit. It amounted to an expensive pissing match played between the Russians and the USA.

My dad was so upset with us over our television watching habits that he tossed the TV in the round file (the trash can) and we read books for years until we pressured him into buying a TV again in the 70s. Books took me on adventures no television program ever had, and to places I might never have known about save for someone writing about it. I began to play football at an intramural level in 1967, and continued to play with great success through high school, where I was awarded with a full scholarship for my efforts. I would have been much happier to get a scholarship for my intellect rather than my ability to play a violent game, but I played it with what at least one college thought was great prejudice and accuracy. I took my football scholarship with great pride as brain scholarships were few and far between then and reserved for Bill Gates and Steve Jobs types, complete unknowns in my day. Microsoft, back then, might have been a word used for erectile dysfunction and Apple was something you ought to eat once a day if you wanted to avoid doctors.

Football, for me, had served two purposes: it got me away from my hometown, and I could get a college education playing a kid's game. Both sounded very appealing to me.

The athletic scholarship system had changed in the late 70s just before I had signed up for the deal. Before, you could not lose your scholarship in collegiate sports if you were injured and could no longer play. A "career ending injury" was given a much broader definition in 1976; meaning if you couldn't rehab, you kept your scholarship until graduation. That's completely different from "not fully participating in rehabilitation," so you lost your full ride and a shot at a college education. In other words, if you had your knee torn off and it was sewed back on AND you could walk, then you should be able to play football, right? I tell you this because athletic scholarships were drastically altered to benefit the institution rather than the athlete, i.e. the scholarship was "performance" based. Performance was defined as anything the coaches dang well wanted you to do. Whatever hoops that were decided you needed to jump or dive through (flaming or not) were subject to a yearly review, with the threat of dismissal if so needed, and that included properly executed ass kissing. No more four-year scholarships in the NCAA. Coach Bradshaw used this change to wreak mental hell on each athlete once a year when scholarship renewal time rolled around. There was no raging against his machine in any form or fashion. He had the upper hand and he knew it. He would threaten us every year, every semester, in every aspect of "the drill," as he called it, which was the life of a football player. No one but a choice few very select ass kissers were safe, and I was not one of the few. I had to make it on ability and grades alone, as I knew I was not on his list of folks to invite over for Sunday dinner.

One of Coach Bradshaw's most hated institutions was the fraternity system he called with great disgust, "know it all, rent-a-friend, drunken excuses for humanity." I was going to violate his most hated rule, I was going to step away from my football "brothers" and enter the slippery slope to hell that was fraternity. The way I saw it, I was leaving a bigger hell behind for a smaller one if his reviews of the fraternal system were accurate. Any other hell-on-earth would be a walk in the park next to the specific brand of hell Coach Bradshaw dished out in generous proportions. I had been a defensive lineman, a starter for my duration in "the drill" and I had taken on dudes that outweighed me by one hundred pounds and had embarrassed them in front of their home crowds when the time came. The frat-rat crowd, by my estimation, would be easy for me since I knew what they might consider to be hell, I called Tuesday.

I only pledged the fraternity at the time when my coach could no longer do anything about my scholarship. The remaining two quarters after the fall season of your senior year had expired and you finished playing ball, you were free. Free from the tyranny that was being a pack mule in collegiate sports. In other words, your eligibility was used up and there was no next year. It was either pro sports or the world, and I chose the World. Truth be known, I had pledged my junior year beginning in spring quarter and had kept it a secret from my teammates and especially Coach Bradshaw. That way, when I had my review after spring training, the frat rat stuff would not be an issue. When fall quarter rolled around, I was a fully brotherized (it's a word…) know it all, rent-a-friend, drunken excuse for humanity and "damn glad to meet ya." By then, I did not give two shits if Bradshaw knew. I caught the major brunt of his displeasure my senior year, fall quarter, while I was playing my last year of college football after the word got out. More on that subject later.

I guess I have Coach Bradshaw to thank for meeting Brian. Without his special brand of tyranny, I would not have extrapolated that joining a frat would be my own way to "stick it to the man," with Bradshaw being "the Man." That is the most positive thing I can say concerning our relationship during those days. We quite simply stood in each other's way of achieving our individual goals. In other words, we hated each other.

I feel that you have enough background on me, so I must tell you a little about Brian. Brian Horst was born in Mobile, Alabama, the third of four children born to Kent and Velma Horst. Brian looked like a mix of the "Shooter McGavin" actor in Happy Gilmore and the fellow with the moving hump in Young Frankenstein, mostly the wandering eye part. He had a terrific sense of humor and was a smart, quick-witted and loyal friend. To say he was a nut was an understatement, like saying "Mr. Peanut" was a walking, talking legume with a top hat and a cane. The phrase "Hey man, watch this!" usually the final words a redneck might utter, was coined by him, I am sure, as he was as fearless as any man I had ever called friend. His parents were the most patient people I have ever had the pleasure to meet and they treated me like a son from the first time we breathed the same air in the same room. They are both true Southern treasures with Mr. Horst hailing from up North and Mrs. Horst being a genuine Southern Belle born in Mississippi. Mr. Horst might not have been born here, but he got here as quick as he could, and that's cool by me.

In my final days at Troy, while waiting for my graduation ceremony to take place, Brian and I were staying at our fraternity house on North Three Notch Street, the main artery running through the city of Troy, Alabama. The fraternity house was a three story mansion with large porches facing the aforementioned street, maybe a half mile from the square. Brian and I were the last to leave the house that spring as I was the only man in our fraternity that was graduating that year. I had squeezed four years of college into five and was just waiting for the cap and gown ceremony to make it official. Brian had stayed behind because he had decided to transfer to the University of South Alabama the following year, and as he put it, Troy would not be the same for him without my guidance. I think maybe his grades and attendance, or lack thereof, might have played a minor role in this scenario too. He also stayed behind because I asked him to and his summer job was not going to start for another two weeks. It would give us time to reflect on our two years of friendship and, little did I know that, it would also lead to what we always referred to as "The Train Ride." The Military used "FUBAR;" Brian and I used "THE TRAIN RIDE."

It was approximately one week before actual graduation ceremonies, classes were over and we had time to just relax and talk, stay up all night, drink and shoot the breeze. One of our frat brothers, Willy, was headed home to Florida for the summer and on his way out, gave Brian and me two one-gallon sized bottles of Crown Royal. I had never seen industrial sized Crown in my life up till then or since, and he insisted it was a graduation present for me. He had won them in a bodybuilding contest I guessed was sponsored by Crown Royal. The bottles were so big the blue embroidered bags that traditionally accompanied each bottle of Crown could double as a toboggan in the wintertime, even for a big headed gent like me. No one asked, but I must confess. A big bottle of liquor seemed like a great prize regardless of the contest you may have won. Brian and I saw our week off as an opportunity to make sure that the Crown Royal was put to good use and were sure we were just the right guys to meet the challenge. I figured it was the very last irresponsible act I could perform without the world's judgment landing fully upon the person I was going to be post-graduation. I was still a college student and I was damn well going to take advantage of what little time I had left holding that particular title. Anything short of speaking poorly about Bear Bryant, George Wallace, or telling a poorly placed Alabama joke to the wrong politician meant I was indeed getting out of College with a real diploma. A printer somewhere had already minted a paper, supposedly made of sheepskin, with my name emblazoned upon it to show the world I had done "it." I was no longer going to be considered a "them"…I was going to be an "us." Of course, that would come after I had walked and put my graduation gown and Mortar Board to its one and only good use.

It was a Saturday and we were up at the crack of noon drinking our breakfast of Crown and orange juice and planning our daily activities. Brian and I always had an agreement and it was this: we never drank alone. If he made one drink, he made two, and I did the same. That particular day it was sunny, about 89 degrees and humid, and I am talking LA humid (that's Lower Alabama to you non-southern types). 89 degrees and 90 percent humidity is like 120 degrees anywhere else in the world but normal for those parts. We had been having a number of on-going conversations during our friendship about politics and sports, and we were trying our best to get some of them wrapped up as we might not be seeing each other for a long while after my graduation was concluded.

Like any small college town, Troy had a set of double train tracks that ran through it from North to South. On that particular day we were keenly observant of all things, one of which was a partial solar eclipse and we marveled at the way the event made everything look. It was as if you could almost see the light waves in the air. The Crown Royal might have had an influence on our vision, but I stick to the former rather than the latter. About that time we were in the process of making one last breakfast beverage, meaning the ice was almost gone. We were sitting on the uppermost part of the old mansion we occupied as a frat. From our vantage point, we could see for miles. We were told that it was used for look-out purposes in Civil War times, approaching carpetbaggers and rapscallions could be seen coming for miles and miles.

Those two groups are now known as the Republican and Democratic parties. I am convinced of that fact after thirty years of looking down into the unflushed toilet that is called national politics. Every four to eight years they swap off who is holding the little silver handle and blame each other for either not flushing or flushing. So, if you are easily offended, the political reference is a way of easing you into what is to come …and that right soon.

The story is just getting started…

Chapter · II

"It's twelve o'clock somewhere"
– Rodney Dangerfield

TOWARDS the end of our final breakfast drink of the day, preparing for the lunch hour (when we would switch from Crown and Orange juice to Crown and RC Cola), a train made its way slowly into town. The Huckleberry Finn in me had always wanted to ride a train the non-legal way and just jump in a box car or on a flat car and ride. I had figured we had almost eight full days of nothing to do, so I was going to suggest a train ride to Brian. Before the thought could leave my brain and make its way through a Crown Royal haze to my vocal cords, Brian said, "Jim, have you ever just wanted to jump a train and ride it to the other side of town just to say that you did?" I just laughed to myself and told Brian, "sure." We agreed that we would make a run for it the next time a train came by. We missed out the first nine times, running full steam from the front porch of our frat house to the loading dock across the street behind the old Piggly Wiggly building. The full run was maybe 1/4 mile from the front porch of the frat house to the ramp leading onto the train cars. It was a serious pull and we never made it on time in any of the tries we attempted. The trains were required to slow down coming into town, baiting the two of us, and then speeding up like the train knew our intentions all along. The truth was, after the proper clearances were given by whatever train gods the conductor answered to, the train sped up. Way up. That fact alone meant we had zero success in getting that train ride we had challenged ourselves to get. We were tired from a full day's running and needed to get dinner. It was our usual meal, steak and potatoes.

We were the two poorest dudes in the whole town of Troy, but we ate like kings.

How did we eat so well, you ask? Well, I'm going to tell you... it's somewhat of a process so hang in there, its coming. When you are poor, I learned, there are two things you must do: (a) befriend everyone that has some sort of authority over beer and food, regardless of how smarmy the store might be (this was Alabama, so bait and tackle were always sold right beside sandwiches) and (b) have a partner in crime, someone to distract the person you'd taken months to befriend. The downside of befriending one of these folks is that you'd get invited to weddings/funerals/family gatherings of people you really didn't want to know. You could always say that you had to go home with your crime buddy/frat brother/etc. to escape the event. I tell you this additional information so you'll understand the process by which two guys kept fed and watered on the cheap.

There was a local convenience store called the Zippy Mart (we affectionately called it the Rippy Mart) down the street from the frat house. There was this guy, Dan, who worked the cash register and was assistant to the assistant night manager. The title really meant he got the shittiest shift on the schedule with no chance of advancement. He was a nice enough dude, somewhat peculiar, and we befriended him as a way to get discounted beer, chips, and whatever sustenance two college boys might need to survive. Dan was a dead ringer for Crispin Glover (Michael J. Fox's dad in *Back to the Future*) with massively thick glasses. He'd usually give us stuff that was damaged, as store policy was to toss out any damaged goods as long as said manager reported it damaged. We initially lived on a steady diet of chips, store made sandwiches and dented beer for our break-in period with Dan. It was amazing how clumsy we could get in that store and the primo stuff you could dent or crush completely by accident. Oh, and I should mention that Dan was as blind as a bat. There is legally blind and, I assume, illegally blind and Dan had to be illegally blind. He wore the biggest Coke Bottle glasses I have ever seen in my life, like I stated earlier. He was not the sharpest knife in the drawer and also not the handsomest either, but we had grown to like Dan. "Dan the Man" we called him and he liked it. He always talked about wanting to settle down, find the right woman, get a single wide on the family farm. Brian and I actually helped him find his wife, a true story told later, and the true love of Dan the Man's life.

One of the ways we made extra money at school (for our social activities) was Brian and I purchased all the food for the fraternity as we always had dinner as a unit at six o'clock. Brian and I cooked the food, served it and cleaned up the fracas afterwards. The job was good for an extra 100 bones each a week for social expenses, and two poor dudes could do some serious entertaining on $100.00 a week in those days. The job was Monday thru Thursday only and the remaining three days you fended for yourself. Buying the food was an integral part of our duties and we strategically befriended the Meat Department manager at the new Piggly Wiggly down the street from our frat house. The Pig had moved from its original location, across the street from the frat house, to a more high-brow location. We specifically targeted the meat manager seeing that meat was the most important part of any meal a dude might attempt to eat. The person with the meat department management job was a pudgy unattractive woman named Suzy. She was a sweet person and she fell in love with Brian almost immediately. Brian had a way of making people like him, primarily by giving them a code name (see Dan the Man) giving them a sense of inclusion. Brian always flirted with Suzy and she really liked it. He'd call her "Suzy the Floozy" and she'd blush every time he called her by that name. If you remember the short portly lady (my daughter said women aren't portly but Suzy was) in the movie *Poltergeist*, she was a wide as she was tall. Maybe. Suzy the Floozy may have topped out at 4'4" tall on a good day at full moon and high tide. I guess it's a good thing her name wasn't Delores, seeing as that'd be a hard name to rhyme, just ask Jerry Seinfeld. Suzy always gave us great deals on our meats for the frat and always made sure Brian and I had a fresh cut pair of rib-eye steaks every time we walked in the store, gratis, just to keep us coming back. We shoplifted the potatoes…I told you we were broke…and she was not head of that particular department anyway.

I am sure that in the last thirty years, you reader(s) have seen *Animal House*. If you recall the scene where Tom Hulce's character gets stopped by the check out girl, the daughter of the Mayor that was going to break the legs of Dean Wormer…

"Looks like you put on a little weight sweetie"-Checkout girl

"Oh, I am pledging a fraternity…."-Frat Dude

"Don't worry, I won't tell"

That's the lead in to this particular part of the story. I must tell it, so here it is for all to see. Brian and I were the shoplifting kings of Troy, Alabama for the last two quarters I was in school. Necessity is the Mother of invention, and, hunger is the Mother of shoplifting. I'm not particularly proud of it now but there it is in black and white. Brian and I had a contest going after we finally crossed over into being criminals and that was who could shoplift the most exotic item from a grocery store. On my life, Brian won as he successfully shoplifted a twenty pound turkey. Not in pieces, the whole thing. It was, I am sure, in the Shoplifting Hall of Fame. Brian was a fairly slim guy, but he could stick his belly out and suck in so he'd either look like he was a lard ass from the waist up or a scarecrow. His particular "genius" was the way in which he pulled off this particular feat. He walked into the grocery store (On the other side of town) with his belly stuck out so far that he looked like he'd swallowed a basketball or was an import from Cambodia. When he went to the turkey aisle, he sucked his belly all the way back in, shoved the turkey perfectly mid way at his beltline and he looked exactly the same going out as he did going in. Yes, a twenty pound turkey. I had managed a full rack of uncut rib eye steaks, the record up to that point, but a full-on Thanksgiving turkey was the winner. At one point we had gotten so good at it that we'd take stuff from say, The Piggly Wiggly, and then go and transfer it to the Winn Dixie. Yes, he'd lift it from the Wiggly and deposit it into the Winn Dixie. Then he'd go in acting like a buyer and take the transferred item to the register meaning he'd then get it for free. The fun part was getting the meat manager to explain how a Piggly Wiggly product somehow managed to land in the meat department of the Winn Dixie. I know it sounds odd but we were bored and it was something to do. At the time it was an adventure, something to laugh at and about, and it would sustain us throughout the years. Brian reminded me once, if you steal a Volkswagen, you get the same amount of time as a dude that steals a Rolls Royce. If the price you paid was the same, we were going to jail eating steak. No hamburgers for us.

One weekend when we knew everybody we associated with was going to the beach, we posted a flyer in numerous sorority dorms (at least the ones with the hot chicks) on campus offering a free steak dinner at the Pi Kapp house. We'd lift fifty steaks, plus the two free ones we'd get from Suzy the Floozy, and we'd have us a party. The male attendee list was usually short with just Brian, me and between 35 and 50 of the finest budget-minded girls on campus. These were complete meals with full courses, salad with all the artsy-fartsy stuff in it, great French bread (folded over they hid nicely) and baked potatoes. And there was wine. Yes, you could buy wine in the grocery stores in Alabama. These events amounted to the best free steak dinner a sorority girl ever tasted and garnered Brian and I an incredible amount of popularity amongst the sorority women. If you could buy it, you could also lift it, and I figured we were like modern day Robin Hoods feeding the poor. I had somewhat mastered the art of the sucked in belly technique also, but Brian was the master. He could come out of a store with four bottles of wine and at least four steaks and not miss a step. He said that the steaks he'd slide up the sides of the bottles in the front as to taper off the sides and give it "a more natural look." Brian was a true artist with a most unusual medium upon which to paint his felonious masterpiece.

So, how did Dan the Man and Suzy the Floozy meet? The Rippy Mart sat almost across the street from the New Piggly Wiggly. Dan, however, worked the late shift, 10:00 p.m. till 6:00 a.m. (prime picking times mind you), and Suzy worked the day shift. They might not have ever met if not for the pressure that Suzy was putting on Brian. She was laying it on heavy and Brian was getting nervous about whatever might come next (Father showing up with a double barrel shotgun explaining that in Alabama, a girl who gives you over twenty free steaks constitutes a "by-proxy" wedding engagement).

I had figured that Dan and Suzy might make a perfect match seeing as they were both "special" if you catch my drift. They did have a full set of teeth between them and Dan was illegally blind, so there was hope. Suzy the Floozy was just looking to procreate, or at least find someone to practice with, so it seemed like a match made in heaven to me. So here's what Brian and I did…we set them up on a blind date. Brian and I shoplifted some of the finest meats (not from the Piggly Wiggly, it might jinx the whole deal) Troy had to offer, red wine, salad, baked potatoes, the works and we offered to serve Dan and Suzy in the Formal Dining room of the Fraternity House. The formal dining table was actually the pool table with a piece of plywood we'd cut to fit the top and then covered with a nice tablecloth draped over it, and let me tell you Martha Stewart would have been proud…it looked spectacular. We had nice dishes at the frat house and wine glasses, silverware for when the parents showed up or we had a formal. The place was dark when they arrived, save for the fancy candles we'd lifted from one of the fancy girly shops up on the square, lit and centered on the fancy eating table Brian and I had decorated.

Brian and I suited up (we actually cleaned up very nice to be such unsavory types) and made the invites. We both lied about the looks of Suzy to Dan and vice-versa so not to scare them off with the truth. The meal went, we thought, swimmingly…although we did have to keep the conversation moving at times (remember-we were acting as waiters for them). The meal ended and Dan and Suzy went their separate ways, exchanging niceties but no perceived Chuck Woolery styled "love connection." It looked like all our hard work and shoplifted fine eats equaled our master plan failed. Or so we thought. The following week we made our usual Rippy/Wiggly visits to try to see if there was a "match" attempting to bring up Dan to Suzy and Suzy to Dan but no spark from either. We thought we had failed until two weeks later. We had made a 1:00 a.m. stop at the Rippy for "dented" items and when we went in, no Dan, no anybody! We waited for a few minutes and I shouted "DAN!!" Well, next thing you know, here comes Dan the Man with his pants practically around his ankles stumbling from the back of the store. When he sees us, he turns back to where he had emerged seconds earlier and said, "It's only Jim and Brian." And who should emerge? None other than Suzy the Floozy herself sashaying like she'd discovered the whereabouts if the Holy Grail! Brian looked at her and said, "You brazen hussy!" the words hanging in the air like a fart at a wedding and us all silent as church mice. Dan looked in Brian's general direction (he was illegally blind, remember?) with a stern voice and told him, "You are speaking to the woman I love!"

The two of them had been inseparable since the blind date. Suzy was worried that Brian would be upset that she had "stepped out" on him, and potentially of losing our weekly meat purchases. Victory was ours. We had caught Dan and Suzy doing the dance of the two-backed beast IN THE RIPPY MART! Dan was so worried that we would tell and he'd lose his job. We parlayed that fear into endless primo dented stuff purchased for a mere pittance, plus our silence. From that day forward Brian and I were in high cotton, Rippy Mart wise, and everything went smoothly for us. At least as far as high carbohydrate based foods were concerned. Our silence was had for dented beer and a premium sandwich with the difference being we dented Budweiser instead of PBR now. Dan the Man was ours and he knew it. Funny thing was, though, if we told (and we had no idea who to tell) of Dan the Man's questionable sexual antics to his superiors we'd have been screwing ourselves out of the sweetest deal we had going.

Needless to say, we were both in attendance at their wedding. Dan had asked us to be his two groomsmen and we complied. It was a huge mistake, looking back on it, as the place was full of some of the homeliest gravity challenged women I have ever seen before or since. A reception filled with liquored up fat women with no sort of moral boundaries, nor dental plan, is not a place for two relatively good looking dudes from "the city" to be hanging out. I am not saying we were the handsomest dudes you'd ever meet, but on that day, we were Brad Pitt and George Clooney and damned prime breed stock. It made for a interesting reception (if you could call it that) for the two of us, getting eyeballed by the all women folk and some of the men folk too, for that matter. I observed that a full set of teeth required at least three women, or four to five dudes. Dental hygiene was not a priority with Dan and Suzy's kinfolk.

The "reception" was a catered affair, with a "pig in the ground" (if you don't know what that means, it'll be revealed later), another as-of-yet unidentified four legged critter on a spit, a giant grill with a hundred or so chickens "severed in twain," all being attended to by a one legged fellow on crutches. He carried a five gallon paint bucket and a mop, keeping all the grilled meats wet with whatever potion he concocted, the smell radiating out over the festivities like your birthday cake baking at your grandma's house.

There was a demolition derby, pitting the two families against each other in beat up station wagons on what looked like a well used dirt race track in the middle of the giant field where this party was being held. There were also guns of every sort present on the hips and over the shoulders of just about everyone from both families. Dan the Man said it was to be a substitute for fireworks, seeing his cousin Jessie was in jail again, and he generally supplied the sky bound exploding entertainment but couldn't be there because of his seventh DUI arrest.

"He'll beat this-un; he's been watching lawyer movies in jail…" Dan said confidently.

Then there was the beer. Keg beer of every sort, bottled beer in giant tubs I assumed must have been used for apple bobbing if kids still did that sort of thing around there. My point is, there were maybe a hundred or so fifty gallon tubs so full of cheap long neck beer there was barely enough room for ice to keep it cold. I asked Dan what they did with all the empties and he matter-of-fact said "we set em up and shoot em later." I assumed that was yet another family style competition planned for the red-neck wedding party Brian and I were attending that afternoon. The only thing missing was Hank, Jr., taking notes for a future country song, based on the current activities and the predictable outcome.

Brian and I grabbed us some chow, served in generous portions by the fellow on crutches in "to go" boxes, amounting to aluminum foil lined shoe boxes. We debated on whether or not to hang around as conscientious objectors, but knew for sure we'd either wind up in the demolition derby…or shot, hung over, maybe married, if we didn't leave right then, sober as judges. We grabbed ourselves a giant tub of beer on our way out, setting it gently in the trunk of the Swinger, it fitting perfectly in the spare tire indention. That crowd would not miss the tub in an hour or so, us noting the number "13" painted on the side. We never figured that one out but guessed it was important to someone. Maybe Dan and Suzy knew a "beer tub guy" and we had just fouled up his system of keeping up with his inventory.

Before we left, we told Dan and Suzy goodbye, wishing them a long and happy life together. Dan and Suzy told us they'd name their kids after us when "kid making time came" as Dan put it. I only hoped that they did not have daughters. Jim and Brian were great Anglo-Saxon male names, but not very good girl names.

We ate some great bar-b-que on our way home, compliments of Dan and Suzy, and we had ourselves to thank for their union, our way of justifying the massive tub of beer we'd lifted from their shindig. We drank the ice cold beer as we drove and threw the empties at signs on the way back. The loser would have to get out and open the trunk to retrieve a new supply of discount wedding beer we enjoyed on our ride back from who-knows-where to Troy and our antebellum frat house digs.

We made the our newest pledges carry the half-full quarter ton tub of beer up to our room when we made it back; it was after all, our duty as brothers…and they were indeed "our" pledges.

Chapter · III

"No story is a straight line. The geometry of a human life is too imperfect and complex, too distorted by the laughter of time and the bewildering intricacies of fate to admit the straight line into its system of laws."
– Pat Conroy (Beach Music)

I FEEL like I need to make one thing perfectly clear here. I am telling this story like a ride on a Greyhound Bus. I rode one once because I wanted to say I had done it. Atlanta to Mobile, Alabama is practically a straight line down I-85 South to Montgomery, I-65 South to Mobile. A ride on a Greyhound Bus is like taking a straight line and driving east and west and back again to maximize the trip for Greyhound. If you have seen the two snakes climbing the probe (I'm not sure exactly what they are climbing), the symbol used for doctors, would be the best visual I can give. The probe is straight there and the snakes represent the route Greyhound takes to get there. I used snakes and Greyhound in the same sentence but I am sure Greyhound is a fine company with no snakes on the payroll other than a lawyer or two. I read *War and Peace* on my bus trip, twice, and my clothes had gone out of style by the time my trip was complete. Take a bus trip and see what I mean. It takes forever.

That was a complicated way to tell you that the Train Ride story is the probe and the other stories about Brian and myself is like that pair of snakes crisscrossing it. I could tell you the straight line story of the Train Ride but I would omit the really funny stuff we had done (or survived) for the two years we matriculated (fancy word for going to college) in the same place. I guess I am giving more words than necessary to explain what Pat Conroy said in the quote at the top of this page. I am totally discounting "Occam's Razor" theory which clearly states that the simplest explanation is the best one. So just keep reading and let it smooth itself out.

The next day was Sunday (chronologically speaking we are on the second day), and we were both weary from running for the train numerous times with failure being our only reward. We were back up on the rapscallion deck, outside of our bedroom and had transitioned to Dixie Beer from Crown Royal to mellow out the hard earned buzz we had slowly built that day. Now it's important to know a few things about Dixie Beer before I continue. Back in the day, Dixie Beer was unpasteurized beer that had a skull and cross bones warning on the back instructing the drinker not to drink, under any circumstances, said Dixie Beer if its contents ever exceeded 72 degrees Fahrenheit or 22 degrees Celsius…period. It stated its contents became poisonous if it rose above that temperature and was then cooled back down, so drink it at your own risk. It was only served in Gooseneck bottles (kinda like the purdy fluorescent light attracting the mosquito to his doom) so there was an element of class and danger to the beer. Just read the label, it was beer below 72 degrees and industrial paint stripper above 72 degrees, making Brian and I the thrill seekers of our day. It was just the way the collegiate mind worked, or maybe it was just the way our collegiate minds were working at the time and under Dixie's influence. Maybe collegiate and mind should not even be mentioned in the previously described process at all but I guess if you are reading this, I survived it.

As a side note and totally off the subject, drinking massive amounts of Crown Royal had led us to a few conclusions. We had agreed that it was ordained that Crown Royal should be mixed with Royal Crown Cola. R.C. Cola was the premier dented can of cola mixer for us that week, acquired after 10:00 p.m. (the beginning of Dan the Man's shift) for silence only and the official cola of the Zippy Mart, for us at least. I am certain that the inventors of Crown Royal never envisioned their fine fancy liquor to ever be mixed with anything other than ice or water, both from some virgin iceberg. I am also very sure that the original purveyors of such a fine mixture never intended it to be distributed in Gallon sizes. The mixing it with R.C. Cola was our brilliant idea. Lastly, I feel strongly that I cannot in good measure mention Royal Crown Cola repeatedly (also known as RC) without mentioning Moon Pies. It is necessary and I have covered that now. Crown Royal and Royal Crown. Royal Crown and Moon Pies. I am sure that Moon Pies and Crown Royal have never been mentioned in the same sentence and the aforementioned connection has never been made in history before now. You are all welcome and "thank you" is not necessary, kinda like thanking the dude who invented the Reuben sandwich. You know, you don't care for any of the ingredients individually, but collectively they are purdy dang good.

Let's move on.

There was a liquor store located up the street from our frat house, and we'd swap steak for two cases of Cold Dixie Beers with the owner. I should point out that Dixie Beer was bottled in New Orleans, Louisiana, a state I'd soon avoid at all costs. Brian and I had wondered if the beer we had been enjoying on the cheap had been delivered in trucks with any type of refrigeration system. New Orleans, mind you, was a good five to six hours from Troy, Alabama if a guy was in "haul ass" mode so Brian and I felt it was a legitimate concern. Considering the warnings of certain death addressed on the back label of each goose necked bottle originating in "coon ass" country, our concerns were, in my opinion, well grounded. Those thoughts had been arrived at along with other pending world issues after two cases or more of said Dixie Beer had been consumed. It really seemed important to us at the time.

Important enough for us to try to catch the Dixie delivery truck in action at the Liquor store for confirmation. We never settled that controversy as we never witnessed a truck with "DIXIE BEER" painted on the side pull up to the door for daytime delivery. Maybe it was delivered under the cover of night, when it was cooler, with the doors up utilizing the "Alabama air conditioning" method…high speed and the cool of the night. We were usually at the Rippy Mart then anyway so we just accepted it and lived our lives.

I guess the fact that I'm writing this is proof of that my petition concerning its relative safety is settled and that the issue wasn't so important back then that it halted our consumption. At $2.99 a case, or our meat currency (two rib-eye steaks for two cases of ice cold Dixie's), we'd take our chances and keep the questions limited. The guy that owned the liquor store was having a clearance sale as college was ending for the year and summer meant a slowdown in his sales. Summertime was his off season and he was dumping his excess inventory. Especially the stuff with fluorescent orange death warnings and skull and cross bones printed clearly on the backs of the bottles. Brian and I had gotten to know him relatively well over time. If you recall our theory of befriending anyone that was in control of alcohol or eats then you know we were "pals" with the liquor store guy. Thank God being a vegetarian was akin to communism back then. He (the liquor store dude) was a meat eater and we had steak and when he had steak, we had beer, even if it might be "kill you dead" beer.

As a sidebar, I have always felt that if God had not wanted us to eat cows he would not have made them taste like steak. I am the staunchest supporter of vegetarians and all they stand for as a group. My youngest daughter tried being a vegetarian once, trying to defend the four-footed steak, milk, and leather suppliers, and I have never been happier in my life as this meant more meat for me at dinner time. She fell off the wagon, as it were, and rejoined the family of carnivores that is her rightful heritage. Cows are the biggest producers of Methane gas and I feel strongly that I am doing my part to save the environment by consuming them every chance I get. Sidebar over and back to the story.

We had made two runs at trains with no luck that morning. Our plan was this, jump the train, ride it to the other side of town, jump off and hitch-hike back. It was a "bucket list" item for both of us if you will and one we'd check off somehow. Those days before graduation Brian and I had been running a de-facto volunteer fire department between us. We were drinking a lot of liquid and we could have put out a house fire single handedly if one arose. Fortunately for us, we had indoor plumbing and no fires to test our mettle, as far as fire fighting was concerned. Let me put this as straight as I can; we could piss over a barn back then. We could just about hit the sidewalk from the upper deck of our frat house and it was fifty feet from our front door. At one point in our busy day we found ourselves at opposite ends of the frat house. A very slow moving train found its way into Troy across the street via the only artery available to a train. Brian and I agreed that regardless of where we were we'd meet full stride, dropping whatever we happened to be doing at the time, to make the train ride a reality. I was in the kitchen in the back of the house (cooking us steaks of course) and I heard the train squeak to a halt. I turned off the stove and ran full speed for the front door. When I hit the door, Brian was right ahead of me trying to fasten his blue jeans from his shortened trip to the crapper. We ran the full 1/4 mile to the train then behind the old Piggly Wiggly onto the loading dock and practically stepped on the flat car. We had made it by golly! We'd ride across town, jump off, hitch-hike back, item checked off and we were good.

It was a slow ride through town and it took about thirty-five minutes to get to the other side of town, south, headed towards Dothan. We discussed the ins and outs of being a hobo and I was singing "The Big Rock Candy Mountain" by Harry McLintock.

The Big Rock Candy Mountain

One evening as the sun went down and the jungle fire was burning
Down the track came a hobo hiking and he said boys I'm not turning
I'm headin for a land that's far away beside the crystal fountains
So come with me we'll go and see the Big Rock Candy Mountains
In the Big Rock Candy Mountains there's a land that's fair and bright
Where the handouts grow on bushes and you sleep out every night
Where the boxcars are all empty and the sun shines every day
On the birds and the bees and the cigarette trees
Where the lemonade springs where the bluebird sings
In the Big Rock Candy Mountains
In the Big Rock Candy Mountains all the cops have wooden legs
And the bulldogs all have rubber teeth and the hens lay soft boiled eggs
The farmer's trees are full of fruit and the barns are full of hay
Oh, I'm bound to go where there ain't no snow
Where the rain don't fall and the wind don't blow
In the Big Rock Candy Mountains
In the Big Rock Candy Mountains you never change your socks
And the little streams of alcohol come a-trickling down the rocks
The brakemen have to tip their hats and the railroad bulls are blind
There's a lake of stew and of whiskey too

You can paddle all around 'em in a big canoe
In the Big Rock Candy Mountains
In the Big Rock Candy Mountains the jails are made of tin
And you can walk right out again as soon as you are in
There ain't no short handled shovels, no axes saws or picks
I'm a goin' to stay where you sleep all day
Where they hung the jerk that invented work
In the Big Rock Candy Mountains
I'll see you all this coming fall in the Big Rock Candy Mountains

---

I might not have permission to post those lyrics, but, it was a song I remembered hearing when I was a kid in the 1960s. It seemed fitting to be mentioned here and the only train song I knew at the time. As a matter of fact, other than "Train, Train" by Blackfoot, this was the only Train song I have ever known. If anybody that wrote the "Big Rock Candy Mountain" song doesn't want it published here let me know and I'll mail you an eraser or a big jug of white out. Or you can just rip this page out.

When Brian and I had finally reached the other side of town, the train slowed down enough for us to just jump off and the bucket list train ride went off without a hitch. When we made our way back to the road, we were standing on South Three Notch Street in a spot we'd see again in a few days under totally different circumstances. It just so happened that another train was coming and was headed back North! It was going slow enough for us to jump on and ride back to the frat house, so we'd get our bread and butter all on the same day! Not one but two train rides and no waiting, hitchhiking or walking. We jumped back on the North bound train and lamented on how this was just too perfect. We were masters of all things Hobo. Right then, we were the veritable kings of the world. Small worlds, and those of our own invent, but kings just the same.

If you recall, I told you that the train tracks ran North and South through town consisting of a double set of tracks with enough space for two trains to pass each other with a little room to spare. If the paint jobs on the sides of the rail cars had been a little thicker, they would have surely scraped against each other when they passed. As we reached our side of town, back at our fraternity house, the train we were riding had sped up so fast that we could not jump off without breaking something attached to our bodies used for walking, holding a beer, or writing.

The Old Piggly Wiggly loading dock that served as the starting point of our odyssey flew by us like Richard Petty on the backstretch at Talladega Motor Speedway.

I had to walk with my cap and gown in a few days. My folks and my siblings were coming, my future wife would be there, and I could not fake a broken leg.

The Train Ride had begun…

Chapter · IV

*"A man who dares to waste one hour of life
has not yet discovered the value of life."
– Charles Darwin, Naturalist.*

AS WE watched the Piggly Wiggly platform disappear into the distance, The Zippy Mart, The New Piggly Wiggly, Troy, Alabama and all things we held dear, I had come to a stark realization. Number One was that NOT EVERY BUCKET LIST ITEM HAD TO BE CHECKED OFF. Number Two was that small voice asking me "what the Hell were you thinking?" and why had I ignored it. I was along for the ride and Brian looked like he was having the time of his life and I was too. We were at the beginning of a trip that would solidify our friendship for the rest of our lives. To clarify, how *long* that life might last, from right then, was up for debate and one whose petition had not yet been settled.

After ten to fifteen minutes of enjoying the scenery in total silence, I had determined that we were traveling between sixty and seventy miles per hour. I determined this by watching the cars on Highway 231 which ran parallel to the train tracks we were traveling on. The tracks connected Troy industrial to all points north and south industrial for the entire state. We were passing the cars we could see from our vantage point and utilized my math superiority to time between mile markers. Sixty clicks on the watch equaled sixty miles per hour. I was doing the calculations because I was figuring that we'd end up in a dirty part of Montgomery, and it was approximately fifty miles away. We'd jump off, walk to the nearest road and a hitch-hike back to Troy, meaning it would still be a trip we could tell our grandkids someday and have a laugh or two on the ride back home. That was the plan and that was the first time I felt like my hard earned college education had come in handy. It was a real shame it had not kicked in just a little earlier, two miles south of the Piggly Wiggly back in Troy. If you are familiar with the way trains travel through the country, they take the straightest path possible with as little curves as possible. Trains also take the most backwoods path to accomplish it goals. Brian and I had only hoped that the train flat car we found ourselves as castaways on was heading towards a city. Montgomery was the next logical stop on the route, and we made plans to try to exit our spacecraft at that point. We made the best of the trip. We talked about all of the things we had done together, future plans, marriage, kids, etc. We also spoke of the things we had done before we knew each other. I feel you should have a better knowledge of our separate antics so you'll have a better appreciation of the Harmonic Convergence that was our friendship for the two years we were closest friends. I'll cover some of the funniest stories Brian shared with me and a few from my past.

The funniest story he told me was about a time just before he had entered college at Troy. He lived in Mobile, Alabama where he was born and raised. He was a "rounder" to say the least. Brian told me about a time when he and one of his hometown friends found themselves in a gay bar totally by accident. He and his buddy had been making the club scene and it was late. I am sure they were intoxicated due to their geographical location and the circumstances of the events earlier that evening that surrounded the outcome of this story. If you have ever heard the phrase, "Nothing good ever happens after midnight," it very much applies to what you are about to read.

Brian was as straight as a country road as far as his sexual orientation was concerned. I know this because of the steady stream of women he dated, so, enough said on that. He and his buddy were just looking for a place to get a cold brew after everything bar related had closed. He said they had been riding thru town and saw a bar with beer lights on. They made a stop, went to the bar, ordered up and proceeded to drink. After the second beer, Brian said that someone started sending beers to him paid for anonymously. He told the bartender to thank the person for the drinks. He figured, free beer was a good thing, the process wasn't broke and he wasn't going to break it. That is until he had to go to the restroom to make room for more free beer. He said he wasn't really paying attention to his surroundings. It was a dark bar, it was three in the morning, and he had to take a leak. When he entered the bathroom, he proceeded to take care of his business in a gentlemanly fashion, not writing his name on anything in "yellow marker." Next thing you know, there was a man standing next to him, too close even for a buddy considering what he was busy doing. The guy asked him if "he needed help holding up his manhood." I can only assume the "guy" in question already had himself a handful by the time the question was being asked, and Brian quickly figured out this was the guy that had been buying him beer. Brian told me he instinctively punched the dude's lights out and was making his way out of the bathroom and the bar. It was then he realized that he and his buddy had found the only gay bar in Mobile. He said he had to fight his way out as the noise of the commotion from his hasty pugilistic restroom exit and the screams of the "meat handler" got the attention of the other bar patrons sporting "alternative" lifestyles. Brian said he was amazed at how hard sissy men could slap, especially if there are twenty to thirty of them at once. He said he got bitch-slapped, bitch-scratched, and bitch-kicked and he knew what it must be like to be in a gang fight with girls. He literally fought his way out to his safety.

Brian did not take this laying down. He told me that, upon his successful exit, a sort of embarrassment came over him. Then anger…then the desire for revenge. His immediate thought was how was he ever going to be able to explain this to his buddies and make it not sound as bad as it sounded regardless of who was telling the story. His buddy that accompanied Brian to the gay bar saw the melee break out when Brian exited the bathroom and high-tailed it out of the bar. According to Brian, this guy was a bigmouth and just short of killing him to shut him up, the only way to make this right was to retaliate against the bar and its effeminate patrons. Brian had circled the block a time or two and had come up with a plan to level the playing field, as it were. He proceeded to go to his buddy's house and retrieved a fireman's hose and the large wrench that could remove the fire hydrant caps and turn the large bolt that would make the water flow hence. His buddy's dad had acquired these items at some point in his firefighting career. After returning to the gay bar location, Brian made his way to the closest fire hydrant, hooked the long hose, rolled it out and had his buddy flip the hydrant on with the wrench they had acquired earlier.

Brian said he entered the bar, in what I can only guess must have looked like scene from a Clint Eastwood movie. I imagined the scene where Clint's character, William Munney, entered Skinny's Bar in *Unforgiven* where Clint proceeded to take out the local posse responsible for killing his friend Ned. With the primary difference being Brian's weapon of choice; a Fire hose with 400 plus pounds PSI of water pressure compliments of the City of Mobile Water and Sewer Authority, and not a bolt action 44-40 Spenser Rifle. When Brian kicked the front door to the bar open and walked in with the fire hose under his arm, large polished brass nozzle and handle in his firing hand shining in the faint neon light, it had quickly become as quiet as confession day at the Baptist Church. He said all he could see was eyes as big as saucers in the darkness of the bar. He pulled the handle back to "wide ass open" (as he put it) and proceeded to hose down the bar from the front to the back. He said there were grown boys being knocked into each other, flipping over each other, chairs and tables flying, neon short circuiting and sparks flying from the beer signs shorting out. He continued his clean up until there was a massive heap of humans, furniture, beer glasses, wine glasses, mineral water glasses, decorating magazines and a ruined juke box full of show tunes and Queen's greatest hits in a massive wet heap in the back of the bar.

Needless to say, Brian had his revenge and then some. Of course, word got out as it made the "word of mouth news" first, then the local Mobile TV news second. Folks knew Brian was the culprit and that knowledge eventually made its way to the local authorities. The Police finally sorted out Brian's whereabouts and promptly arrested him. Restitution was made by his loving and immensely patient parents, I am sure. Brian had the opportunity to tell his side of the story and it's telling must have been as effective as the fire hose he held that night. Lore has it that the local politicians made sure he did no time as the bar was not supposed to serve alcohol after a certain time, and it was a gay bar (sorry, you dudes that care—it's what they were called back then), not cool with the Bible belt crowd. The truth was that there were probably a lot of folks attending the bar that did not want their identities known…like some of the same politicians or their rich friends.

There was not a single person who had brought charges against Brian for his revenge fueled antics. The way Brian told it, so matter-of-factly, he had become a local hero of sorts fighting for God and Country, as it was after all, the South. I am sure he did not pay for drinks or meals in Mobile for a good while.

He had dodged a bullet that would now get you strung up by the ACLU and every Democrat within a thousand miles of Mobile, Alabama looking to get ahead politically.

I cracked up knowing he was telling the truth…

Chapter · V

At this point in our journey we had somewhat of a competition going. What we had done and how crazy or stupid the deed was seemed more important than winning or losing was concerned. Truth was, we were just sharing stories and who won or lost didn't really matter. It was a beautiful day, about 72 degrees and the wind was blowing about 72 miles per hour based on my mathematical calculations of our speed. We were in the back country now, peeling away from civilization as we had come to know it, as Highway 231 faded off into the distance. I was not sure if Highway 231 was curving away from us or us from it. All I knew was that I hoped the train didn't come to a halt way out in the sticks. It would have been a hell of a trek to get back to the place where the road curved away from us (or us it). I assumed we were not headed for Montgomery based on my brief stint in the Boy Scouts and a touch of common sense. Our trajectory was telling me that the movement of the sun meant we were heading northwest. It really did not matter where the train was headed, we were headed there with it, like it or not. Montgomery was due north from Troy and we weren't headed there. I was anxious to leave Troy behind, mind you, but just not this way.

My return volley, story-wise, was this particular jewel. It is as true as I remember it and there were witnesses.

I drove a 1965 GTO in High school. It was a work in progress I had purchased with the help of my dad for $500.00. Men should not love inanimate objects, but I loved that car. The only reason I had sold it was to finance a trip to work a summer job in Lake Tahoe, Nevada, the summer between my junior and senior years in college. I miss that car but the summer spent in Tahoe was more than worth it. Things were different in high school back then. Way different than now. In 1978, any car was a great car, and my GTO was my great car. My best friend at the time, Stuart Adams "Stu", and I worked on both of our rides every chance we got. After football games on Friday nights we'd meet at the local Pizza Hut, do our civil social duty, and head directly to his house to turn wrenches. We'd then head to the local drag strip late that same Friday night to a place known as Lower River Road. There we'd bullshit, bet, and drag race until the wee hours of the morning. It was a prime spot to race, one perfectly straight two lane black top road completely deserted and no houses anywhere close and we often had between thirty and fifty cars doing "run what you brung" races. Back then speed was expensive and how much money you were willing to spend determined how many races you won. I can sum it up by telling you that the local speed shop had a sign hanging in it and in bold print it said:

"SPEED IS EXPENSIVE, HOW FAST DO YOU WANT TO GO?"

My GTO had a Ram Air III 400 big block with a turbo 400 transmission with a "his and hers" shifter. A 3:73 Posi rear end rounded out a good combination and we had a lot of fun with it. Stu had a 427 cubic inch big block Chevy motor in a '69 Camaro, 4-speed with a 4:56 rear gear and it would outrun the word of God and radar. He had it painted silver with black Z-28 stripes and it was upholstered in hounds tooth check in black and white by the only Hispanic in the state of Georgia at the time. Let me tell you that "mutha" would scream. It was a tin can with a giant motor. His dad was an old school racer and knew every trick in the proverbial book. Stu was a hell of a driver and he drove that car like he had stolen it. The only person I have ever seen shift a four speed faster and more efficiently than him was his mother. That's a story for another day, but, trust me…it must have been a genetic trait she passed on to him.

In our travels, we had figured out how to make our cars backfire like a cannon going off. It was simple; you rev the motor up, and then keep your foot on the gas pedal while turning off the ignition key. You'd then let off the pedal while turning the key back to the run position. The gas would build up in the cylinders and when the spark plugs re-ignited it was Katy bar the door. It let out a boom so loud it would wake the dead for a twenty mile radius. As a side bar, it also shot flames out the dual exhaust pipes a good fifteen to twenty feet making it all that much cooler and a great way to stay entertained back in the day. We would ride through neighborhoods at night, blowing our bombs off at all hours of the night making dogs howl for miles around. I had gotten so comfortable with the scenario I would do it riding past kids on the playground and people walking down the street. Even the elderly were not spared the bone jarring explosions. There were times I was sure that some of victims actually jumped out of their clothing from the sudden sonic boom. I have achieved "Old Fartdom" now and I swear I would have chased myself down and whipped my own ass for doing something like that. Dang punks with nothing better to do.

One particular evening, my buddy and I were riding in his '69 Camaro, making the cruise around the McDonald's and the local Strip mall. We had spent the previous two hours doing "the bomb" thing. That particular night, we had pulled into the Bonanza Steak house right next to the McDonald's. We were exiting the car when all of a sudden ten or more cop cars pulled up around us, blocking our exit. Blue lights flashing and guns drawn, we were asked to exit the vehicle by more deputies than I imagined it took, and ordered to "surrender your keys and ID and come with us." Needless to say, the McDonald's and surrounding parking lots were full and cruise night was in full swing. There was no denying we had been taken by the Police and where we might be headed. We were then transported to the Sheriff's office where we waited for what might have been an hour for justice Douglas County style. Soon enough Sheriff Earl Lee, quite possibly the biggest and baddest Sheriff in the United States of America at the time, walked into the office we were sitting in and told us in a southern drawl that he needed to question us concerning "blown up mailboxes" in *his* Douglas County. Sheriff Lee was at least six foot six and carried a .44 magnum at all times. "Damaging a mailbox was considered a felony in any state in the USA," he told us. He then proceeded to produce picture after picture of exploded mailboxes in his county and he was sure he had his culprits. I hereby swear, as God is my witness, we never blew up any mailboxes and that was on a short list of things we didn't do for fun. My dad was a Postal Executive and the mail delivery paid for dinners, showers, and everything else I enjoyed under my mom and dad's roof. Blowing up a mailbox was like stealing my own car. It was considered blasphemy in my house and something I'd have never attempted. I also knew Sheriff Lee had us by the proverbial hang downs. Now I'm not saying we might not have committed an unsolved petty crime or two in our young lives, mostly involving racing or fast cars, just not this particular crime. We sat quietly and did not say a word as the best Sheriff to ever watch over a county spoke. He did not get a confession out of us and he was not going to get a confession from me about blowing up mail boxes. Understand now, he absolutely could make it stick if he so desired, so he moved on to plan B. He escorted us to his beautiful 1974 Pontiac Catalina official Sheriff's car. Police Brown, no markers and the fastest four door car (or any car for that matter) this ole boy has ever ridden in. Rumor had it that Sheriff Lee had busted a drug dealer passing thru Douglas County on Interstate twenty driving a 1974 Super Duty Trans-Am. After confiscating said vehicle and incarcerating said dealer, the car became property of the County of Douglas, State of Georgia, Earl Lee, Sheriff.

I must tell you now that what you are going to read next is purely from the heart of a car dude, of which I am. The Pontiac Super Duty 455 cubic inch engine was the last of the bad ass engines produced by General Motors. It was one of the most prolific hand assembled pieces of Muscle car history to ever sit between the fenders of a GM car, or any car for that matter. Not an all aluminum ZL-1 Corvette engine or an L-88 Big Block mind you, but the very last of the pre-smog motors to see asphalt in the seventies and the most wicked engine produced for a Pontiac past the formidable, over the counter only Ram Air V. Super Duty Trans-Ams from 1973 and 1974 sell for between seventy to one hundred thousand dollars today just to gage value for you folks needing a gage. To say they were a rare breed automotive-wise was an understatement of epic proportions. To have a Super Duty engine from one meant a Trans-Am was sitting somewhere without one. The presence of this engine, and the rarity of it, was legendary for any car guy.

Sheriff Earl Lee was a devout Pontiac man and knew what he had in the Trans-Am he had confiscated. He had the SD 455 engine immediately swapped into his personal police cruiser of which Stu and I were about to go for a ride. I learned firsthand exactly how fast a police car with a Pontiac Super Duty engine would go that memorable cool evening. He placed us in the rear of the police car where we were lectured for a good hour and forty-five minutes straight. All while the honorable Sheriff Lee drove at breakneck speeds on the freshly opened I-20 extension that connected Douglasville and Georgia to all points west of Atlanta. I-20 was a divided four lane and was a straight shot to Alabama and eventually California if necessary. I-20 was so new it didn't have much traffic on it for a few months after it opened up for business. It gave the Sheriff a broad and effective pallet upon which he would paint his authoritative picture. He lectured us on citizenship, God, Country, not scaring old ladies, and small children with exploding tailpipes, and how he would cast us down with the sodomites in his jail if we ever "Fucked with him inside of *his* county again." He knew we were just back firing for fun, but, he had numerous complaints of two cars that looked exactly like ours "fleeing the scene" whenever loud explosions were heard. I mentioned breakneck speeds earlier and I should clarify that fact. I was on the passenger side rear seat and I could see over Sheriff Lee's shoulder. His speedometer went to 120 miles per hour. It was an automatic, and, the orange fluorescent pointer that told you how fast you were traveling was spun all the way around past the 120 mark to the D (P R N D 2 1) on the indicator. I estimated we had been traveling between one hundred fifty to one hundred seventy miles per hour on the straight-a-ways. He drove the entire trip with one hand on the wheel and the other he had propped up on the bench seat, mostly looking at us, over his shoulder and not at the road. He had the heater wide-ass open and it was hotter in the back seat of his car than the peanut oil in the deep fryer at Hudson's Hickory House on a Friday night. I reminded him one time that he might want to pay closer attention to what was in front of him rather than what was behind (us in the back seat). He asked me, in a voice tinged with sarcasm, if I had any other useful pointers he might utilize while being Sheriff and I said "no sir," keeping my big mouth shut for the remainder of the important lesson he taught that night.

I was sure that the best route to take was to agree with everything he said, keep my mouth shut, and carve his warning into the highest walls of my brain. Sheriff Lee ran the cleanest county in the state and most criminals took the long way around Douglas County during his long tenure. I never exceeded the speed limit after that particular visit with him and he let us go with no tickets. He didn't need to as far as I was concerned. I had a clear understanding of how politics worked and who was in charge 'round there. I'm convinced our Sheriff extended the full measure of his Southern hospitality that evening, with the added fact he was a football fan, and my buddy and I were "cut loose" with this warning: "His name was Earl, this was his county, and what he said, went…period."

When we were re-deposited by a deputy back at the Bonanza there was a crowd waiting for us. We had agreed that we would have to keep mum. Small town rumor had spread that we were asked to be undercover cops by the bigger than life Sheriff. It was a full on lie but we did not confirm nor deny the rumor, playing it out to its fullest extent. I told one guy, "If I tell you I'll have to kill you," before that phrase showed up in the movies. I'm not saying I invented it or even used it first, but if the truth had gotten out that we had collectively crapped our pants in fear of going to jail that night, we'd have been ruined as tough guys. I have never been so scared in my life. I was a cool customer that night but on my insides I was screaming like a little girl sitting in the front seat on the Great American Scream Machine at Six Flags over Georgia.

Over the years, I'd see Sheriff Lee, long after my days of mischief had ended. He'd always greet me kindly and start our conversations with these words "Jimbo, you and that God-damned Adams boy keeping your asses out of trouble?" I'd answer, "Why Hell no Sheriff Lee, gotta keep you in a job." And we'd both laugh like we'd never exchanged those exact words the hundred or so times after our long-ago high speed learning class. I was the smallest class I'd ever sat in, four seats, four doors, 455 Super Duty, one teacher and two students. I can assure you, I learned more on that trip than 12 years of school and five years of College.

Brian and I both laughed loud at the conclusion of that particular story. It was his turn and we were streaking towards God only knew where with no end in sight…

Chapter · VI

BASED ON the watch ticking in my mind, we had been riding approximately one hour. The train we were riding would slow down at times, and then speed up with what seemed to be neither rhyme nor reason. I estimated that the train had slowed down below thirty five miles per hour only once and that was in downtown Troy. We had begun a competition with stories from our pasts being the wall upon which we would compete. Pissing the highest up a wall was one silly way that men settled things since pistols at dawn would get you "three hots and a cot" in the local jail. It's funny how men can make a competition out of just about anything and Brian and I had the undeniable advantage of time to test that theory.

Brian reminded me about a certain girl he had dated in our Troy days when we had first met. We were pledges and just beginning to sort each other out, personality wise. He had been initially afraid of her rejection and was quite nervous about asking her out on a date, much less the frat formal we were required to attend every year. She was quite a beauty with a father that was protective beyond all reason and measure; like any good father should be. This father was so protective he would agree to pay for her college education on the sole condition she attend the local center of higher education, Troy University. I can only guess she was itching to get out of her hometown but she knew the only way she'd get an education beyond high school was to "go local" and on her father's dime. She and Brian had dated off on for a while, mostly off, and apparently Brian's antics were well known by her parents due to the constant snooping by her father. Brian explained to me that this particular girl's father so disliked him that he would rarely let them out of his sight. I knew Brian and loved him like a brother but I would not have let him date my sister or my daughter. The crack of dawn was not safe around him and I knew that the father's concerns were well founded. Brian was a charmer. He could talk the Pope out of being Catholic if he could get a few minutes of face time with him alone and Brian happened to be in Vatican City (lucky for us Brian was mostly heathen and the rest Methodist). Let's move on shall we…

Brian told me that the girl's father insisted that he eat weekend meals with him and his sometime girlfriend's family. Before he would agree to let Brian take her beyond the confines of the large spotless home, Brian had to endure her dad's every examination. Brian told me he hated it primarily because the father in question would use every opportunity, be it big or small, to belittle him. It's important to know the father was a relatively successful business man and his museum-like antebellum home was his proof of that success. He was a perfectionist and attended to every detail of the home no matter how insignificant. He was constantly warning Brian that he was a person of questionable character and a reluctant guest in his home at best. One particularly hatred-solidifying evening, Brian was informed that the entirety of his collegiate education had lesser value that the clothes the sometimes girlfriend's father happened to be wearing that particular evening. Whenever Brian ate with the host family, the father always pointed out to him that he was eating with a silver fork reserved for his daughter's future home and husband, making it crystal clear that Brian would not be that man. Brian was raised a southerner and did not dare rebut the father as this would unleash the full force or her father's ire towards him, killing whatever chances he may have had with the daughter completely. It made me realize later that Brian was quite the cool customer and a force to be reckoned with. Brian also told me that his "girlfriends" mother was a closet alcoholic. It was probably her only defense against the constant judgmental tirades she must have endured daily as his wife. Brian said she was very flirtatious with him, once offering him the keys to their cottage on Dauphin Island if he would come when she was there by herself. He knew it was just amusement from an intoxicated and frustrated woman. To top it all off, the daughter was so repressed by her father's constant control that she would have mated with the first man with enough balls to take on the hyper-possessive control freak father. I think, in retrospect, she was hoping that Brian was that man but it was not to be. I had only realized the full force of this man's dislike for Brian when the daughter had invited Brian, me and one of her sorority sisters to attend a semi-formal dinner at her home, hosted by her mother and father. The occasion was a medium-brow affair in that you didn't wear blue jeans but khakis with a nice long sleeve button down shirt, pressed of course, and Dockers with socks. Our attire seemed to be the official "frat rat" uniform of the day, not just for us, but for every fraternity man I knew. The Izod (now Lacoste) alligator was as fancy as it got then and we were the veritable fashion plates of our day.

Upon our arrival we realized Brian's initial mistake was he had worn a pink button down purchased by the daughter whose father and mother were hosting the affair. As soon as we had cleared the massive leaded glass front door the father started in on Brian. The father was as kind and welcoming to me as if I were a long lost brother or someone who had won the lottery and owed him money. The tension was so thick in the room you would have thought we were playing "Marco Polo" in a swimming pool full of chocolate pudding. I truly did not know how Brian kept from cold cockin' this ass-hat minutes after we had arrived, but I appreciated his ability to restraint his emotions. I instantly disliked the father, not only for the way he treated my friend, but for his general dislike for anything or anyone he could not control. I have omitted the most important part of this particular visit in that when the father commented negatively on the pink shirt (salmon was the color printed on the label), Brian clearly stated that the shirt was one that he would surely approve of. Both the color and manufacturer were similar to those he had seen the father wearing. When the father pressed him on the issue Brian stated that the daughter had purchased the shirt for him specifically for this occasion and to insult him at this juncture was to insult his own daughter. "Holy Shit!" was the only thought I could muster. The father went on a tirade, with all guests present, that would have made Scarlett O'Hara blush. His displeasure was not only aimed at Brian, but his daughter as well, making a complete and total creep out of himself in the process. He was good at it, the making an ass of himself part, obviously a seasoned pro.

Both the mother and the daughter broke down in tears and quickly exited the room. Their attempts to suppress this anal-retentive control freak (with narcissistic rage) had failed, and their only recourse was to totally leave him in the hot spotlight of his extra "Y" chromosome induced psychotic tirade. To say the event had taken a turn for the worst was an understatement. We had not even lifted a fork and the night was already a complete disaster. The father then asked if he could excuse himself to go and try to fix the problems at hand leaving me, my date and Brian standing in the formal living room of the beautiful antebellum prison. The question (more of statement than a question) he asked was rhetorical in nature, as you certainly were not going to stop this train wreck of a man from attempting to control this most unfortunate of situations he had created. Brian kept his cool and had only asked to be excused to visit the restroom. The father pointed him to the facilities and Brian quickly found his way there.

It was maybe fifteen or twenty minutes later when our hosts returned. Both of the women returned with perfect make-up and obvious swollen eyes from the tears of embarrassment they had shed while away from the carnival that had become this dinner party. The father then invited us all into the formal dining room to enjoy the feast that his hired hands had prepared for us. The meal and all it courses served that evening were fabulous. Every course was a culinary delight and each course was met with anticipation only exceeded by the next. The father minded his manners for about three courses when he felt like the quality of the meal had smothered the memory of the events that had transpired earlier that evening. Sorta like covering a cheap cut of meat with good gravy. He did not, however, let up on Brian one bit. Brian excused himself twice more during the grinding courses that had been accompanied by endless jabs and spears thrown at him for the duration of the meal. I had figured that Brian was truly in love with this girl as no human being in their right natural mind would have signed up for a lifetime of this store-bought hell. I knew he and I were going to have a very serious conversation after this event to "check his oil level" concerning what he was buying into. A long-term permanent relationship with this girl would mean marrying the father, too. Separation from him would come only with his death or murder, both of which could be arranged.

After what seemed to be a lifetime, the meal had finally reached its conclusion and we retired to the veranda on the back of the house for drinks. We were outside for a few minutes when the smell of what I thought was a dead animal wafted outside to where we were standing. The father immediately excused himself to see where the odor originated and quickly and rudely ordered some of the hired help to correct it immediately, if not sooner. The smell had invaded the entire house and had made its way to our location smelling like the fecal matter of a very sick zoo animal. The odor reminded me of when the elementary school I attended blew out the septic system and we had to miss school for three days until repairs were made. I lived five miles away from the school and I could smell it from there. It smelled like a fart soufflé (pronounced Suu-flay in English).

We were quickly dismissed by the father, obviously embarrassed by the events that led to the abrupt end of the festivities at hand and promised that he would invite us over again when the problem had been corrected. Brian and I had that serious talk I had mentioned earlier that evening and he stated that he was not in love with the daughter and had no other plans concerning her and him. The father had become, what he called, a lesson in dealing with assholes and Brian was not going to allow the dad to get the best of him. I had to ask Brian how in the world he had planned any sort of revenge and he simply stated that he already had his satisfaction in the matter and that was that. The funny part of this story was that I was with him just about all the time as we were plebes requiring constant fraternal togetherness, learning the "in and outs" of our chosen Greek fraternal organization not allowing time for revenge of any sort, at least as far as I could tell.

For the next two weeks, we'd drive to school passing by the girl's house both coming and going and every day there would be a septic tank truck with massive hoses and suction devices manned by fellows in what appeared to be "Haz-Mat" suits, and an excavator digging up the front yard in two places. I assumed the workers were replacing the pipe that connected the homes plumbing to the city sewer system or Roto-Rootering out prehistoric plumbing...or both. Each day seemed to bring more and more experts to try to alleviate the incredibly awful smell that would not go away. At one point, we even saw moving trucks outside the home removing the furniture for what must have been a thorough fumigation of the beautiful residence. This went on for about fourteen days and soon enough; the family was back in the residence.

Brian had completely cut off contact with the girl who lived at the home for obvious reasons. I had assumed he realized what a hopeless cause their relationship was, and would always be, if the father remained on this side of the dirt and she and Brian dated. I spoke to her at the on-campus student center and asked her what had happened at the house. She said they had the smell of feces all over the house and it would not go away regardless of how much money the father spent trying to make it stop. She said it had gotten so bad that they moved into a hotel while the father attempted, unsuccessfully, to make the smell go away. After two weeks or so, it just went away by itself. She said it was her father's full time occupation to make the stench go away and it worried him more when it went away by itself. She said she had enjoyed the vacation and made good use of his smelly diversion. The shit smell in the house had taken all of her father's energy and she took advantage of the time out of his spotlight and did things she rarely did, like live free. She stayed out till all hours of the night and she and her mother stayed on Dauphin Island weekends and just had a great time bonding. It was what would be a liberating time for both the daughter and the mother in more ways than one. In the two weeks during the house clean-up phase, the mother stopped drinking and gathered the courage to leave the control freak father. She then hired a lawyer and cleaned his clock financially. The daughter later went on to live with her mother, post divorce, and enjoyed what I am sure was a happier life than the one she was doomed to have suffering under his tyranny. The last we heard the mother and daughter had moved to Birmingham and the daughter attended and later graduated from Samford University.

It was only months later that Brian told me what he had done to get his revenge on the asshole father. We had gotten to know each other very well by then and I had remembered it, inquiring about the whole revenge thing during one of our Dixie Beer weekends. It seems that when Brian had excused himself the numerous times during our dinner party, he had been busy executing a plan to which even I had to tip my hat. Brian had visited three separate bathrooms in the lovely antebellum home that psycho dad so lovingly stood watch over. In his visits to the porcelain facilities Brian had taken his revenge in the most covert but effective of ways. It seems that Brian had an upset stomach whose relief usually accompanied the number two. If you recall the scene in *Stand by Me*, when Will Wheaton's character Gordy LaChance was telling his story to Chris, Teddy, and Vern by the campfire, concerning the revenge of "Lard-ass" Davey Hogan and the preparation Davey used to wreak his havoc (The Barf-O-Rama) for the years of ridicule the town of Castle Rock had showered on him all just for being a blimp. Brian ate enormous amounts of Zippy Mart type fare (before we met Dan the Man) and prepared for his revenge. He did not have diarrhea mind you, it was all solid and carefully prepared for longevity, industrial type poop generally used for flaming bags on doorsteps at Halloween.

Brian's revenge came in what he called a "high tanker dump." My son's generation calls it the "upper deck" crap. He had removed the porcelain lid covering the vertical tanks on the toilets and had quite literally taken a dump in the water tank. It would not be something someone would find immediately and the constant water movement in the tank would keep "it" ripe (for lack of a better term) until it worked its course and dissolved in about, say, two weeks. Every time the toilets were flushed, it stirred up the contents and the whole house smelled like the inside of a Port-a-John after a hot day at an Alabama-Auburn game. The "Iron Bowl Revenge" as we came to call it, and the single most non-destructive revenge I had ever heard of. I was now friends with a mad genius.

It was brilliant. I knew then Brian and I were going to get along marvelously.

I laughed until I almost threw up when he told me of his perfectly executed plan. I still laugh about it to this day and it has been almost twenty-six years since this event transpired. He had the upper hand in our story telling and the train had not slowed down at all, so it was my turn.

"Train, Train…Take me on out of this town…."
"Blackfoot Strikes" title track, 1980.

Chapter · VII

AS OUR train sped onward for destinations unknown, North of where we originally started our journey, the competition continued for best story telling. It was my turn and I figured that a good football story was at hand. There were many stories that could fill volumes of books but I will reserve a few of the better ones here.

When I was a freshman from the big city of Atlanta via Douglasville, Georgia, I was indoctrinated to the "low country" (not an insult) that was the wiregrass of Alabama. Every year our football team had a barbeque where the freshmen were responsible for the hog that was to be cooked "in the ground" style. For you neophytes, that meant that a large pig or a bigger hog was procured (more on that later) and a big pit was dug. Hickory, oak and other wood was piled up bonfire style and a big fire was started, primarily to have an excuse to drink beer and secondarily to produce coals that would be shoveled around the beast to slow cook it southern style. Believe me here, drunken dudes that can bench press a small car get hungry when large amounts of beer get consumed in a short amount of time. Usually the festivities began the evening before, as the freshmen were in charge of the event to the benefit of the seniors on the football team. I was assigned to the "procurement" committee, which actually meant we were the ones responsible for getting the meat.

Three others and I made the trip with another dude, aptly named Bubba. It seems to me that every story that involves trains, beer, barbeque and football is ordained to have one, if not two or more Bubbas included, or you can just about bet it isn't true. There were four, count 'em, four Bubbas on my football team at any given time. This was, after all, Alabama, where there were more Bubba's per square mile than any other place in the known universe. Every year we'd have at least one Bubba lose his eligibility due to grades or lack thereof, pregnant girlfriends (yes plural) back home, parole in the summer time running over into the regular season, or even death. The Bubba's continued to re-populate the football team when one went astray, away, to jail, or on a rare occasion, graduated. The Bubba of the day and the one mentioned here was one that actually stuck it out and graduated in seven years. It was a four year bachelor's degree, but who was I to judge the higher education of this or any other Bubba for that matter.

On this particular trip, Bubba One, as we will refer to him from this point forward (because there were three other Bubbas around at the same time and intermingling Bubbas seems inherently wrong) was our chauffeur and pilot. Now, these were hardcore Bubbas I am talking about and ones whose names on their birth certificates said BUBBA. Not a nick name from being named Theopolis or Dontrez, but pure hard core, southern white trash, double wide trailer, down home Bubba's. Some of them were Bubba the third and I assume by now, twenty-seven years later, there may be Bubba the fourth or even fifth. I guess you get the gist of where I am headed with this. These boys could "skin a buck and run a trot line" as Hank, Jr. put it and I reckoned it must have been written in their genetic code. Bubba One drove a jacked up four wheel drive Ford F-150 and he had two guns hanging in the gun rack in the back window. A shotgun "for up close meetings" as he put it, and a thirty ought six he used as his primary hunting rifle. This particular Bubba made his own rounds (bullets, to those of you that don't know better) in his dorm room and was by all accounts a hard core outdoorsman.

I was riding "shotgun" and my three cohorts were riding in the back of the truck in the bed. The deal was each person, other than seniors, paid ten bucks to cover the costs of keg beer and other expenses like plastic cups for consuming beer and plates for eating the cooked pig. Our job was to go and "pick up" the Sow that was going to surrender her all for our shindig. I had asked Bubba One where we were going to pick up our critter and he explained, "We get 'em from all over. Usually, we get 'em from various pig farmers that inhabited the area. It depends on how much we drink before the event." I came to know what that meant in the most personal of ways in a very short amount of time. We had driven about twenty miles out of town towards Brundidge, south, towards Dothan. We were on some serious back roads and darkness had fallen, thus raising my suspicions as to the legitimacy of the hunt. I asked Bubba again about where we to acquire our pig and he plainly told me that, "We have gotten a number of pigs from the same farmer we are about to visit" and, "he (the farmer) usually wasn't up late but trusted us to pay him after the party was over and the money was counted." Just as soon as I was about to cry "bullshit," Bubba hollered "we are here…get ready!" We rounded a sharp curve and proceeded to run right through a barbed wire fence holding some of the biggest hogs I had ever seen before or since.

I will say there was one exception, Hog-wise, that I will share with you now concerning hog sizes. In high school I played football with, and owe my B in Physics my senior year to, a fellow named Jessie. Jessie had the biggest head of any human I have ever met. I was a veritable "melon head" myself, clocking in a 7&7/8's bucket sized noggin but ole Jessie was the proud owner of a head that was easily a 9 & ½ or bigger. His head was so big that in the tenth grade playing Junior Varsity ball, our coach could not fit Jessie properly with a football helmet. His solution to that particular problem was simple, he'd just remove all the inside padding from the helmet and handed it to Jessie telling him "if you want to play, this is what you will have to wear." I was flabbergasted at the time, even as a tenth grader, knowing Jessie was as tough as a two dollar steak and would flat knock your dick in the dirt (a compliment in football circles) utilizing his head as lead. He did not question his circumstances, as far as head size went, and helmet limitations certainly wouldn't prevent him from participating in a sport he loved. I must say that every time Jessie would hit someone I was concerned he might not graduate from high school. Why? We were all coached from a very young age to "lead with your helmet," meaning your head and the helmet strapped on it was what you used with when you set out to cold-cock an opponent. I swear there were times when poor old Jessie would hit someone and come up cross eyed from the impact. I said earlier that Jessie was "tougher than a two dollar steak" and I meant it…there was never one occasion I recall in four years of being his teammate that Jessie didn't knock the tar out of someone and not get up. In retrospect it would have been the same for Jessie if he had just played without a helmet as there was only a 1/4 inch layer of plastic between his head and whoever he was tackling. I can truthfully say that Jessie was as tough as any person I had ever played football with or against, and that includes college football too.

I should finish covering the "Big Hog" portion of this story by telling you that Jessie's dad raised hogs for a living. Jessie carried a picture of his dad, in overalls, standing next to what I thought was a baby hornless rhinoceros, but in actuality he was standing next to his prize pet hog. Jessie's dad was six foot tall and, in the picture, had his arm extended straight out to his side, level, and resting upon the back of the humongous animal he called "Larry." The funny part of this story was that Jessie's dad wore a belt buckle that said "HOG" on it and it was clearly visible in the picture. His dad also was never seen without his overalls on even at football games and that was cool by me. I had never seen a set of overalls worn with a belt before or since as Jessie's dad had pioneered the look. I challenged Jessie as to the authenticity of the picture and he humored me by agreeing to take me to his farm and show his dad's portly swine pet to me. Seeing the massive hog changed the way I feel about pork forever and I knew the sheer size of this critter would turn most gentiles away from pork faster than converting to Judaism or seeing sausage get made. One slice of bacon from Larry's backside would have raised the collective cholesterol of an entire days worth of Waffle House patrons. To say that Larry the Hog was huge was an understatement and Jessie told me Larry had weighed in at just under 1,800 (that's eighteen hundred) pounds and would come running every time his dad whistled for him. That enormous hog barreling towards us like some massive, shaved, overweight dog changed my life in some strange way. I've never felt the same way about a pet, and, the thought of that massive hog crapping on the floor inside of my house was a recurring nightmare I had for a while.

To round out this story and somehow get back onto the interstate that is our original story, a few years after we had graduated, a friend (whose name escapes me) and I saw

Jessie working in a Krystal Hamburger joint toiling in lower management. After our standard greeting we asked Jessie if he would accommodate us with "discount" (meaning free) burgers. Jessie immediately told us "NO." I remember telling Jessie how it was shame that one of our classmates had done so well, working himself into a respected middle management position so soon, and yet denying his former teammates who "bled the same blood in the same mud" a discount on food. I remember telling him, "Jessie, you've become a success now and you've up and got (are you ready for this)…the big head." I must make it clear too that I genuinely liked Jessie and we all got a good laugh out of that comment. Jessie still didn't cut us any slack on Krystal's finest offerings and maybe I should have kept the "big head" thing to myself, but it didn't matter anyway, as Jessie was not coming off any hamburgers for us that day. Jessie is now a valued and key employee in an exceptionally large corporation.

As Bubba One rammed his way through the fence, he leveled his thirty ought six and fired a perfect head shot between the eyes of the biggest hog in the pen, just after he slammed into the enormous pig with his front bumper. It fell to its knees and was doing its death dance, squealing in protest, as we attempted to gather him up Bubba One screamed at us to "Load that big son-of-a-bitch in the truck!" When the three dudes in the back did not move quickly enough he grabbed his shot gun, levered a round into the chamber, and fired it over the heads of the four of us as I had exited the truck and moved towards the gunshot and bleeding porcine beast. This was a good nine hundred pound pig and, as God is my witness, we heave-hoed that big sucker in the truck in less than five seconds as our adrenalin was pumping like a freshly drilled oil well. This was a very important point to know as it had become very obvious we were uninvited ne'er-do-wells from that point forward in our quest for all things pig. The next thing you know, the lights go on at the front porch at the farmer's home and shots started ringing out as we hauled ass away from the point of our felonious pork grab. We were traveling at least one hundred miles per hour down dirt roads with the headlights off and I must say it was a religious experience. You very much called on whatever God you believed in for protection, and your faith would increase exponentially, after successfully power sliding around each turn. I know mine did. Bubba One drove that four wheel drive like Junior Johnson, running a load of moonshine through the hills of North Carolina at night. His driving was what I considered at least, an art form. A lesser form of art, but any man has to acknowledge genius when he sees it. Bubba One never placed both hands on the wheel at the same time and drove mostly with the back tires sliding, accelerating, utilizing the emergency brake to aid with full speed turns with such proclivity that I could only marvel at its purity and grace. A time or two, he drove with his knees and loaded his shotgun with his two free hands, just in case we might have a close encounter of some unknown kind. He did this while carrying on a conversation with me about the weather. This guy was cooler under pressure than the other side of your pillow, with an equally austere conscience. He was as guilt free as a new born baby.

The events of the evening also told me that Bubba One had passed this way before and may have very well been from the area. I never got a clear understanding of his exact place of origin, but understood full well he was as "country as a run over possum" and definitely from these parts. In one fell swoop he had made four full scholarship athletes into felons, a requirement in Alabama if you wanted to maintain full card carrying Bubba status. It was a glimpse into what a local good ole boy did when he was bored or there was a party needing to be populated with chow. We all had a great time at the barbeque, us pig getters never mentioning to anyone the great price paid for the "guest of honor" at our felonious feast. Pig procurement was an indoctrination of sorts, for a select few freshmen we discovered later on, and I have never, ever discussed the events that evening to anyone save for these words written here. Maybe there is a Bubba (or four) still on the team carrying on the tradition of countrifying city boys "Hog procurement committee" style.

The train had not slowed down one bit and I had one more "Bubba One" Football story to deliver before Brian got his turn...

Chapter · VIII

THE TRAIN had not slowed down at all and I still had the floor. I had broken out the Big Guns and this story would make Brian have to dig deep to top it….

It should be especially noted that Bubba One, the same Bubba from the hog procurement story, was also the gentleman that single handedly and inadvertently brought the full force of the ASPCA down upon the university, the athletic department, and especially our trainer, named "Doc." It was three years later, my senior year and first quarter in school as a card toting member of the Pi Kappa Phi brotherhood, football player, and generally righteous dude. The football team had a pep rally planned at our stadium and we were to play our most hated rivals, Jacksonville State University. Jacksonville State's team mascot was the Gamecock. If you recall Head Coach Charlie Bradshaw hated fraternities and sororities wholesale and Pep rallies were purely a place where fraternities showed up collectively drunk. The Greeks raised all matter of unbridled hell in support of themselves first and the football team, or whatever event had purposed the meeting, second. Troy University had the most awesome of marching bands, aptly named "The Sound of the South" in attendance, and the entire school had turned out in support of our efforts that particular year as we were in contention, once again, to win our conference title.

One thing I can honestly say about Coach Bradshaw: The man was driven and could produce winning seasons as proficiently as Hershey could produce chocolate. We, as a team, never had what one would call a losing season, save for one lone year, in my tenor at Troy. We were winners, anything short of that was unacceptable. Any arguments to any authority figures by disgruntled players concerning Coach Bradshaw's terroristic and sometimes unstable methods of producing win's was outweighed by the phenomenal amount of decisive victories he produced and the number of "paying butts" he put in the seats. He could "rip your head off and shit in your neck" as he put it, and get away with it without question. But he knew how to win.

We needed a theme, as it were, for the game and for the pep rally at hand. Bubba One, now an assistant coach, had come up with what he thought was a brilliant idea involving a fighting game rooster, chewing tobacco, and the public humiliation of our most hated rival's mascot. The frats showed up that day with signs saying "Trojans cover the Cocks" and other rude, and what I thought were witty, slogans that involved thinly veiled observations regarding the male genitalia and condoms. It had set a tempo for the rest of the day and what occurred later. I had earned the right to enjoy the rambunctiousness as I was a full blown Frat Rat Football player and this was our last game of the season and my last college game ever. That fact alone made me happier than a fat man winning a year's supply of honey baked ham. I was elected team captain by my teammates much to the dislike of our illustrious head coach. I received a very warm ovation from the crowd in attendance due to my dual status as frat/football dude and more than likely my dashing good looks (but I digress). When my name was announced my frat brothers screamed and hollered for a good ten minutes without so much as a second's break. I had asked them to scream for me just to piss off Coach Bradshaw and it was effective. Screams of "Big Jim, Big Jim, Big Jim" went on for what seemed like days led by my pledge brother and closest friend Brian with shouts of "Pi Kapp, Pi Kapp" thrown in for good measure. When Coach Bradshaw was finally was able to speak he could hardly be heard over the raucous inebriated screams emanating from the home crowd. He handed over the microphone to me, all the while giving me the look of death (I mean my death; he never sweated, ever), thinking I might have sway over my new family of Greeks. I can only assume he thought I had somehow orchestrated the events, exposing his obvious inability to control the crowd at hand, and his hot displeasure radiated off him like he had rheumatic fever. To say Coach Bradshaw liked control was akin to saying beans liked making you fart. He was not a happy man when he looked me square in the eyes and said, "Your public awaits you."

I said all the right things that a good football player should say, reminding the crowd that victory was unsure save for their participation and presence. I had watched World Championship Wrasslin' a time or two, and had even seen it in person in Opp, Alabama, where it was held in the same location as the annual Rattlesnake Rodeo. When I attended the wrestling festivities in Opp, to my amazement thousands were in attendance. I watched as the wrestlers worked the crowds into a frenzy with words alone. Preachers had done it, pro wrestlers did it, and I could do it too. Depending on your geographical location the "Poor Man's Passion Play," as my dad called it, was played out in all its "Good versus Evil" glory on football fields and in wrestling rings hastily erected in VFW's across our great land, and this was my chance to stir up the crowd.

I had convinced the attendees that the Jacksonville State University Gamecocks were the Yankees of our day, veritable northern aggressors in disguise, moving south to try to refight the Civil War one more time, taking one football field at a time. The Gamecocks were coming to take our women and children, farms and homes, and they were going to do it on the gridiron. The Troy Trojans were the only thing standing between total annihilation of each person there and the southern traditions they held dear. Sweet Tea would disappear from restaurant menu's everywhere, hockey would become the sport of choice, Coca-cola would forever be called "pop" and our beloved "grits" would forever be replaced with Cream of Wheat. The crowd had bought the entire line of bullshit I laid out hook, line, and sinker. We were the good guys and saviors of all things Southern. I received compliments on that particular speech from, of all people, Coach Bradshaw. Brian said it was the biggest load of horseshit he had ever had the pleasure to hear and was glad to have been a witness to its effectiveness. "It's a curse" was my smart-assed answer back to my now best friend and partner in crime, Brian Horst.

After the niceties had been delivered, and before the late fall chill had beaten the Pep Rally attendees to a stiff, frozen numbness, I witnessed one the most awe-inspiring things I had ever seen in my entire life. Bubba One had procured a genuine Fighting Game Rooster for the activities he had planned at the conclusion of the Pep rally. As I write this I wonder where one might acquire a gamecock at the drop of a hat and I am sure it was a non-issue for Bubba One. I also wondered if any shots were fired during his procurement of the critter. The gamecock Bubba One "found" (as he put it) was an exact duplicate of the mascot that adorned the sides of our most hated rival's helmets increasing the effectiveness of the planned events. You should know that the pep rally was held in our stadium outdoors and it also served home to our track team. The football field was encircled by an eight lane Olympic style running track utilized in spring when track was in season. The long jump pit was on the home side and the sand pit used for landing was approximately five feet from where we were standing, just to the right of where I had previously spoken to the home crowd.

Before I go further I must explain our team name, the Trojans. Troy University had been called the "Red Wave" for all the years up until the year before I had arrived. Our team had mirrored the Alabama Crimson Tide's football program in every aspect. We ran the same offensive schemes and defensive schemes and it was well known that the one and only Bear Bryant and Charlie Bradshaw were long time best friends. It was rumored that their friendship extended back to the "Junction" days and The Bear had called Coach Bradshaw, and I quote, "The meanest son-of-a-bitch he had ever met;" documented in the autobiography of Paul W. "Bear" Bryant, and more in depth in "The Thin Thirty" by Shannon P. Ragland about Bradshaw's days at the helm of Kentucky's football program. I could attest to the out and out meanness of the man first hand, but I still respected him, concurring with Coach Bryant's and Mr. Ragland's assessments. In Alabama, Bear's autobiography was the bestselling book just this side of the Bible. The Trojans remained the Red Wave until, according to local lore, a major prophylactic manufacturer had moved into town and made a major endowment (it's what it's called I swear) to the College. From that point forward, we were the Trojans. The year prior to my arrival the team sported a logo exactly duplicating the logo of said rubber company on the sides of the helmets worn by its participants. It must have been one hell of a donation as far as I could tell. Thanks to the powers that be, whoever they might have been, my years on the team we just had "TROY" painted on the sides of our helmets. I guess it was a good thing Kotex or a douche bag manufacturer had not made a donation to the school making the same mascot requirements…but I digress.

The aforementioned long jump landing pit had been prepared by Bubba One as a holding pen for the Game Cock he had purchased or stolen earlier that day. The pit itself was surrounded by chicken wire and the Game Rooster was brought in a bag and thrown into the pen. This was after Bubba One shook the sack with its irritated contents spilling out in what must have been a terrifying site for a male chicken or any other manner of fowl that day. Bubba One had managed to place a paper bull's eye of sorts on the back of the Game Rooster and had concocted a great plan. It was amazing how the redneck mind worked and I had only hoped that Bubba One had not majored in Marketing as this was my chosen field. I did not want to compete with him for a job post graduation if this stunt worked. The idea was to have ten guys with "Chaws of Tobacco" surround the pit. The object was to have each man try to spit on the game rooster with tobacco spit and the one hitting the bull's eye was declared the winner. He'd receive two free tickets to the upcoming football game with all the comforts afforded therein. The agitated Fighting Rooster was running for what he thought was his life (if chickens have a thought process, and, survival is one of those thoughts) all the while making it nearly impossible for anyone to hit said target and win. The charade went on for what seemed like an eternity with the crowd, at first, enjoying the festivities at least as much as spitting on a replica of our rivals mascot could deliver. But the mob grew restless quickly, as mobs usually do. What seemed to be a novel idea quickly became an exercise in the absurd based on the disapproving stares of the sorority girls. Every Greek lettered southern belle sported matched jerseys and color coordinated hair ribbons that day. It was their way of designating their collective yet individual affiliation according to what sorority they had pledged.

The show was getting old fast.

What happened next will never be forgotten by those in attendance and will be seared in my memory forever. Doc, our trainer and team Doctor, was a wild man from Louisiana and most likely insane. He had left the LSU Tiger organization by request of Coach Bradshaw and had flourished at Troy. To say he was a unique individual was like saying the Sistine Chapel had a neat painting on the ceiling. This guy was a complete loose cannon, always marching to his own drummer, but a brilliant doctor. I was standing with a glazed look on my face all the while watching the debacle that had become the Gamecock tobacco spitting contest. I almost jumped out of my skin when Doc came running by me, screaming at the top of his lungs, "Gamecocks must die!!" He cleared the hastily erected chicken wire fence with the ease of a high hurdler war whooping and grabbing the Game Rooster with one hand in what appeared to be one continuous motion. He then proceeded to swing the terrified chicken over his head with his forefinger locked tightly around the neck of the defiant Gamecock. He continued to scream, war whooping at the top of his lungs swinging the bird faster and faster all to the absolute horror of the sorority girls and the delight of every male in attendance, save for some of the guys in the band.

The next thing you know Doc snapped the head of the Gamecock off, sending its headless body flying into the crowd of horrified and fear frozen sorority girls. It was obvious to me that Doc had done this before at some point in his life and was no stranger to the procedure. The screams of the girls have never left my memory banks as I witnessed the melee that ensued. It was friggin awesome.

I must pause here to reflect on what I call "a learning opportunity." Over the years I have heard the term "he/she/it was/is running around like a chicken with its head cut off." I learned firsthand what that particular phrase meant and I considered myself an eye witness expert from "Pep Rally" day forward. I could, if needed, be called as a professional witness to any headless chicken activities or any occasion where a headless chicken might have reeked it's mindless terror on an unsuspecting crowd regardless of how large or small it (the crowd or the chicken) might have been. I could also say to any person (usually a mother talking about a small child) using the phrase casually, "Nah, I've seen a chicken with its head cut off and what it can do. Your kid is, at best, running around like a chicken with its head firmly attached and not causing nearly as much damage." I had acquired what one might consider a Doctorate in headless chicken, with a specific emphasis on Gamecock. I realized then I had been in Alabama way too long and needed to get back to the big city, sooner rather than later.

The Gamecock went wild and headless throughout the crowd spewing blood out of its neck and clawing everything in its path. I have never witnessed a bigger riotous stampede, sorority girls running over each other (affiliations be damned, it was every man/woman for themselves) and band members scattering like marbles dropped on a hardwood floor. It was chaos akin to the final scene in *Animal House* where the Delta's wreak havoc on the homecoming parade benefiting Faber College. There were passed out sorority girls with chicken blood covering their clothing laying everywhere from the stampede of Greeks avoiding the crazed and headless fighting rooster. Some girls fainted from what they had just witnessed, as delicate constitutions forbid witnessing animal sacrifice. I had become light headed with awe and reverence purely from the audacity of what Doc had just done. It was incredible to see and I am a better man for having been privileged to witness it. This was not, in any way, akin to Texas A&M's stealing of The University of Texas' mascot "BEVO" a massive Longhorn Steer. The story goes that A&M stole then barbequed Bevo before the much anticipated football game out of hatred for its interstate rival. It was intended to "fire up" the Aggies football team for the big game but had quite the opposite effect. Texas beat A&M like "it owed them money." This was one small chicken and a couple a thousand people to feed. Snapping its head off was the right thing to do, in retrospect, as two legs, two wings, two thighs and two breasts were not going to satisfy this shocked and hungry crowd.

I, and the entire football team, stood in awe as the events unfolded before us. I even had to ask the co-captain standing next to me if what I had witnessed actually happened. It was as amazing a scene as I had ever witnessed in my life up to that point. The ASPCA got wind of it almost immediately and I am certain that the college paid a hefty fine with a promise of someone's head having to roll (namely Doc's). Doc got fired for that stunt and he immediately disappeared from campus. The newspapers showed up wanting an explanation of the events and it indeed made the national news. I guess the College's condom fund must have gotten raided to cover the fines laid down by the Government for that stunt.

Doc went back to LSU and remained there until he retired. Over the years I would see him on TV, standing on the sidelines or attending to the injured warriors on the gridiron. Every time I saw him I laughed at his audacity and the balls that man possessed. He had single handedly produced a cock that indeed needed covering. This time it was covered with Troy University's endowment money instead of rubber.

Doc was indeed "the Man."

It was Brian's turn…

Chapter · IX

BRIAN HAD the tiller and delivered a few stories that involved both of us. The Train we were riding had sped back up and was still heading due north. There wasn't a lot we could do about stopping so we just reflected on the past few years and laughed deeply as events flooded our memories.

During the pledge phase of our friendship we knew we were sorting each other out in more ways than just drinking. We challenged each other to do anything that was a traditional pledge duty with flair and style. What it really meant was we were going to push every limit we possibly could, all the while pushing the outer limits of the patience of the brothers charged with our fraternal education. There were numerous physical challenges we faced and our collective goals were to shatter every record achieved up to that point, all with a fresh and cocky edge. One of the very most challenging physical feats was the pledge course run. It was a weekly event separating the "real men from the boys." I had just come off four grueling years of physical training under the watchful eye of Coach Hannibal Lector. To say I was physically fit was an understatement. I was a 275 pound freight train that could bench press 400 pounds and run for hours.

Training was a mainstay in my football career. In 1980 the outdoor heat index hovered like a gnat at a picnic: in the 115–119 degrees for most of the summer and fall. To say it was hot was a like saying the Titanic was a really big boat. I have said it before but it bears repeating, Coach Bradshaw believed with all his heart that "sweating was a complete lack of discipline" and (I actually heard this in a movie in later years), "Water was for washing blood out of game uniforms." These exact phrases were repeated by Denzel Washington in *Remember the Titans*. I thought Mr. Washington might have been channeling Coach Bradshaw in the movie and I got cold chills when I heard the words. Bradshaw never allowed water breaks of any sort during the grueling four hour practices filled with running, hitting, and scrimmage drills so intense that some players totally dehydrated and would collapse on the practice field.

On one specific occasion we had a player collapse in the middle of a scrimmage. It royally pissed our psychotic Coach off to the point he ran down off the massive 200 foot tall hill he perched upon daily when the scrimmage portion of our day had started. From his vantage point he intermittently barked orders and insults with the cadence of a Marine Corps drill instructor and the smoothness of a seasoned auctioneer. He physically dragged the player off, by his heels, to the side of the field screaming at future Gamecock killer Doc to "revive his worthless ass or send him home to suckle at his momma's tit." On one particular day that year, heat beating down hard enough to fry bacon and us making it to the end of a particularly grueling day of practice, we were rewarded with running 100 yard sprints. We had no less than four players quit in one day. It was not a record for quitters; however, as there were many times in the first days of our training we'd lose almost 50 souls in a single day. Words like "grueling," "cruel" and "insane" were regular phrases quietly uttered to describe the intense heat and immense physical efforts put forth by the survivors. (Coach did not care…he figured if you couldn't survive it then just go home to your damn momma!). It was during two-a-day practices, and his single objective was to trim down the team to a more manageable number, thus eliminating the "wanna-bees" and "girl-friend-missers." We called those first two weeks "90% days." It was not unusual for us to have over 300 "walk-ons" (non scholarship players) show up in an attempt to extend their former high school gridiron glory for a few years, or in most cases, days and sometimes hours. We would lose between 85 and 90 percent of the walk-ons and at least 20 percent of the full scholarship freshmen athletes that mistakenly left girlfriends back home or just could not "gut it out." Heading back home to a girlfriend sounded better that being called a pussy (code name for quitter).

It was hotter than a jalapeno enema that year and I remember it well. Two-a-day practices, both four hours each, stretched the physical and psychological limits the human body and mind could endure. One hundred and twenty degrees outside with 90 percent humidity, wearing sixty pounds of equipment, made the separation of "doers" and "don't want to do-ers" simple. There were days I would lose forty pounds or more per day and I was not nearly the highest loser. It was all water weight and would be quickly replaced at training table meals via drinking two or more gallons of liquid per day. To have said you survived was an accomplishment only recognized by its participants. Most of the mountains I have faced in my life pale in comparison to my years playing football at Troy. I remember watching *Band of Brothers* and seeing what the heroes represented there meant when one man said, describing one brutal winter after he had returned home, "It's cold… but it's not Bastogne." Surviving the five years in Troy's athletic system in no way compares to the sacrifices made by the "Greatest Generation" as Tom Brokaw so accurately named them, but I can tell you I have met many footballers from bigger programs yield the floor to me, shaking their heads in disbelief, when I told them what I and my teammates endured and ultimately survived. We could "Eat bullets and Shit Tiffany Cufflinks" as Bradshaw would say. We were meaner than a cotton mouth rattlesnake with an incurable dose of jock itch and nothing but fangs to scratch with.

After two grueling weeks of hell on earth the band would show up with all the flags and twirlers and all would be right with the world. One of the primary reasons I loved the Troy University Band was simple, if you were not drop dead gorgeous, you would not be in the Sound of the South band. The majority of the females represented left behind boyfriends dismissed with the "I just want to be friends" technique, code for "I am going to College and meet some new dudes." Their eagerness to meet new "friends" was met with the hospitality of true Southern Gentlemen, or something like it. Imagine red blooded football players with nothing to do but sweat, puke and practice for twelve to fourteen hours a day for two isolated weeks. Add 225 lovely band beauties to the mix and see what happens. There was enough testosterone, as Lynyrd Skynyrd put it "to float a battleship around" as I recall. To describe the results of mixing that many lonely dudes and that many beauties would be ridiculous and decorum prevents listing the results here. There's only one shade to that particular gray.

Troy, as a university, rewarded all fifty newly minted "Junior Misses" representing every state in the USA (and Puerto Rico) with full scholarships just for being beautiful, most with average to mid-level intelligence. That meant that, at any time, there were 204 beauty contest winners on campus at all times as each year, fifty-one (remember Puerto Rico) fresh beauties made their way to the Troy campus. The awesomeness of the Troy University experience (at least for a dude) could be expressed in sheer numbers. Troy's available on-campus housing was as unequally balanced as my two year old grandson Jonah trying to tackle Bo Jackson or Hershel Walker in a football game, but in a good way I mean. There were nine girl's dorms to one guys' dorm, signifying an overwhelming 7.9 to 1 girl to guy ratio. It was incentive enough to "gut it out" in two a days and akin to pure heaven, setting aside the hell a ball player had to endure to get there. The term, "There are no one-sided coins" come to mind when I reflect on those days. Pure hell on earth practices then eight beautiful girls to one dude. Life, as we knew it, was good. Cue the music.

Brian and I would run the 2.4 mile "pledge course" at least twice and sometimes four times a week. It encompassed a circuitous route throughout the city of Troy similar to the route I previously described when telling about the Greyhound Bus trip. I was slap in the middle of my football spring training when I was a pledge and nothing any full blown frat rat brother was going to throw at me was going keep me from succeeding. Brian and I would purposely upset a brother or incorrectly identify whatever year the Pi Kappa Phi founding fathers got together over single malt scotch, invented the men's club we had all pledged allegiance to and sworn secrets never to tell anyone about least we surrender our very lives, with a nifty secret handshake to seal the deal. We always complained about the pledge course like Brer' Rabbit pleaded with his captor Brer' Bear "to please not throw him in dat Briar patch." Running the pledge course was always administered as punishment to both of us and we liked it. We mastered that run like a fat man mastered an all-you-can eat buffet. It was part of a master plan Brian and I had hatched for months.

It had gotten toward the end of our spring school quarter and Brian and I had prepared ourselves for what we lovingly called Hell Week. It was by all accounts, a week of peace and calm accompanied by candlelit dinners prepared by the brothers. Moonlit nights of reflection of all that we had learned and mastered over the three months we had pledged Pi Kappa Phi. I am sure anyone with a brain knows that is a big ball of manure. Hell week was the Brothers way of giving us hell via sleep deprivation, starvation and physical punishment all as a last ditch effort to rid the brotherhood, once and for all, of the low rent no good Yankee loving sons a bitches that were the pledges. Brian and me represented two of that species. Truth be known, they needed the dues.

Brian and I were encouraged, by the brotherhood mind you, to make our mark as pledges and that was exactly what we intended to do. Brian and I had planned our final pledge course run with a style and flair that would not be soon forgotten by either the Fraternity we had chosen or the other fraternities on North Three Notch Street. The Delta Chi's, Lambda Alpha Chi's, Theta Chi's, Sigma Delta's and Omega's all had frat houses on the same street we were located on, with three hundred feet of separation between each antebellum mansion, all claiming to be "The Best." I could not understand why the frats couldn't get along. We all did the same stuff. Drinking, partying, and chick chasing being the primary pursuits we all shared. Oh yea, and I forgot about the brotherhood part, a point I should emphasize now for good measure.

Brian and I carefully planned out our last and most notorious pledge course run. After this last run we would never navigate the now familiar course as pledges again. Here's what we did. We had planned to bring the initiation festivities of all five fraternities located on North Three Notch Street to a dead standstill and simultaneously divert all attention away from the actual guilty party—us. We accomplished that goal and then some. Brian and I had gone through the whole "double, triple and quadruple Dog dare you to do it" scenarios and had settled it as do-able, consequences be damned. Brian and I had become proficient at daring and insulting each other with everything from momma jokes, i.e. "Your Momma is so fat she broke her leg and Sausage Gravy poured out" and "Your Momma is so fat when she hauls ass somewhere she needs to hire a moving truck and some movers," and my personal favorite, "Your Momma is so fat she has a gravitational pull and a smaller fatter woman in orbit around her," to who could consume the most liquid refreshment in the shortest amount of time. It was male bonding 101 and is still a class taught by men to this day in some form or fashion. We had gotten very tight, and always had each other's back. I guess it is something that dudes do. We never sat in candlelit circles pledging fraternal love (covered as long as your dues were paid) or kept diaries to exchange with our pledge brother outlining the nice things they had done for you written therein. If I have to explain it you wouldn't understand anyway. Just ask any dude currently or previously in a frat.

The run was afoot and we were ready.

Brian and I had engaged the help of the day-time manager at the Rippy Mart to help accomplish our never to be forgotten last pledge run goal. We were being timed, as everything was a competition among dudes and the lowest time posted on the pledge course came with a four hundred dollar pot to be split by the person or persons beating the timed run record. Brian and I were going to go to Florida on that money and we had prepared in the best way possible. Every pledge put twenty dollars into the pledge course fund and the pot was split fifty/fifty with the brotherhood using half to buy beer after we had ran the course and completed the secret ceremonies that followed. The other half had been populated by the fifty or so brothers that had pledged over the past few years and had not won the pot. The last guy to win it was a cross country runner so for him it was like hunting in a baited field.

What happened next, I must say, is probably repeated in hushed whispers and given as warnings to pledges instructing each newbie in what not to do when leaving one's mark. Brian and I had made ourselves ringers to win and this is how. Before we began, we hid clothing at various and specific points along the pledge course. Our plan, if successful, would re-write what "leaving a mark" meant as pledges. It was more like a skid mark in a pair of silk boxer shorts your wife would give you for Valentine's Day. As we ran off into the darkness, North up Three Notch Street, we ran to the Zippy Mart and to the bathroom where we stripped off all of our clothing. We proceeded run the entire pledge course totally buck-ass naked. We wore running shoes, sunglasses and our birthday suits only. We hid clothing along the route in case the police came hunting the insane "nekkid" runners. If the possibility of being captured arose, we'd dart into the woods or behind houses where we had hidden clothes, then sneak our way back to the house. We also parked Brian's car 1/3 of the way into the pledge route and my car 1/3 further down on the route as a precaution in case making a quick get-away was necessitated.

All the frats were in full secret meeting mode by the time we had made the first 2.1 miles of the course with home within site. The last part of our plan would involve the other fraternities without their knowledge. It was not so late that the streets were deserted. North Three Notch Street was the North/South artery running right through the center of Troy. The city police department was located more towards the Troy campus than the downtown of Troy and the University was approximately nine miles apart. Brian and I made damn sure we were spotted by locals every chance we got. The police were on high alert as they knew that frat hell week was in its full final swing. They (the police and the other frats) had been lulled to sleep as the authorities issued warnings of retaliation if any fraternity got out of line. Up to that point, everything was as calm as a prayer meeting at the Lutheran Church and the police had all but convinced themselves that their threats were sufficient enough of a weapon to stop us.

We ran through the town square and cut down each street that made up the pledge course. On the final three tenths of a mile, we heard sirens blaring and had not needed to clothe ourselves with the shorts and shirts we had hidden along the course nor drive the automobiles we had carefully placed on our route in case we were at risk of getting caught. We made sure that we ran up the front porches and around the backs of each fraternity house on Fraternity row with the exception of our own House. There had been numerous sightings by the locals and each told a different tale as to which fraternity had put their pledges up to such a notorious and tasteless deed. When we passed our house we had broken the course record in enough time to back track in the woods after we'd run back to the Rippy Mart and clothed ourselves in the same clothes we had departed in.

We ran into the basement of our fraternity house where our awaiting brothers prepared to indoctrinate us into the brotherhood. The wails of police sirens filled the air quickly followed by knocks at our front door. The police were simply warning us, as it were, that there were nude joggers from what they suspected was a fraternity (other than ours) as no one reported seeing any nude speedsters running up our front porch or behind our house. We went upstairs to the front porch to see the five other fraternities being questioned on their front lawns as numerous calls had been received with the callers saying they saw nude runners going into each house. The cops were pissed to say the least and we were never even suspected in the crime. I'm sure that every policeman in Troy was in attendance that day. There were at least six cars in front of every Frat house on Three Notch Street. Blue lights flashing and questions being dispensed to innocent frat members called from the solemn initiation services that had been disturbed by the local Law. There was law enforcement patrolling on the backstreets tracing the route Brian and I had just completed. Our Fraternity was held up as examples of virtue and we were as guilty as John Wilkes Booth. Post initiation, the brothers told the story about our pledge run for years to come. Of course, we didn't tell the brothers the truth about our deeds until after we were fully initiated and paid some dues to seal the deal.

Brian and I had pulled it off. One of the only times I passed through Troy after I graduated and after I had married my wife, we were headed to Dauphin Island to visit Brian and his fiancée to spend some time together. My lovely bride and I stopped by the old fraternity house and I met some of the pledge brothers of that year. I asked them about the pledge course, if they still ran it and how much the "pot" was up to. They said it had been won the last time in 1983, spring quarter, by two guys that were rumored to have run it nude. The pot was up to over 1,300 dollars and our winning time had not been beaten. As a matter of fact, they intimated that no one had come within two minutes of breaking the record Brian and I had set. They speculated that the runners must have cheated, as no one could have run it as fast as the scantily clad pledges had done. I never told them that I was one of the runners. It didn't matter anyway, as "time is the enemy of memory," and it wouldn't change the truth about our accomplishments that day.

We ran the full course, had shattered the old mark set by a cross country runner, and had truly left our mark. Mission accomplished. Brotherhood was ours and we were in.

We had a hell of a time in Florida that week.

Brian had another story to share and I was more than willing to yield the floor to him. He reminded me of that Florida trip we took with the spoils of our pledge run victory and what happened while we were there.

Chapter · X

*"Money can't buy happiness,
but it sure makes misery easier to live with."
– Unknown*

BRIAN AND I had been train riding for what seemed like days when in actuality we had only been riding for a few hours. We were approaching a small town and the train had slowed down below forty miles per hour. We adjusted what we thought might be "survival speed" for jumping off the train we had so unwittingly mounted, all in a quest to say "we had been there, done that, got a tattoo to prove it." The primary problem in this scenario was the tattoo' in question was going to be quite possibly a large surgical scar (or scars) acquired after we jumped into the veritable rock quarry that lined each side of the train tracks. We had the advantage of speed to help us clear, maybe, the giant rocks called appropriately enough "Rip Rap." But speed was also our enemy in this circumstance as not clearing the giant and menacing rocks would make certain things that God and Doctors intended to stay inside our bodies be introduced to the ugly outside world. A multiple compound fracture was not the kind of thing neither Brian nor I was looking forward to explaining to our families' much less total strangers in a town located God only knew where. I had determined the name "Rip Rap" came from the "new ass" that would be ripped from jumping into rocks the size of the ones we needed to clear to successfully exit our extended and unexpected jaunt through the lovely Alabama countryside. There had been no care taken when shaping the rocks at whatever satanic rock quarry that manufactured the bone crushers that lay beneath us. I still had to walk for my diploma in less than a week and unless Troy University would consider moving the graduation ceremonies to a hospital wherever I might be staying, and not walking or crawling to the podium was not an option I even remotely considered.

I figured if we jumped and had indeed been knocked stupid, the first folk to find us might be hobos, carnival people or circus folk as trains were the chosen transportation of the day for people in the aforementioned professions. Now I must state that I personally have no problems with, nor prejudices against, any of the three groups I mentioned earlier as I am sure they all have some very fine qualities as human beings. I have eaten many a po-boy sandwich in my life, the name credited to the hobos back in the depression era, and I was sure "hobo sandwich" just didn't have the right ring to it. I have been to a number of carnivals and, well, the paid help there just creeped me out. Anyone with enough dirt under their fingernails to start a good tomato patch while frying funnel cakes with those same nasty hands isn't the kind of folk I choose to hang out with on any sort of regular basis. And besides, if you were found knocked out near the train tracks by a bunch of "carnies" you might just wake up as the Bearded Lady's new boy toy or worse. Circuses? Barnum and Bailey was a quality outfit by all rights and might be able to find us something to do. And the Circus did make a swing through Atlanta in January of every year, so Barnum and Bailey Circus might not be so bad to work for if pressed into duty. I'm certain that elephant pooper scooper was a job with a revolving door and the requirements were simple. I could just quit the circus when it hit my hometown and put Brian on a two week Greyhound Bus odyssey, sending him back to his hometown of Mobile, Alabama. Ok, Ok, I am just using the previously described scenarios to give you an insight into how my brain was working when I wondered what the hell we were thinking by jumping a train. For all we knew, the train was heading to Canada and telling my folks and my future wife "I have decided to travel with the Circus/Carnival/Hobo's" sounded much more palatable than "we jumped a train not knowing where the hell it was headed and now we are God only knows where—maybe Canada."

After considering all the options before us, maybe with the exception of joining the Circus we had decided not to jump, take our chances and just keep on riding. What the heck, I had five plus days until I had to consider what excuse I might need to come up with if I didn't make it back in time to walk in the graduation ceremony. I was a college grad now regardless and I had learned in at least seven of my core classes how to bullshit someone. It was a class taught by necessity and I was good at it. I was getting a diploma if I walked in a ceremony or not. I had majored in Marketing with a minor in Finance and Psychology, and my degree had "BS" at the beginning of it. It was proof positive I had a degree in Bullshit. Every time I see my College diploma I remember that specific time I thought of it. "BS in Marketing" was printed in black and white on my diploma. I was at ease and all was well in my world. Brian was just going with the flow and was not even considering a graduation ceremony anytime soon. He was still in charge of the story telling and he was ready. We sat back down on the open rail car and were the kings of all things free.

After winning the Pledge Course pot totaling $400.00 dollars, Brian and I headed for the Sunny Beaches of the Redneck Riviera known as Panama City Beach, Florida. Summer season was in full swing and rooms were nearly impossible to rent in some of the low class dives that populated the beachfront back in the day, before Thomas Drive. The Hi-brow street (Thomas Drive specifically) was populated by numerous hi-rise condo complexes. It had made enough sense (and money) to developers and city politikkers (work with me) driven by the potential for increased local revenues, and graft, to run the "Mom and Pop" motels out of business. Having been the mainstay of Panama City Beach for nearly eighty years, running the Mom's and Pop's out of business by raising property taxes made good sense to the greedy politicians. This foul deed eliminated the family motels for the sake of the hi-rise money makers that were Beach Front condominiums and put the small guy under.

Brian and I tried but could not find a place to stay. Our fall-back plan then was to go to the fancy-shmancy (it's a word) part of town and just rent us a place for three to four days instead of a week. Eating was not an issue for us as we hit every grocery store on the way out of Troy stopping at both Rippy Marts, the Piggly Wiggly and the Winn Dixie in town before we left for the sunny beaches where we enjoyed the spoils of our Pledge Course Victory. We found a condo complex and rented a place on the top floor only for a few days as luck and our limited funds took all but $50.00 of our running money. Most of the bars in Panama City had drinking contests and Brian and I were more than good enough to compete as each contestant drank for free. Plus you could get mixed drinks made with cheap swill that was "aged on the way there" and that suited us just fine.

We had a great time that first day and had gotten so intoxicated we invited a few of our closest friends (we had just met) that evening to come back to our condo to share in the spoils that was our high dollar top floor Ponderosa. We had invited maybe ten people but had forgotten in our collective inebriated stupor that ten people will tell one person each, and those ten might tell ten more. Next thing you know, we have 75-100 warm bodies in our palace and the party was on. I remember some of it as the week was young and most folk had brought some sort of liquid refreshment with them. We had filled the bathtub with a de facto punch by the name of "Oobeedo" or "Purple Jesus" as I have heard it called a time or twelve. Basically it was every cheap clear liquor one could find, twenty to thirty packets of grape Kool-Aid and enough sugar to make the entire Mormon Tabernacle Choir into insulin dependent needle jockey diabetics. It was cheap, tasty and very effective. To say it fulfilled its requirements as an inexpensive party starter was a complete understatement of massive proportions. I figured the two names, Oobeedo and Purple Jesus, got the names by utterances made after consuming too much of the recipe at one sitting.

"What's your name son?" the policeman asked the inebriated college freshman…

"OOOOBBEEEEDDDOOOO."

The second name was probably derived from the hollow promises made to our savior if he (Jesus) would just let the offender survive the experience of being tanked on the Purple liquid. "Oh Jesus, I swear on all things sacred I will never do this again if you will let me survive and don't let me puke again." I've done it, you've done it and most every college student who has ever drank the aforementioned punch in its entire, oh-so-covert ass-kicking glory had done it also. We've also made the promises to Jesus to spare us the hangover and nausea that accompanied the deadly grape flavored elixir. Immaturity in one's spiritual walk will do that. Of course, one never intended to keep the shallow promises made from desperation to the King, because that's what young indestructible people do. You would just drink half as much the next night and all would be well. You do remember, don't you?

It only took one night at the fancy hi-brow condo complex and only one party for the Panama City Beach Police to visit to get us evicted from our fancy temporary digs. We were told by management that the balance we paid up front would be, and I quote, "mailed to us pending a thorough inspection of the premises minus cleaning and repair fees." In other words, we were out on our butts and we did not have a dime to our names. We considered protesting the punishment, but the local law looked as if it were going to side with the management that day. We decided we would hang around for a few more days as we might run into someone we knew. We had about twenty bucks left from the fifty we started with the night before. All of our inexpensive hi-brow food was eaten by the ravenous intoxicated crowd that had collectively gotten us thrown out of our fancy room and we had not spotted a single soul we knew. Brian and I had decided late that second evening (after we had been tossed by management) to either sleep in his car and head back to Mobile the next morning. Or just grab a bag of Cheetos and two cokes from the giant Coke machine located in the Family Area of the Condo Complex we had been booted from and leave town right then completely defeated. Soft drinks (I knew why they were called soft drinks-see the Oobeedo/Purple Jesus explanation for what a hard drink was considered) were cheap at the condo as the machine catered to a more family type crowd.

It was settled. We would go to the Stop and Go food mart (Florida's equivalent to a Rippy Mart without illegally blind cashiers) across the street from the Motel Hell that had kept our hard earned dough; we'd purchase a big bag of crunchy Cheetos (as the cheese puffs were akin to cheesy farts if you were hungry and needed to fill some hungry belly space on the cheap), grab two canned drinks at the condo drink machine and head back to Mobile. We had fought the good fight, run nude, and we had been whipped.

We had decided one kick-ass night and two days at the beach was good enough for us. We had stayed up all night so that was, to us, the equivalent of almost seven days of fun. Seventy two straight hours, divided by sixteen hours (the average time humans stayed awake in a day not under the influence of Oobeedo), equaled four and one half days. We had packed almost five days of fun and frolic into two days, based on the math, and we were satisfied. We had lied about our names when we checked in anyway because we figured we might get into some mischief while there. I think Brian gave the address to the Gay Bar he had hosed down as his home address and I am sure the owners would wonder who Dickey Johnson and Johnny Dixon were if a check showed up there. Those were the names we'd regularly use when attending any festivities, uninvited, or when names were required for registering, signing in or guest lists and code names for the two of us.

I had purchased (yes purchased) the Cheetos and Brian was going to walk to the Giant Drink Machine that would contain the last liquid we were going to consume in our short-lived trip to the beach. It would leave us about seventeen dollars for gas to get back to Mobile if needed. Brian walked to the giant machine, and when I say giant it was the biggest Coke Machine I had ever seen up to that point in my life. He dropped the fifty cents required into the slot and pressed the button, waiting for the familiar clunk.

Nothing. Not a thing.

The damned place had taken our "running" money, shortened our hard earned vacation, and now it was going to steal our cans of chilled refreshment reserved for our trip home. To say Brian and I were pissed was like saying the United States Marine Corps liked to go and kick ass when called. I saw Brian push the button again with zero payout. I got out of the car (like it was going to do some sort of good) and marched over to the thieving drink machine. Brian said "maybe we'll just put the second fifty cents in the machine and it will drop both of our drinks." I agreed and he then deposited the second two quarters into the massive quadruple sized drink machine and nothing came out. It did not even make any internal ratcheting sounds like it was attempting to deliver us the cold nourishment we had paid for twice. I might have even split my drink with Brian if one had been dispensed after the second set of quarters had been dropped. I figured the first set was his and he was a Mountain Dew man. He was, after all, from Alabama. I was a Coca-Cola man myself; being from Atlanta and home of "Sweet Georgia Brown" as the song went, and nothing else would do. If you could picture two Mountain Lions whose sphincters had been rubbed raw by a freshly picked corn cob you might get a small glimpse of how upset we both were at that particular moment.

I reared back and kicked that drink machine with such force you'd have thought I was kicking a field goal in the Super Bowl with time running out and my life savings on the line. The only thing I got was a sore foot, as I was wearing Flip-flops (fruit boots as my father-in-law called them), and nothing else beside my Ocean Pacific Shorts and a tee shirt. Brian reared back and hit the face of the machine so hard the lights went out on all four panels of the offending machine. We stood there, in the dark, for a few seconds and then it happened. All of the small lights that designated "empty" popped on for every selection given on the machine. The machine apparently had a short circuit and we were just throwing our money down the proverbial drain. We had concluded we had been ripped off and it was just the way things would have to be.

Motel Hell - $351.00 (I added the dollar we'd just lost), Raw-assed Mountain Lions - Zero.

We had turned to walk away when suddenly Brian turned back to the machine and full force kicked the front of the giant empty box, I assume, for good measure. Then it happened. The door to the giant machine popped open just slightly. We stood there in silence as Brian opened the door to what was the proverbial "Pot O Gold" at the end of the proverbial drink machine rainbow. The giant double machines were in actuality one massive machine that had a feeder system that was an engineering marvel for its day delivering all the drinks in the machine to one solitary chute. I estimated, as we did not hang around for very long, the quadruple machines held at least 2,000 soft drinks. The best part was that it was completely empty of drinks. Yes, I said the best part. When the door wobbled open we looked down at the base of where the money landed inside the machine and there were double two-foot square by two-foot tall stainless steel boxes with handles on top, both filled to the brim with quarters. It was, by all accounts, a leveling of the playing field in our summation and our field was leveling out one shiny quarter at a time. The dill weeds that owned and managed the massive drink machine had not serviced the empty box that week. It was obvious that the giant twin steel treasure chests full of twenty five cent doubloons would be emptied every day or so. Or, in this case, maybe the machine was serviced when someone complained to management that the drink machine had stolen the unwitting purchaser's money, thus alerting the management of the empty drink box. I guessed that whoever was supposed to service then refill the massive drink machine must have forgotten to lock the huge front doors on the massive thieving drink machine. I also assume they then got re-assigned to another duty leaving our condo refund in two large containers. That's my story and I'm sticking to it.

We knew our credibility was shot with management, so we were fresh out of luck in that department, meaning we kept the drink machine being empty thing to ourselves. To tell you that Brian and I pondered telling the condo management team of their misfortune concerning the busted drink machine would be a stretch. The girl had revealed her bounty to the two guys who, by all accounts, had just been ripped off by the same management team that kept our hard earned pledge course running money. We grabbed the two massive square buckets and considered it restitution, knowing we were never going to see a refund, ever.

We hauled the twin treasure chests to Brian's car and had to lift each one in the trunk one at a time with both of us grabbing the handle on the top. We decided not to hang around for very long, as we figured there was about three hundred and fifty dollars of quarters, give or take, and we would happily consider ourselves (the condo and us) *even* at that point. We decided to drive on to Mobile, cash in our "winnings" as we called it, and go to Gulf Shores for the rest of the week. Brian had a good friend who had a small house at the beach and he'd surely rent it to us for $350.00. Brian's parents were out of town when we arrived making it easier to count the quarters without explaining where they had started life and how they found themselves in our possession. We counted for eight straight hours and had weighed the quarters on the bathroom scales in his parents' living room. They came in at a stealthy two hundred and twenty five pounds apiece.

There was six thousand dollars and change in quarters in the two stainless steel buckets that day… six grand, more money than Brian and I had seen up that point in both of our lives combined. Brian and I hit every bank in Mobile, Spanish Fort, Daphne, Foley and Gulf Shores cashing in our quarters a little bit at a time so as not to raise any suspicions. We had reasoned if we took our $350.00 for the money kept by the condo and returned the balance, we'd be in some seriously deep doo-doo so we just let it go. I also guessed the management team at the condo complex refilled the massive drink machine four or five times before the quarters were removed, and it stole from us on the right day or the wrong day depending on one's perspective. For Brian and me, it was the rightest (it's a word!) day of our lives.

Brian and I lived it up for the rest of that week in Gulf Shores. We rented the nicest top floor condo in Gulf Shores, Alabama. We ate filet mignon for breakfast, lunch and dinner, all paid for (yes, paid for this time) complements of a nameless condo complex in Panama City Beach with a faulty drink machine and a penchant for booting out paying customers. One night in particular we bought drinks, for four solid hours, for every living soul in the Florabama Bar. If you've been there you know what I mean and where it is. We were the kings of our day and we shared our good fortune with every person lucky enough to clear the door to the beach bar dive on the Florida-Alabama line. It was one of the best weeks of our lives.

It was my turn…

Chapter · XI

THE TRAIN we found ourselves on had finally begun to slow down to the point we could exit safely. We had entered a train yard of sorts, evidenced by the tracks on either side of the tracks our train rested upon. When we entered the yard we could hear other trains and just as we were going to exit, two trains came along both sides of ours, heading south, to points unknown. They were not traveling at a very high rate of speed, but there was barely enough room for the trains to clear each other, much less Brian and me jumping off. We were literally stuck. It had become a Greek tragedy of sorts. Two dumb-assed Frat rats jumped on a train and could not get off for love or money. It had become so funny to us we figured we'd just have to adapt to living on a train car. Takin' a leak was going to be easy, but, well, you know the rest. Anyway, we did not bring any food with us, so none in, none out. Cool.

We sat back down on our rail car and could feel the train speed up. We were on for the long haul and we knew it. It had become a joke of sorts with the both of us silently thinking of how stupid this whole thing was. It was ordained, I guess, knowing the two guys that would at least try anything once had met their collective Waterloo. "What the Hell," I thought to myself. "I'm here, my best friend is here, and I have graduated." Brian reminded me that it was my turn at the podium and I was ready. I was reminded of one of the many characters I had crossed paths with in my time at Troy playing football.

I feel like I cannot go further until I mention a fellow named Jessie Clyde Wallace, Junior, the Third. This particular fellow was a teammate of mine and probably the quickest human being I have ever met. One "for instance" during a game we were playing, Jessie was called for an off-sides penalty. If you don't know what an offside's penalty is, put this down and go back to whatever you were doing before now. Usually Coach Bradshaw would withdraw you from the game in order to give you an ass chewing of massive proportions, with your loyalty and family lineage (or lack thereof) questioned, which he did in Jessie's case. I was lined up right next to him and I was right at the point of snap, looking down the line at him and the ball, and I was sure he had not been off-sides. It was not critical, as it had no effect on the outcome of the game, but Bradshaw had his rules and inside those rules were perfection of execution at all times, anything less was unacceptable. In watching game films the following Sunday I had maintained he was not off-sides and upon close examination of the films, Coach Bradshaw had to apologize to Jessie in front of the entire team, as he was indeed not off-sides. Bradshaw had chewed me out after the series of plays terminated, as I was to tell Jessie if he lined up in the neutral zone and to instruct him to "check his line," code for "back up some." I had made it clear that he was on sides and I had looked. He mustered a half hearted apology to me, lackluster at best. The film had revealed clearly that Jessie had beaten the snap to the quarterback and sacked him for a loss, but the penalty that ensued gave them a first down and Bradshaw came unglued, screaming like a banshee at Jessie and anyone else he could make eye contact with. Jessie was that quick and Bradshaw, from that day forward, used Jessie's quickness as a lesson. Jessie's feat was uncanny. He was a genius at quickness, and he was a character. The dude had beaten a snap to the quarterback and the quarterback was under center. Trust me, in football circles it was quite an incredible feat.

On one occasion, at a practice that was particularly hot, we had six players pass out at practice. We were allowed to take a seat and remove our helmets, which never happened. We figured Bradshaw had some bad news to deliver to us. Maybe he had spoken to God and his son Jesus was about to return, or the heat had gotten to him also. It was the heat, stifling to say the least. Bradshaw had told us that for the next few days we'd get a sit down (no water break, of course) for five minutes to recover a bit from the intense heat. It had a neutral effect, as there was no shade, but at the very least we got to sit still in the thick airless heat. It was the third day of practice in the "five minute sit down" rest period and it was so hot that I was hallucinating, or so I thought. Here's why. It was as silent and still as a funeral during the five minute periods and all present took advantage of the time. That Wednesday I was sitting in the "Ghetto," as my brotherly teammates called it. It was what they referred to any meeting, meal, anything where the black teammates I played with congregated. I was an Atlanta native, clearly understood and could speak jive fluently, and I was always welcome in the "Ghetto." As a sideline, I can truthfully say my team had no racial conflicts whatsoever. Bradshaw made it to where we needed each other to survive and molding and melting us into a team was how he kept us close and tight with each other. We were too tired to not like or at least tolerate each other. We had all survived a common enemy: heat and Coach Bradshaw. It was a calculated, effective tool, the heat and extreme physical exertion used by Bradshaw, and it worked perfectly.

On this particular day, we had all just sat down and I had counted to about ninety (a minute and a half) when next thing you know I see Jessie Clyde Wallace Junior the Third pass in front of me in his typical quick blur. By the time I had counted to ninety three (three seconds later) my mind processed the fact that Jessie Clyde Wallace Junior the Third was holding a brick! He had a regular sized red brick in his right hand and had "laid it upside" a brother's head for reasons yet undiscovered to anyone, save Jessie, at that point. Now the commotion that ensued was spectacular to say the least and spelled the end of our five minute sit down's. Apparently, Jessie fancied a particular female and another one of the "Ghetto" brothers had taken an interest in the same girl, likely to aggravate Jessie. She had been Jessie's steady girlfriend and he was not going to have anyone mess with her. He had asked kindly for his teammate to back off and leave the girl alone. Pride and testosterone proved to be a bad combination for the offender in a big way. Jessie had given the last warning he was going to administer to the offending teammate and had clearly told him, "I'll get you when you least expect it." He made good on his promise. I was exhausted during the five minute sit down period, and as I said before hallucinating (or so I thought), when I thought my mind saw Jessie with a red brick in his right hand. To say Jessie used the brick effectively is like saying a thirteen-year-old boy could effectively make good use of a subscription to Playboy. He split the offender's head open wide, enough to see "clean through to the other side" as one of the other brothers put it. Jessie got in three swings before the other tired sitters processed what was going on right then. The head of the offender got busted open like a cantaloupe or a watermelon falling off a ten story building onto concrete. Jessie's punishment was so effective the offender never returned to play again purely from embarrassment. The punishment Jessie dealt that day was secondary to all concerned and we, as a team, agreed the offending dude should have backed off from Jessie's love interest. Oh, and none of the brothers ever said or looked at Jessie's girl again. He was such a good player he ran stadium steps as punishment for two weeks after practice and that was it. We lost the privilege to sit for five minutes after that incident. Bradshaw said we obviously had better things to do with the time, like run the massive hill he usually perched himself on, so that's what we did. "What the Hell," I thought. It fit the way things usually went in those days and we all accepted it. Resting only made you weak and Lilly-livered.

Ok, I cannot let this pass without explaining a few things that had occurred to me after the "brick upside the head" incident. Later that evening, Jessie made his usual stop by my room for his usual,

"Hey Big Jim, can I have two pieces of bread?"

"Sure Jessie…"

He'd leave and about five minutes later another knock on the door,

"Hey Big Jim, can I use some peanut butter?"

"Sure Jessie…"

A few minutes later, knock-knock…

"Hey Big Jim, can I have some jelly too?"

"Sure Jessie, just come on in and make a PB&J for both of us."

I enjoyed those talks with Jessie over peanut butter and jelly sandwiches. After the events of that day (the bust a dude upside the head with a brick day) I asked him as soon as he knocked on the door to just come on in and make us both a sandwich and let's talk. Jessie explained to me the circumstances leading up to the events of that particular day. I had listened intently to his story and at the end I was glad Jessie called me his friend. This was a guy not to be messed with and everyone knew it.

My one and only question for Jessie and one that no-one had even considered was,

"Where in the wide, wide world of sports did you get a brick?"

I wondered if he had hid it.

"Nah," he said, "because the dude I waxed never sat near me and I figured if I had been toting a brick, a coach or someone else might question me." We agreed on that point. He knew everyone present would be tired and not paying close attention to anyone or anything. I pressed him again on the brick. Here is what he said...

"Big Jim, I am not the smartest man in the world and I know I will probably work in sanitation management (be a garbage man) or something like that after I get out of here, but I am going to have a wife and children and be a good father when the time comes. I met this girl; she loves me and wants to marry me after we get out. I tried to tell Dexter to leave her alone but he just wasn't going to listen to my warnings, so I had to make a point with him. So here's what I did. On my way to practice I passed the gymnasium and they were re-bricking a wall where a door and window had been added. It was simple, Big Jim, I just picked up a brick and took it to practice and busted Dexter up side his dumb-ass head."

"Where did you hide it, Jessie," I asked him.

"Simple, I hid the brick in my crotch. When the time was right I took it out and ka-blammed his simple ass up side his head with it."

Jessie had practiced for two solid hours, warming up, stretching, calisthenics, hitting drills and scrimmage with a brick between his legs right below his family jewels. Two hours, man. Sweet Jesus. I was in the greatest shape of my life and would barely survive the intensity of the practices we had endured daily. Jessie "hid" a seven inch standard sized brick in his crotch for two sweaty hours, all the while waiting for the right opportunity to crack the skull of the man that was messing with his girl. I had to respect that. Any dude that has ever been in love could respect that. I knew someday I'd meet a woman I'd have to love that much

I guess you might wonder why I call him Jessie Clyde Wallace Junior, the Third. It's because he called himself that on national television in front of the entire NCAA division

II college football watching world. If you have seen the intro's in some games where they allow the starters to introduce themselves, each giving name, major and home town you get the picture and the set-up. When Jessie's time in the spot light came up he said,

"Jessie Clyde Wallace Junior, the Third. Crinimal (yes C-R-I-N-I-M-A-L) Justice. Mobile, Alabama."

He caught every sort of hell imaginable for that particular incident for the rest of the time I knew him at Troy, but in the nicest of ways. Every teammate called Jessie the "Brick House" after that, referencing the head bustin' episode. I called him "23" for second and third (Jessie Clyde Wallace Junior (2) the Third (3)) knowing we had become good friends and I appreciated his loyalty. After Jessie completed his stay at Troy, he contacted me about being in his wedding. He was going to marry the girl he'd busted the dude upside the head over and he was as happy as his last day playing for Bradshaw. He told me just to give him my measurements, shirt, shoes, pants coat and he would handle ordering the tuxes. When I arrived, I went to pick up my tux for final fitting and I must say the tux was the most incredible shade of purple I have seen before and since. He said he had chosen purple because the tux rental place had never rented the Purple Tuxes and he'd be the first user ever and would get a massive discount. Purple patent leather shoes, shirt, cumber bun, bow-tie, everything. It looked like a Parliament Funk-a-delic convention and concert all at once.

A purple damned tuxedo with purple everything to go with it. The only word I had was this; awesome. There was so much purple present it would have given the artist formerly know (and now currently known I guess) as Prince, a woodie.

The funniest part was that I was the only white dude there. I was it. I was called "Ummgawa!" by all the other groomsmen and they laughed about it and so did I. I finally asked,

"Why 'Ummgawa?'" and one of them told me,

"That's what the natives called Tarzan in the Tarzan movies"

I know now that the correct word was "Ungawa" meaning "Go" or "Stop" as used in the old Johnny Weissmuller movies by Tarzan himself when barking orders to the natives, but who was I to argue? I smiled and I went with it. I was honored to be there and was treated like royalty. Jessie had indeed become a Sanitation Engineer, and when he and his new bride left the church, parked out front was a shiny new white Garbage truck (complements of the City of Mobile Sanitation Department) with shiny new silver garbage cans tied to the back. He and his bride climbed into the giant white truck and drove away into what I hoped was the life he described to me over peanut butter and jelly sandwiches.

Jessie Clyde Wallace Junior, the Third, was sure of who he was, what he wanted, and the life he was going to enjoy. I always thought of him as a great friend and a unique individual. There might even be a Jessie Clyde Junior the Fourth or Fifth by now….

We both got a great laugh out of that story and I had another…

Chapter · XII

"Humor is a means of obtaining pleasure in spite of the distressing effects that interface with it."
– Sigmund Freud

I WAS still at bat, as it was, and I had a few more short but good ones to share. It had become obvious to us both the ride was not about to end anytime soon so we'd just talk 'till the damned train ran out of gas, tracks, or just flat out derailed. It's what illegal train car passengers do to pass the time.

My Dad told me one time, "Son, crap in one hand and wish in the other and let me know which one gets full quicker." This meant I could wish for the train to stop, the train company to have the utmost of pity on us (exercising the stupidity/mercy clause) and hire a limousine to take us back to Troy. That particular wish fell in the empty hand, or the "wish" hand. The two of us happened to be in the "dookie" hand and it was completely by our own doings.

Brian Horst was the very man who thought this whole scheme up in the first place (giving me the ability to blame him for it, more on that to follow). I never questioned him as he was the most loyal friend I have ever had. But, he had indeed mentioned (out loud, I just thought it and kept my trap shut) the whole "Train Ride" concept, thus allowing me the right transfer all blame to him. It was Brian's idea, and he was by all accounts insane, so all of this was his fault.

OK, so it's obvious that everything I have written in the above paragraph is bullshit. We were equally to blame for the mess we found ourselves in this day but I thought I might try the curve ball at least once. I'd blame him then he'd blame me for this mess because he and I had a very basic rule we exercised regularly and that was we'd blame each other for everything that went wrong regardless of origin. It was a blood pact we made and one we both got hundreds of miles out of when in use. Late for a date with the girlfriend? Brian made me late. Got a paper he had to finish and missed a date? Jim broke my typewriter. Even if it was true, we agreed it was the best way to put someone off. Twain also said, "Honesty is the best policy- when there's money in it." I tend to believe that in most cases, especially when the "transfer of blame" card must be played or money is involved.

Truthfully, I have told my friends all these 30 plus years later, "Listen, I will be your most loyal friend, but I am going to blame a lot of stuff on you and I expect you to do the same." Try it and see what I mean. As a courtesy you should, on rare occasions, tell your friend what you've blamed on him in case your wife and his happen to meet at the grocery store. Saying you were helping a dude with a brake job while you were both watching college football or racing or baseball or the final four means it is was important to establish set alibis for you and your fellow scapegoats. I didn't think it up; it just is and has been in the guy rules of friendship. It's a dude thing, and I figure if you are reading this then you are neither a sissy nor a canyon yodeler. And more than likely you are not a dude that uses "nor" in a sentence very often either.

Somewhere around the beginning of my football career, we had an occasion to travel to Texas to play a game against Texas A&I, a division 1AA school. They played the likes of Texas, Texas A&M and SMU and they were some ole big beef eater Texas boys. A&I's football team were also one of the dirtiest bunch of SOB's this writer ever played against, other than Southeastern Louisiana (I'll tell that story later). It was hotter than ten Hells on A&I's football field, but us Troy boys were used to it. One hundred degrees for five hours straight was also known as Wednesday to us. We actually enjoyed games because we'd get water every now and again, so as not to violate the NCAA's rule on making liquids available to players playing in over 90% humidity. Bradshaw knew the "big boys," i.e. the NCAA, were watching him and he'd comply with the rules to the letter when he knew he had their attention.

I had never played football against guys that did not "sprecken zee doich" or speak the King's English but that day would definitely be the exception. I am certain I did not spell "sprecken zee doich" right but I must again credit Mr. Twain when he said, "I don't give a damn for a man that can only spell a word one way" even if it's German spelled wrong. What I am saying, in so many words, is that we played against Mexican football boys that were meaner than a future bride at an overcrowded wedding dress clearance sale. These fellas had the rashy ass for a victory and the only way to accomplish that goal was to whip our butts, and rules be damned. I speculated if you made a call to the Department of Immigration and Naturalization Service our team would have won by default that day as ninety percent of A&I's team would have been on a bus back to Guadalajara.

I said earlier Texas A&I played all the big boys and suffered some Texas sized ass whoopin's that year. They had played four homecoming games (not their own mind you) and the season was not half over with yet. I guess you can play your homecoming game as your second or third game if you want too but it told me something about A&I more than their opponents. All I knew was this; these boys were upset and were hungrier for a victory than a fat man on a liquid diet eyeballing a double-cheeseburger. It was the fifth or sixth game of their season and WE were their homecoming opponent. I must tell you now that it was a tremendous mistake to do what they had done. Coach Bradshaw never allowed us to be scheduled for a homecoming game ever. Why?? Because he was sworn to beat the ever lovin' shit out of you and embarrass you in front of your moms, dads, girlfriends, and whoever else you wanted to impress, if you had the misfortune to schedule us in the aforementioned slot. It went bad from the beginning and it got exponentially worse for our opponents as the game progressed.

The rules stated that when an opponent travels to your town to engage you in battle, it is an unwritten (it might have been a written rule somewhere, but not that day) rule that you made comfortable accommodations for your opponents. This basic requirement was intended to ease the burden of the traveling team. This meant having a place to relax with air conditioning and a nice pre-game meal, usually with protein and some carbohydrates to burn during the game. We, on that day, had flown in and were going to play the game and fly back that afternoon. No big deal. It meant the accommodations part for them would at least be simple. The arrangements A&I provided were simple alright. To say we were treated with very little respect was an understatement. When we arrived at the airport, we were met by the ricketiest old smoking bus with no A/C, a driver that could not speak our language, and windows that would not roll down. I could see Bradshaw getting pissed right away meaning I could see him building his case for a pre-game speech to beat 'em all.

When we arrived at the stadium, we were directed to what appeared to be an old Quonset hut but a lot bigger, maybe a Quonset building having no ventilation, no place to rest and, of course, no air conditioning. We arrived hot and sweaty (which we were used to) and basically were lead to the old cow barn to prepare for our contest. As far as a pre-game meal went, a golf buggy with a pull behind trailer loaded with small white boxes arrived about three hours before we were to warm up. Inside those boxes were meals that would appall a starving man, much less athletes expecting a decent pre-game meal. There were two pieces of chicken that were tougher than weathered shoe leather. A baked potato that had been baked by sitting in the sun for a few hours, along with some coleslaw that was so warm it might kill roaches. As God is my witness, I remember the meals as if it were yesterday, sometimes seeing them in a bad dream. I was convinced the chickens that had "given their all" for the meal I was looking at had died of natural causes rather than having been slaughtered. They were probably run to death then cooked or forced to cross "The Road" endlessly until death in some ill-fated chicken Hell.

It was that bad.

Coach Bradshaw never said a word. The warm Cokes we got later were the proverbial icing on the cake. Coach Bradshaw did not say much before, during or after the warm-ups preceding the massacre of which we were about to engage. He was as quiet as a preacher and solemn as a judge in the pre-game speech, which for him was a rarity. I was ready for a hum-dinger cuss fest that might decide where a fellow would wind up after he died. One of those judgment day cussin's that might be brought up at the White Throne in front of your maker after you'd met your end.

Coach Bradshaw was so filled with rage he could barely speak. His pre-game speech was so lackluster it was almost a disappointment; he said a few words and ended it with:

"I'd never treat a guest with the kind of indignity with which we've been treated, men. My plan is to beat these boys one hundred to nothing."

When we huddled up just before the game was to begin, he said just two short but poignant sentences, *"I love you boys. Remember the God Damn Alamo*!!" Inappropriate as Hell, but effective for the circumstances and terrain, plus, the "love you boys" part was a downright lie.

We punished those poor A&I guys like they had kicked our grandmothers. To thoroughly beat Texas A&I into humiliation was Bradshaw's goal that hot Texas day, and he was exceptionally effective. We ran every play we had in the book, a few he made up on the spot, and never let up until the final whistle blew. What happened at the end of the game was what blew my mind.

I feel I must offer this mental pallet cleanser as a side note before I move forward with this story. Consider it the mint sorbet of this story; served just before the best part of the meal, and a mind clearer for sure. At the end of the third quarter, one of my teammates, David, a Yankee redneck from Cocoa Beach Florida and one of the best defensive ends I have ever watched play the game, was complaining about stomach cramps. He would drink water intermittently to try to ease the cramps, but the water combined with the heat only made his condition worsen. I asked him if he had a stomach virus and he confessed to me he had actually eaten the nasty, pre-historic pre-game meal the fools we were playing had provided. My position coach came to us and warned us not to consume any part of the pre-game meal in fear of catching something incurable before our contest. David was hungry and he thought "what the hell," he'd eat it and let his stomach fight it out, French-Canadian Yankee Florida redneck style. David was one of the rare walk-on's that attained a full scholarship after much hard work and perseverance. He was not going to abandon his position for anyone or anything and that included the squirts or puking.

On one memorable play, we had clobbered an opposing player with extreme prejudice and David had gotten piled upon, finding himself at the bottom of the stack (the worse place to find oneself in the college game). Next thing I know, the opposing players are cussing in Spanish and scattering like wildfire with David on the bottom of the pile wide eyed and not moving. I thought he was injured. Eye gouged out, scratched from asshole to appetite, bitten, something. I walked over to him and all I smell is the most awful sick stomach shit odor I have ever had the displeasure to have to endure. I asked him if he was alright and he whispered, "Jimbo, I have shit my uniform, and I am not getting up. Call the trainers over and tell them to bring the stretcher."

They hauled David off the field, took him someplace where he could "hose off" and fix his problem, returning after a few minutes with the smell of hot ass lingering in his uniform. He had dirty Sanchez-ed the Sanchez's.

I happened to be standing near Coach Bradshaw when the game clock was counting down. As the timer reached ten seconds, I could see that something was about to happen based on the way Bradshaw positioned himself. Traditionally, we had two Alabama State Troopers to escort us at every game, and this was no exception…yet. I watched intently…ten…nine…eight…seven…six …as each second ticked off the clock, Bradshaw's stance became more like that of a sprinter preparing himself to run a race. He got sleeker and more focused as each second ticked off… five…four…lower and lower, arms positioned to run a sprint…three…eyes squinting…two….muscles tight and fists clenched…one… Referee blows his whistle ending regulation play.

And it began.

Coach Bradshaw took off running like he was shot from a cannon toward our opponents' sideline. I have always been a people watcher and that day it paid off in spades.

He caught everyone on our sidelines off guard, with the exception of me, since I knew how pissed off he was and his pre-game promise of total annihilation. I saw this coming when the rickety bus pulled up when we got off the plane. I bolted also, running just a few yards behind him. He was an old man but to this day I would not mess with that Marine, and he was on a mission whose end only Bradshaw knew. He was running, full stride, towards the Texas coach for the traditional meeting and shaking of hands at the fifty and I looked ahead at the Texas coach who had no idea what was coming. As we drew closer I noticed the other head coach smiling and extending his hand to congratulate Coach Bradshaw on his decisive victory.

It was a tradition in college football. It was a more public tradition of good sportsmanship, akin to two prize fighters hugging after a hard fought bout. It was also an unwritten courtesy, kinda like the home team taking care of the visitor's pre-game accommodations.

Coach Bradshaw caught the Texas head coach under his neck with his right hand and proceeded to roll him over backwards with such proficiency that the Texas State Troopers thought he might be trying to kill the coach they had been assigned to take a bullet for. I was there and, I swear, the two troopers unsnapped their holsters and had their hands on their service revolvers out of instinct. The two Alabama State Troopers did the same, I guess because the Texas boys had unsnapped theirs. I stood in silence waiting for the next words or deeds that would follow this unpredictable scene. Somebody was about to get shot and I was right there to witness it. Bradshaw had the Texas A&I Coach pinned down by his throat and there were a total of four pistols with their holsters unsnapped and hands on right there on the fifty yard line after a football game! Bradshaw said with a cold chill in his voice that usually spelled death for the hearer shortly thereafter and went something like this,

"If you no-good-mother-fucking-sons-of-bitches ever treat us or anyone else like we were treated today, I'll beat your asses 150 to nothing if we ever meet again!!" He delivered that warning with the ease of a seasoned drill instructor and the confidence of a preacher at a revival, warning his audience about Hell if they didn't straighten up and live right. The opposing coach never uttered a word in protest; he just laid there and took his punishment with Bradshaw's hand securely around his throat. I'm convinced now, looking back on it, that any sound made by A&I's coach meant Charlie Bradshaw, USMC, would have presented him with the business end of his wind-pipe, showing him the asshole end just seconds before his demise.

By then there was a crowd of 120 players in a tight circle and every one there knew he meant it. We collected ourselves and rode the smoking bus back to the airport where we flew back to Troy. We beat Texas A&I 87–0, still the worse ass beating that team had ever taken.

The only two people that were cheering for us that day wore guns, had unsnapped (meaning they were ready to draw and fire if necessary) unexpectedly, and had matching Alabama State Trooper uniforms. Hell, even our cheerleaders did not attend the game, more of a budgetary issue rather than a precautionary one, and I guess that was a good thing for them at least. We had steaks waiting that evening when we returned to Troy, compliments of Coach Charlie Bradshaw himself, the toughest screw to ever walk a sideline in college football. There was no hero's welcome for us, typical in division two football, but what I witnessed that day would have gotten any coach, save for Bear Bryant, fired. I choose to think, that on that particular day Charlie Bradshaw did indeed love us.

Remember the Alamo indeed.

Chapter · XIII

AS OUR seemingly endless train ride continued, Brian had his turn at the "microphone" for lack of a better term, and he had a good one. We had, in all actuality, only been riding for about an hour and twenty minutes or so, but it seemed like a long time to two dudes heading to who knows where. I guess it was just my small voice inside telling me, "You complete and total dumb ass…it's probably a very good idea to keep this one to yourself for a while if and when it ends."

Millions of thoughts raced through my head: Did God exist and did he intend for this to happen? Can a Reuben sandwich be made with anything besides corned beef? If the Venus De Milo had arms, would she be famous? Why "corn-on-the-cob" wasn't just called corn, and "corn-OFF-the-cob" given the special title?

After Brian and I became full-fledged brothers in the frat, we felt free to create as much mischief as we could muster short of getting kicked out. We did, after all, need a place to sleep. On a few auspicious occasions, Brian and I had a contest going to see who could (a) get a picture made with the fattest girl at a frat party (b) who could "Gator" the wildest and not break any bones, (c) who could come up with something we had never done before and not get ourselves mortally wounded or killed and (d) who could consume the most beer, oysters, steak or anything else that required any degree of measuring, just short of pissing up a wall, to ultimately declare a winner? Brian and I were the right guys for the jobs and we were always ready for the challenge.

To start with, my frat threw the wildest and most legendary parties in Troy University history. The parties attracted more women than hair on a blue sport coat. If you recall, the girl to guy ratio was an impressive 7.9:1 and that did not account for married dudes, dudes with steady girlfriends, and, well, guys that liked other guys. That made the actual ratio more like 13:1 or more. It was heaven. It must be said that I feel strongly concerning the "to each his/her own" rule. I liken it to vegetarians. I fully support vegetarians. More steak for those of us that can truly appreciate it! Anyway, shoplifting heads of lettuce was pointless (Rolls Royce vs. Volkswagen). The women of Troy, and Alabama in general, were spectacular to say the least. Man, oh man, it was one of the greatest things I loved about the South. We made sure that all the good looking women were served complimentary drinks and lots of them. Most times this helped with bringing forth the "relaxed moral code" for the hardcore and late-staying party chicks.

I must stop here to clarify a term I learned in college. It's one that I heard over and over and it actually sounded like a legitimate college degree. It was described as the "MRS" degree. This was where a father and mother sent their lovely daughter to a college to find a husband. I am not kidding you here. I was stunned when I first learned of the phenomenon and then came to recognize it as absolute truth. I won't say that all young ladies did it, or were forced into it by their parents, but many were on that track. I dated an awesome looking girl one time and I was invited to meet her parents by her on the second and last date we ever had with each other. It was a spooky realization as she showed up in some of the weirdest places after I told her that I was not interested in her. Her dad even called me and asked me if I thought something was wrong with her. It was here that I learned the full effect of the "MRS" degree and its truthful existence. I answered her dad with the most careful of words as he loved his daughter, but he had no idea of the fervor in which she was trying to fulfill her husbandly desires. The conversation I had with the "MRS" degree girl's dad was my first and last. The day a guy learns of the mysterious "MRS" degree it changes his hunting techniques forever. This was after all, L.A. (Lower Alabama) and free steak was not the only thing that could find a guy staring down the wrong end of a shotgun.

Coach Bradshaw always coached us to keep our heads on a swivel. Now you might wonder what in the hell that had to do with what we are discussing here. I will tell you it means a whole lot. The term meant numerous things that I later related to in life. My first experience with hearing the term (used about me) came in my first college football game against the Fort Benning Doughboys. We were playing a team that consisted of dudes that were in the Army and the only qualifications for being on their football team were—could you fog up a mirror, and were you willing? That was it. They had both young and old dudes on the team.

When we went to play, we looked like a million dollars in our warm-up drills. Our execution was perfect before and during the game which we won handily. Bradshaw would have it no other way. I was traveling on the team with the big boys, almost unheard of back in those days. I had made the Varsity team as a freshman and was proud of it. My uniform was spotless (I say that because it would not last very long) and we had lost the opening toss and were kicking off to the Doughboys. I was on the kickoff team and you basically had to be a kamikaze pilot with a helmet on as it was a virtual suicide mission and injury minefield for its members. One would basically run wide ass open down the field trying to break the wedge formation containing the man running the pigskin. Again, if you think wedge formation is your skivvies in your crack, go back to redecorating and forget this story.

I was prancing down the field running towards the pre-described wedge formation and, WHAM!! I got the tee total moose piss knocked out of me from my blindside. This was my first play in college sports and I thought it was going to be more like Rudy sacking the quarterback in his only play from scrimmage at Notre Dame. I barely remember the hit. I was focusing on the wedge and did not yet have my head on a swivel, as Bradshaw so perfectly put it. I learned that day that a 42 year old man with the willingness to play the college game could be as hard as a blind man attempting to do calculus on an Abacus. I do remember seeing back down the field, in mid air, before I hit the ground and the old dude telling me,

"Bet you didn't think an old army soldier had it in him did you, sonny?"

I had learned the distinct difference between youthful exuberance and old age and treachery. The old dude even helped me up and was kind enough to aim me towards my side lines as not to embarrass me too severely. I truly did not remember my own name he hit me so hard. It was the third quarter before I fully realized I was not in high school anymore. He hit me so hard that when I came to, my clothes had gone out of style. Why do I mention it here? We always watched film of the game on Sunday afternoon following game day. When this particular film was about to begin, Coach Bradshaw began with,

"Today men, we are going to learn early what the term 'keep your head on a swivel' means."

It was the opening play of the opening game of our year and the film was as crystal clear as hindsight usually proves to be. It showed me getting my ass handed to me by that old man who called me sonny on that first college play this old boy ever played. It was a sterling example of what not to do as it was played repeatedly for grinding salt in the wound purposes for me and instruction for my teammates. He pointed out the fact that the old man helped me up and aimed me to my own sidelines. He finished it with,

"Welcome to college football, Jim Hall."

OK, OK, so you are wondering how in the Hell does "keeping your head on a swivel" and talking to a girl's Dad relate to each other? I am about to share that knowledge with you now.

Be on the lookout.

Peripheral vision has more than one meaning. Anticipate everything you have knowledge of. Be aware of oncoming trouble from every direction. If you keep blinders on you will get your ass cold-cocked like I did and, unlike me, hopefully yours will not be caught on film. Not just on the field of play but in life also. If you are going to date a girl you'd better find out how big of a gun collection her Dad has and if he worships the ground she stands on. If he does, be careful, very careful. If he doesn't worship the ground she stands on…run like a bat out of Hell. Dads whose daughters have been sent to acquire an "MRS" degree are on a mission from God. A smart man will recognize it quickly and avoid it. Sometimes a blind squirrel finds an acorn, i.e. he is able to circumvent the "MRS" degree even after he finds himself in the quicksand of the vortex that is an Alabama girl's pursuit of a husband. Absorb this knowledge and live. Don't, and live married.

Here, what I have come to learn, is the very most important relationship question a man will ever have to answer in his relationship with his wife or girlfriend, and quite possibly the central point of every question he may have to field for the rest of his natural married life. I have marveled at its simplicity and complexity. It's a "duality of man" type of question and one for the ages.

"Do I look fat in this?"

Every man's handling of this question will determine his future happiness if he intends to stay with the asker of said question. We've all been asked this at one time or the other. You are on dangerous ground so be careful. Short term, or maybe long term, celibacy is at risk. Answering too quickly is as dangerous as saying,

"Yes! You do indeed look fat in that!"

She will think you are panicked. Waiting too long to answer and it's long, cold showers for you my friend. I have devised the perfect answer even if I am lying my ass off.

"Do I look fat in this?" she asked.

"No sweetie! I'd look fat in that, but you? Well, you look like a million dollars!"

Feel free to claim this answer as your own but be careful of how frequently you use it or variations thereof. Remember to keep your head and its contents on a swivel at all times.

On the night of the biggest party of the year, Brian and I had a bet on who could have a picture made with the least attractive and most gravitationally challenged female in attendance. I was a goal-oriented young man and wanted to win the contest as much as Brian did. I had baited the field as a precaution by inviting Suzy the Floozy's sister to the shindig, as she had taken an extreme liking to Brian after the wedding ceremony for Dan the Man (our Rippy Mart buddy) and Suzy. Brian was a charmer (regardless of where we were and how pretty or ugly the girls were) and it had apparently left somewhat of an impression on the heart and mind of Suzy's sister. I must make it clear that Brian was the hands down winner of every "picture made with a fat girl" contest we ever had. I knew to control my alcohol intake on these contest days and it was the first true sign of my maturity I can recall.

I was working the bar. It was a giant wooden table with Oobeedo punch in a 75 gallon aquarium with a fifty gallon aquarium full of the purple death right next to it. I filled Suzy's sister full of the elixir and always aimed her towards Brian. Honestly, I probably was not as truthful about Brian's feelings towards her when I was pumping her full of swill and aiming her towards her toward her unsuspecting target. I guess it was akin to cheating but, what the Hell? The game was afoot and he'd do the same to me. He always found the photographer and had a "cheek squeezer" picture made with her. Now I will tell you that she was a good 275 pounds and could hold her liquor. I recall her crossing the line of tipsy to drunk (after a good two gallons of purple Jesus) and she wanted her man…Brian. She actually got to where she would bull rush any female that talked to Brian for more than five minutes out of unfounded jealousy. Poor Brian was so lit he did not know I had primed her for love, with Brian being her target. At around midnight the hard cores were all that remained and Large Marge was snorting like a cow in heat. Usually when we wanted the party to end we just turned up the heat in the party room and that was as effective a party ender as the cops showing up with pepper spray. Brian and Large Marge were slow dancing (he was in full grip of his faculties at the time) and he was hell bent to win the picture with a fat girl contest.

And win he did.

I turned the heat up. Way up. I could see her turning green around the gills and Brian was bound and determined to win the prize of a case of ice cold Dixie Beer (that we always split; remember, we were poor). What happened next was too perfect to even hope for. Brian was slow dancing with Large Marge and she unexpectedly but predictably puked all over him, the dance floor, the walls and I think even the ceiling. This was thick purple industrial puke too. I am talking purple projectile funk from the belly of the whale with what appeared to me to be at least two pepperoni pizzas mixed in with it. Brian slipped in it and, to his horror; she fell on top of him. I threatened the photographer's life if he did not snap off multiple pictures of the mayhem. It was the single funniest thing I had ever seen up to that point in my life. If you have ever seen something so funny that it made you go limp and lose your breath before you even made a single sound then you have an idea of how funny that event was. Brian woke up to 24 of the coldest long neck Budweiser beers a human ever drank. Dixie was not good enough to cover this bet and I gladly handed over the finest cuts of meat to our liquor store friend for the case of suds.

The last thing I recall about that night was having to call Suzy to come get her much bigger sister from the frat house dance floor. She brought with her six or seven of the biggest humans I have ever seen to carry her out and tidy the place up. The scariest part was how quick they arrived. I guess it was her cousins, as I faintly recall some of the faces from the wedding. They were friendly enough, willing to hose down the room she had blown chunks in and we let them. They had cleaning supplies and did a yeoman's job cleaning up the evidence from the events that transpired that evening. It was almost like they were cleaning up a murder scene to keep a relative from going to jail. Destroying the evidence before the cops could show up.

Brian kept his head on a swivel from that day forward. I was the old Army Soldier he had to keep a look out for and now he knew it. It made life more interesting, I must confess, and he would get me back in the most satisfying of ways.

This train ride was getting better…Oysters, "gatoring" and new stuff to do came next.

Chapter · XIV

It had been getting hotter and we were moving much faster as we continued traveling north. We started to speculate about whether or not our kids, wives and family members would even believe us—if we ever told them about the train ride. It didn't matter as the train was riding on its prescribed way and we were helpless to change its course. But, we were the architects of our own misfortune and had no one else to blame.

My stomach had started to growl and it reminded me of a contest of sorts that Brian and I had on a weekend we recalled as Oyster Fest. Our Fraternity had had an oyster bake, basically another excuse to party and get, as my ghetto brothers put it, "get tow up from da flow up"… that's "get tore up from the floor up" for my non-jive speaking readers. These social occasions were mandatory for all. Brian and I had been designated as procurement officers for the soirée and were charged with ordering the oysters and beer (no Dixie or PBR mind you, were talking the good stuff: Keg Miller and Bud). We had a defined budget, but Brian and I were somewhat connected in the food and alcohol area. This was our biggest party of the spring quarter and every sorority and GDI girl (non-Greek affiliation; AKA-"God-Damn Independent") on campus was invited. It usually meant that our frat of seventy dudes would be matched with over 500 (not all at once mind you) gorgeous, thirsty co-eds showing off their bikini bodies. I will say we put more effort into that particular outing than any other we had during the year. We used the gathering as a vehicle to strengthen our numbers and it was effective. We usually invited between twenty five and thirty five prospective pledges (rushees) and got them knee walking drunk, then lied to them about how great being a Pi Kappa Phi was. On that particular day, it was friggin terrific to be a member. College was like anything in life, it is what you make it and Brian and I made it good every chance we got, in our own private sorta way.

Brian and I manned the oyster shucking table which meant we stood over two very large tables and shucked oysters for beautiful women all day. Brian and I had a system worked out. We'd feed oysters to a select few chicks and then get them to feed us cold beers in exchange for a steady flow of the oceanic snot-locker innards that waited inside a mollusk shell. I liked oysters, but not better and never in place of a great, or even mediocre steak. I could take 'em or leave 'em (the oysters) but in this case it was a way to get ice cold Miller High Life on draft and check out some purty dang good lookin' women., We also used the party as an excuse to dig a giant water filled hole in the back yard of our house with a massive water slide off the upper rear deck as a chute of sorts down to the water filled pit. We literally transformed the back yard into a college-boy paradise of beer, oysters and hot chicks, all motivated to slide down a five story slide that could rip the chastity belt off a King's daughter into ice cold water. Drunk. Shall I go on?

This party went on for what seemed like days, but really lasted until either the cops came, the beer ran out, the oysters ran out, the chicks all left or any combination of the four. Brian and I had a few girls we were "Big Brothers" to. This meant that for some odd reason (maybe lots of oysters and beer) they had selected us to be affiliated with their particular sorority as adjunct male members of the clan. I was deeply concerned, as I would question any organization that had us as members. Brian and I were always ready for a good time and the party girls we knew could hang with most men and out drink most bikers. There were two particular girls, Patty and Samantha, who were the coolest. They were both beautiful and we were all just friends. They were fun to hang out with, had wealthy parents, nice cars and loved Brian and I like brothers. Pat and Sam were like Brian and me in some ways, inseparable as friends and always looking for a way to make life more interesting. The biggest difference is that they were well funded by loving fathers that did not send them to school to meet a husband. I had met both Pat and Sam's dads and they both were Troy football fans so they knew me first by my skills on the field and by friendship of their daughters second.

Breaking here for just a moment, I must pause to explain a military term that my Father, a Marine, and Coach Charlie Bradshaw both called "Mutinous Glances." I used to hear about them from my Dad when I got old enough to have the passing thought that "I can take my old man." Every young dude goes through this phase. It's akin to suicide if you pursue the thought beyond its logical end. Letting go of the thought of takin' out the old man, fueled by youthful testosterone and blatant stupidity, is the first true sign of intelligence. A mutinous glance is any lingering derogatory look by a subordinate showing displeasure concerning orders given. In other words, copping an attitude when you don't agree with something your dad has told you to do OR not to do.

Let me share with you that I was not one of the smart fellows that passed on challenging my dad to his rightful throne. It happened one Saturday morning after a long lengthy night out with my hometown buddies. I had come home from Troy in my sophomore year (the term sophisticated moron comes to mind) and was in the best shape of my life. I was benching over 400 pounds and could squat 700 pounds easily. I could also run like a deer and all day if necessary. On one memorable Friday, my Dad gave me the order to be "high and tight, 6:00 am cutting grass." My Dad was not a military junkie as far as his dealings with me or our family. He was never a *Great Santini* dad, ever. The Marine Corps had such a strong effect on him, as it does most men who have been in the Corps. He never let go of the military way and its influence on his personal and business life were as beneficial as a college degree. I saw it as a very positive thing for him.

After my long night that ultimately led to an early morning arrival to my bed, I was awakened by the sound of the lawn mower running. This was not good. I had a great relationship with my dad, but he had his rules and I lived in his home. I had dang well intended to cut that grass and I flew into my shorts, shoes and shirt in seconds and down the steps I went out into the yard where my father was making quick work of the task at hand. I waited at the edge of the driveway for my father to make a pass at the end of the neat straight rows he was painting with the lawn mower. It was a beautiful day and I remember it so vividly because of the lesson I learned that day. Don't mess with Marines regardless of their age, height, weight or perceived intelligence. I stood a good foot taller than my Dad and outweighed him by a better seventy five pounds. I asked him to hand the lawn mower over to me and I would finish the grass cutting duties. He glanced up, did a perfect military style 180 degree turn and headed back in the direction he had just come from, ignoring my request with a curt smile and a passing glance. Not a mutinous glance mind you, but a glance that said,

"Go back to bed you dingle berry."

I was instantly pissed off by his calm nature. My body language went from friendly and inviting to an "I can take you old man" stance. I was twenty and knew better. I had considered it a time or two when I was 14 and stupid, maybe once when I was 18 but thought better of it. I shoulda been smarter now, at the ripe old age of 20.

When my dad passed by me again I was standing kinda-sorta in the yard so he would have to maneuver the mower around me and not foul up his neat pattern. When he got close enough and hesitated, I grabbed the mower by one hand and sternly told dad to let me finish the damn yard. He looked at me and calmly told me it was OK, he'd finish the task and I could go back to bed and sleep "it" off, which further pissed me off. He had both hands on the mower handle. I took my right hand and placed it on the outside of his right hand and with my left hand I slid his hand so I had full grip on the mower. I gave him the one and only mutinous glance I have ever given him saying:

"I am up, I am pissed, and you are gonna let me finish cutting the friggin yard!"

And then it happened.

In a blur, I was down on my back in a pretzel hold with my legs bent over myself with my knees basically on my ears and what appeared to a be a nut sack hanging in my face. I was going to bite them out of anger but I realized quickly they were mine. My 190 pound Marine father had just felled a 270 pound freight train (yours truly), dropped him like a used prophylactic and humbled him to the point of hollering for mercy. He never let go of the lawn mower. He could twist my pinky finger and every part of my dumb-assed body racked in pain. I had been formally introduced to what the inside of a can of whoop-ass must have looked like. He smiled and let me up. I was sore as the underdog in a prize fight after that particular lesson, never forgetting to never mess with a Marine, especially my own personal Marine, ever again.

Mutinous glances also are used by fathers when their young daughters pass into womanhood. I have two lovely daughters now and when I catch older men staring at them I whip out the industrial strength mutinous glances. I do it when younger boys look at them too. I love seeing the scared looks on their faces and the smell of pee.

Let me get back on course here and back to Pat and Sam. When our oyster party ended, Brian, Pat, Sam and I were riding in a new Pontiac Trans-Am Sam's father had bought her for her 18th birthday. It was red as whore's lipstick and fast as greased lightning. It had T-tops and they would ride everywhere with them off. There was a particular hill that we would jump on occasion and you could get some serious air if you went fast enough. It was really a cross road that dropped off on both sides so it was easy to accomplish. The four of us were riding after the party with me in the front passenger seat, Brian and Pat in the rear, with Sam driving. She asked if we wanted to jump Bandit Hill, named for Smokey and the Bandit, and we were along for the ride so we agreed. The first jump was at thirty miles an hour or so, decent jump and major stomach butterflies. The next jump was at forty five miles an hour and I tell you we got good air and a great landing. Sam had gotten the bug and wanted to jump one more time. As we approached the jump, the side road that intersected the jump had a car coming on it and no stop sign. I warned Sam of the oncoming car, but instead of stopping and restarting the jump, she floor boarded it so as to outrun the potential disaster coming from our left.

Burt Reynolds would have gotten an erection if he could have witnessed the jump we made. We hit the jump at eighty five miles per hour. I know this because I glanced at the speedometer when I told her to slow down. We launched like we were shot out of a cannon. We were so high off the asphalt that I had come about halfway out of my T-top catching myself with my out stretched arms to keep me from coming out of the airborne vehicle. I looked over Sam, noting the demonic smile she had on her face. She was just as far out of her T-top as I was out of mine, with the exception of her holding firmly to the leather wrapped steering wheel. In my peripheral vision I could see Brian and Pat squished up in the rear seat compartment. When we hit the pavement, all hell broke loose.

The car landed nose down first and then slammed onto the black top with a force so strong that it broke the two front alloy wheels away from the car, the hood flew up, front spoilers flew off and my door opened by itself. It must have been a sight to behold; but, save for us and the crossing car; no one was there to see it. The other car just kept on driving and we had traveled a good 110 feet in the air before crashing to a stop.

We pushed the car off to the side of the street as best as we could, walked back to the frat house, and Sam, as cool as a cucumber, called the Troy police and reported it stolen only after she waited a few hours to make the whole thing look right, as she put it. She had trashed a brand spanking new car with a little less than 450 miles on it and did not even blink an eye. When her dad came to see about the whole incident, he drilled Brian and me with the skill of an FBI agent on the trail of a serial killer. I realized then that whoever married Sam had better watch himself and hoped someone, maybe Sam's dad, might give her future husband the "keep your head on a swivel" speech out of mercy, or as a warning. I am sure Sam's heartbeat never got above normal after she committed her felonious ride. She never blamed any of us, casually wiped down her prints from the steering wheel and door handle, and later called the cops. Her dad suspected foul-play, but the Troy cops' investigation proved that Sam, Pat and Brian and Myself were indeed attending a party at the Pi Kappa Phi frat house at the time of the crime. Everyone there was so wasted they could not remember if we were there or not. Fraternal unity rules states that you cover your brother's ass whenever called upon.

Her dad used many mutinous glances on us after that episode too. I wonder if he was a Marine too, or just a dad watching out for his good looking daughter… or both.

Chapter · XV

THE NEXT day, after the Oyster Fest and the total wasting of Sam's car, Brian and I had a great idea cooked up and we were eager to implement it. I figured we'd just been passengers in Sam's felonious trashed out red Trans-Am adventure and had been quizzed nearly to death, so why not. To top it off we'd dodged more mutinous glances from Sam's dad than any two innocent dudes should have to handle in one afternoon. It was a difficult task, covering Sam's ass and our own and maintaining our innocence while never breaking eye contact with Sam's dad. It was Sunday, known as "the Sabbath" to any respectable six day a week heathen hailing from those parts. Most of the folks nodding off in church were either hung over or tired from late night activities generally reserved for college age sinners like Brain and I. We both knew better than to darken the door of any church back then. We figured our presence alone might cause its roof to cave in, jettisoning us into some double secret Hell as punishment for all the other unconverted sinners getting killed because of our attendance, Old Testament collateral damage style. I figured any preacher could recognize us, inside or outside of church, as two dudes needing redemption of some sort so we stayed clear of the house of God. We reckoned it was part of a preacher's job description, recognizing sinners and converting them over, if you wanted "it" or not. We avoided the church so we could get as much of the other "it" out of our systems now, and be better folk later. That theory was a sound one, but only if our "jumping off" spot didn't sneak up on us both unexpectedly, like it usually does. We survived the aforementioned interrogation with flying colors and made sure Sam knew she owed us for keeping her malcontented backside clear of trouble.

Pat had a sweet car too, so she and Sam still had a nice ride until Sam's dad replaced her car after the insurance paid off. I still maintained that any guy that married Sam was in for the ride of his life. I believed she could commit murder, pass a polygraph and shop for a new pair of shoes the next day with her biggest concern being whether or not the shoes matched her purse and belt. Her dad obviously knew he had a Jezebel on his hands in Samantha. She was as wild and beautiful as the crimson tide that grew in the medians between Alabama interstates, but could bullshit better than any human I had ever met. I thought a little differently of her after the Trans-Am incident, though not in a bad way mind you, but different just the same. I never let her position herself behind me or let her get out of my peripheral and I never bent at the waist if I dropped anything around her, if you know what I mean. I kept my eyes on her at all times whenever we might find ourselves in the same room or in the same state for that matter.

When Brian and I made it back to the frat house to crash out that evening, we had gotten the idea that we could keep on drinking the cold Miller and Bud keg beer as everyone had dispersed or passed out at the antebellum mansion we lovingly called home. Most of the guys who were still awake could barely remember their own names much less stop us from our appointed rounds, meaning screw with them as much as possible. Brian would sometimes use the opportunity to ask to borrow money from the drunken brothers as, in his esteemed opinion, it was indeed better to receive than to give. It wasn't stealing if he asked to borrow it and the lender didn't remember the loan so all was well. We figured it was a good way to express brotherly love and give the borrower the pleasure of loaning money to forward our mission. It was the primary reason I never got out of control due to excess liquid consumption, and for good reason. My wise Dad told me to always keep your wits about you and maintain a modicum of control in all situations and Coach Bradshaw taught me to keep my head on a swivel. Both of these pieces of advice combined applied in a big way concerning this situation. Passing out with money in your pocket was the fastest way to make honest broke men dishonest. That class is called justified blame transfer 101.

I felt at times I was Brian's designated driver *of life* for the time we went to school together, but I also knew he had my back regardless of whatever situation might arise. I was the older dude and it was all good as far as I was concerned, as Brian and I were the proverbial Dean Martin and Jerry Lewis of our day. It never mattered how crappy any situation got, Brian could make me laugh in the middle of a tornado or a forest fire.

After much searching (the place looked like an armed jungle incursion had been fought there) we discovered there was one remaining keg of Miller High Life. In truth, we had strategically placed it where it could not be easily seen and used later as an emergency keg if needed. We planned to have a small gathering the next day (the two of us) and maybe a few others if they wanted a little "hair of the dog" to help make life a little easier to bear. We also rounded up about twenty dozen oysters from the various and sundry serving tables scattered about the festival grounds behind our frat house and planned to make a good meal that evening. One particular bunch of oysters sat in melted ice and was a little on the warm side, so we decided to ice them back down and eat anyway. That would prove to be a huge mistake as Brian and I ate the ripe oysters leaving none to waste. Later that evening we both started to feel crappy, sweaty and feverish, with a heavy dose of nausea and the atomic squirts tossed in for good measure. I puked so hard that I actually choked up something chewy and really bad tasting like a cross between corn chips, sweet and sour sauce and peanut brittle. I swallowed it because I realized it was my own butthole (not really but you get the picture), so you'll know how sick I was. Brian and I drove to the college infirmary which was managed by the nursing staff from our heralded nursing school located conveniently on the main campus. He and I got a four day rest from the warmed-over, bacteria-laced oyster food poisoning we had so stupidly invited upon ourselves. We drove no faster than 15 miles an hour to the on-campus infirmary as we had to stop to puke, primarily from the warm oyster bugs that were taking a giant dump in our stomachs and secondarily from the motion of the car we were driving. When we finally made it to the infirmary, we had to crawl from the car to the door, and then crawl to the nurses' desk to proclaim our separate, but similar, illnesses.

During that time Samantha and Patricia came to visit us, sneaking in pizza and beer (I don't know how mind you) on the fourth and last day of our visit. While we enjoyed our private party, our nurse walked in the room, paused, then declared us well and dismissed us with great speed. When we left, Brian and I each had a set of hemostats, scissors, bandages and a few good sets of scrubs to wear around campus to remind us of our stay. We were not dopers so we did not know what to do with most of the paraphernalia we had confiscated. It just seemed like the right thing to do at the time so we did it. The scrubs were cool though, and I rotated them into my wardrobe from that day forward. I think Brian did too; difference was he told folks he was pre-med, which they believed, and that was cool by me.

The next week, we were sawing away on the remaining keg of beer we hid in our room and came up with a brilliant plan. I asked Brian if he had ever car surfed. Car surfing was where one individual drove, preferably in reverse, while the other stood on the hood or roof of the car purely for the thrill of it as a challenge to one's manhood. I had learned of car surfing when I was just a lad in high school with the three guys I primarily hung out with. My three best friends in school and I all were in the same grade so we grew up together from the seventh grade until graduation scattered us to the four winds. I will confine the car-surfing portion of this tale to Brian and me, but I will share a funny thing that happened to us while we were still young and did not know better. Oh, it involves trespassing, near-death and scaffolding, so just read on.

It was the year between my sophomore and junior years in high school and a new way to divide one's loyalty was about to blossom in the small community I lived in. A 125 year tradition was about to be broken; a new high school was about to be built, a true sign of the growth my county experienced due to the completion of the new interstate (the very same interstate one I had gotten the ride from Hell on from the sheriff for allegedly blowing up mailboxes) and the increase in population from the thruway. Our new school, Lithia Springs High school, was under construction and off limits to all but the construction crews working therein. This amounted to a gold plated invitation for my squad to go inside and have a look around. The school itself was so big you could drive a car around in it, which we also did without damage, and got a good laugh out of it. In the gymnasium "area," which was all you could call it then as it was not complete, we found a massive, roll able, two story scaffolding that begged to be used for something other than its intended purposes. We figured one guy could climb all the way to the top of the scaffolding and stand in the center while we all manned a leg of the scaffolding at the bottom. We'd then unlock the wheels, spinning the scaffolding in a circle with the man on top challenged to keep his carcass on by trying to center his self on the platform. It really seemed like a great idea at the time and a brilliant way to fill in the blank spot between breakfast and lunch.

On that particular day, we had a fifth amigo wanna-be named Andy, and he was the first to climb up the two story twenty-five foot high scaffolding used to paint the ceiling of the gymnasium. It was ironic as Andy was the most cautious of the five of us and it (his caution) was the primary reason he did not get quicker acceptance in our group of four. Agreeing to at least try anything stupid and dangerous was like an American Express card; it was a sign of membership in our little club and membership had its privileges. I think we rode Andy pretty hard about being such a pussy when it came to being what we called adventurous, and I think in retrospect he was definitely the smartest of our bunch. Of course, all hindsight is 20/20 and everyone can pick the winning lottery numbers after they have been dropped, so we'd just tell Andy to shut his cake-hole and stop his whining. As Andy climbed up to the top of the scaffolding he told us to give him a minute to center himself on top so not fly off too fast, a request we basically ignored. We hollered up to him that he had thirty seconds and he'd better hurry up and stop with the caution crap. In fifteen seconds we started pushing the scaffold in a tight circle with the four of us, all linemen, manning each wheel. We had taken the precaution of sweeping the floor to clear the path for the scaffold as we were sure if it hit any object on the floor and toppled over, somebody was going to the hospital. That would be a bad thing as it was government property and we were indeed trespassers. I was amazed at how quickly we were able to get the scaffold with its twitchy passenger up top moving when we took all that into consideration.

Within a minute we had the structure moving as fast as our legs could run, and I mean run wide-ass-open. I think we had run in the circle for about thirty seconds when we heard Andy holler,

"Slow down, I'm losing my center on the platform!"

Hell, we just thought it was signal to run faster so we ran faster. Andy hollered louder,

"I'm slipping…slow down damn it!!"

We ran a little faster, with Andy protesting all the while in a half screech, half holler that made fingernails on a chalkboard sound like elevator music. We finally had reached the end of our endurance, which seemed to us to be a good ten minutes, but more likely about two.

Andy was hollering while we just stood back and watched the scaffold spin, amazed at what we'd created. I must say it now that the scaffolding must have had a great set of ball bearing wheels as it did not seem to slow down much after we stopped pushing. Next thing you know we hear Andy scream,

"I'm sliding off!"

We look up and Andy is hanging onto the spinning joyride, fully extended, and hanging on to the outside of the rigging. He was all the way off the scaffold looking down at us, eyes as big as two fried eggs, knuckles as white as Crisco shortning, in sheer terror and hanging on for dear life. The scaffold was still spinning really fast but everything seemed like it was in slow motion at that point. We all chuckled for a second and then rushed to attempt to slow down the scaffold so Andy could make a safe exit. It was like trying to enter a revolving door and if you timed your entry improperly you'd get your bell rung or knocked on your ass then run over. We could slow Andy down then we could ride him for screaming like a little girl.

I reached my leg of the scaffolding first with the others to follow as we were sure that if one person attempted to slow the spinning structure down it might topple over. All of a sudden we heard Andy scream,

"I can't hold on anymore!!"

When we looked up at Andy, fully extended, he let go and I swear he flew like a Frisbee off the top of that scaffolding. Andy had gotten what appeared to be good air as he traveled at least thirty five feet out from his point of launch. It was his high trajectory and the speed he was spinning that contributed to his distance traveled. He landed with a splat, face down, and did not move a muscle after he slid in the dust for another good twenty feet. The four of us looked at each other, and I am sure, simultaneously said,

"Oh shit, Andy's dead!!"

We could not even walk over to where Andy was laying motionless. So, we did the next best thing and did what most dudes would do when faced with the consequences of something that proved to be exceptionally stupid, such as death by scaffolding on government property.

We ran.

I mean we ran as fast as we could, outside to where our car was parked to formulate a plan on how to either fake Andy's death or come up with some alibi to keep from being convicted of murder. We had been standing there creating an alibi, all four of us injecting our limited knowledge of covering up a dead guy's ending for a good five minutes when we hear someone coming from inside the school. We again prepared ourselves to run, as we had made the trip to the school in Andy's '65 Mustang. It would fit that Andy might have decided to end his own life by first spinning then climbing up the scaffolding and lastly flinging himself off all by himself. It was all we had and we were going to run with it.

The next thing you know, out walks Andy who asked us,

"Why in the Hell did you guys run?" all the while slapping dust off clothes, unscratched and un-dented by his flight.

"Who's next?" he asked.

We said we thought we'd heard someone in the building so we split to see who it was. We were lying sons-of-bitches and cowardly deserters to boot. Andy had officially become the fifth amigo that day, but only after we made him buy us all barbeques for being such a pussy.

Note to self: stay off spinning scaffoldings on guv'ment land.

Brian and I had consumed a good portion of the remaining keg of Miller (not all of it mind you, just most of it) and the sun had began to set and the car surfing idea was fresh on our minds so we made a go of it. Brian went first and never got over 35 miles per hour like the girl he was. I did not want to be responsible for calling Brian's mom and telling her he had gotten injured standing on top of a car I was driving while *he* was intoxicated. Brian did a roof surf, hood surf and a trunk surf all while I was driving down Three Notch Street in reverse. My turn came and Brian took the wheel, excited by the new activity he learned from his big city friend. We started up past the Piggly Wiggly building speed and headed straight for our house, in reverse of course, so we could turn into our driveway or the Wiggly parking lot just in case we might be seen by the local law. I am not sure how long a jail sentence might have been for car surfing, but I am sure the local law might come up with something suitable if we were caught, and toss in a resisting arrest, night-stick beat down for free.

I had made it to the top of Brian's birth-control mobile of a car, a 1972 Dodge Swinger, tan in color with a disco era (it was 1983, the last breath of the most hated era in all of music) interior that was surely approved and possibly designed by Elton John or any member of the Village People. It was a dependable car but it repelled chicks like a toothless man with bad breath and a serious dose of unwashed ass, or "hot butt" as we call it these days. We were just getting up to speed on my surf when, all of a sudden, Brian sped up without any warning. I am sure I sounded like the aforementioned Andy on top of the scaffolding, but I was screaming like a titty baby while perched on the roof of Brian's Dodge. I slipped then landed on the hood of the car and all I could see was Brian laughing his ass off holding the steering wheel. I spun and grabbed the only thing I could reach, that being the windshield wipers, designed to only hold five ounce wiper blades. Brian proceeded to turn, in reverse, into the Piggly Wiggly parking lot and the centrifugal force of the turn slung me off with both wipers still in my sweaty hands. Holding onto the wipers proved to be my folly as the turn slung me around to the passenger door and sat me, ass down, onto the asphalt. The biggest problem was it sat me in the path of Brian's turning car and the passenger front tire ran my legs over about mid-calf. I was wearing shorts that day and the process left two perfect black tire tread marks across the fronts of my legs. I sat there dumbfounded, not saying a word when Brian jumped out of his halted chariot and ran around the side of the car where I sat. His eyes were as big as saucers when he looked at my legs and his adrenalin must have been pumping as he lifted me up and slung me into his car. I outweighed him by a good sixty pounds but it did not seem to matter that day as we were headed back to the infirmary where we had just been admitted the week before for oyster poisoning.

The nurse on duty just snickered when we told her the lie about how I got the two tire tracks across my legs. I didn't break anything, mind you, and I couldn't get a word in edgewise when Brian was driving like Junior Johnson haulin' a load of moonshine through the North Carolina Mountains, trying to get me to a doctor. I walked in under my own power to the infirmary. The imbedded black rubber from the tires stayed imprinted on the fronts of my legs for a good month and a half and the ladies loved it. Brian had the opportunity to tell the car surfing story many a time in the six weeks that elapsed after the incident. We'd even embellished it to incorporate saving errant puppies or kittens and small, innocent children as part of the reason for my injuries, depending on present company and if we needed a sympathy beer.

We didn't car surf anymore after that day and there was not scaffolding within fifty miles of Troy, Alabama so we were safe.

For now.

Chapter · XVI

THE STORY tell*ing turned to Brian, and we had numerous laughs as our unplanned trip continued. Brian reminis*ced of a time when he and I went to Atlanta, my home town, and the adventure we shared there. Our trip was a great time of reflection for us both and I knew and he knew we needed this one big story before I left school, got married, and got serious with life. Time has a way of murdering memories, or keeping them on life support, depending on the strength of the characters involved and the bonds strengthened by events shared. We had a long weekend in Atlanta and Brian was reflecting on the events surrounding those four days.

Before I begin, I must tell you of the art of D&D, dine and dash, eat and run, chomp and stomp and numerous other names and acronyms used to describe the act of eating at a restaurant and hauling ass out the door without paying. Leaving a generous tip was always mandatory for the waitress as there was always honor among thieves, and looking back on it, we were, well… honorable thieves. Brian and I always committed this crime for the adventure of doing it and not so much for the act of removing oneself from a restaurant with unpaid food in our belly. We always left a tip big enough to cover the bill and transferred the final decision to the waitress to make it right. It may have been the wrong way to handle the situation but we enjoyed the exercise and the circumstances involved in the D&D act. If our waitress did a crappy job, we'd leave a small tip and haul ass anyway, but a tip just the same.

On the weekend I brought Brian home to Atlanta we were staying with my brother at his house in Douglasville. We planned to hit the big city of Atlanta and see what kind of trouble might await us there or we could cook up on our own. We told my brother about the numerous D&D trips we had made, and for some strange reason he wanted to see one in action so we agreed on a time and a place and made the date. Brian said "your brother is some kind of voyager…" I was going to correct him by saying "Voyeur" but I just let it go. I understood what he meant and the closest thing to anything French for Brian was fried potatoes. Anyway, our plan was simple, go to a busy restaurant, order big, leave a great tip if the waitress was a good one, and do the D&D shuffle. A simple plan was hatched with a perceived good ending. It is important to know that when we left a tip large enough to cover the meal it was a self protecting insurance plan of sorts. If we were to get caught, we'd say we paid at the table and did not realize we had to pay at the register, placing us in the clear.

This particular weekend, however, we were exceptionally light on funds so we were leaving a good tip and that was it. We had decided on a number of bacon and egg outlets on a particularly classy strip of road named Fulton Industrial Boulevard. This road was a good eleven miles long and lived up to its name as it was the industrial hub of west Atlanta. It was a divided four-lane and home to everything from UPS to Budweiser, strip joints to hotels. Fulton Industrial had it all; it was constantly teeming with semi-trucks and their drivers, to factory workers and the warehouse workers that the truckers fed with their bounty. There were cheap chain restaurants lining the expanse of the road, from Waffle House to Denny's, all fast food sit-down and eat chains serving breakfast and everything else 24 hours a day, seven days a week. Not even Christmas and Thanksgiving were sacred on Fulton Industrial Boulevard, as the "stuff" had to be delivered constantly, shelved constantly, then moved to their designated retail locations constantly, holidays be damned.

We had agreed to meet at a Waffle House near the interstate (I-20, the road that ran from Myrtle Beach to California and through my town of Douglasville), and it was the biggest Waffle House I have ever seen. This particular Waffle House had a seating capacity in the 125-150 range. If you've ever been inside one, they usually hold no more than fifty occupants. This Waffle House had at least five cooks and twenty-five waitresses at all times slinging hash browns 400,000,000 ways, eggs, cheese burger plates, coffee, and of course, waffles. It was a cash cow for the owner, and surely one of the busiest Waffle Houses in Atlanta and possibly the southeast. Brian and I ordered our regular, T-bone steak, eggs scrambled with cheese, large grits in a bowl, coffee, and a giant slice of the chocolate pie to finish it out. It was the most expensive thing on the menu (in keeping with the VW versus Rolls Royce rule Brian had taught me) occupying the greasy dive's extensive yet budget-minded board-of-fare. We had about six bucks between us, equaling what would be a great tip, and we sat down before our feast just as my brother walked in and found himself a seat near the front door and cash register. He ordered his food and waited for the festivities to begin. He situated himself so he faced us and it enabled him to watch our every move. Brian and I ate our meal, enjoyed our coffee and our pie, then left our tip and had planned to make a covert but speedy exit. That was the plan and it had worked smoothly every time up to this point. This would prove to be the one time we had invited an outside observer and he happened to be one who could not keep his enthusiasm in check while we were planning our exit. That person was my brother, George.

I must take a minute to tell you of my brother. He is my elder and the good example I never got around to following. He is a genius by every right, I.Q. in the high 170's and the single smartest person I have ever met. He has an exceptionally dry sense of humor, my favorite kind, and we have had a number of on-going conversations that have lasted fifteen plus years each, sometimes resumed by just a word. It's amazing how two guys can get roughly the same amount of ass whippin's (he got a two year head start on me, but I outpaced him quickly), eat the same food and breathe the same air, suffer under the same tyranny, and be so completely different. That's my brother and me. He's a great dude that I love dearly, but on this day, I was certain that I wanted my brother to retroactively fill an infant's grave.

Here's how it went down. We left the generous tip after the meal as planned. The restaurant was relatively crowded but you could still get a table if needed, meaning the majority of the wait staff was occupied with the business at hand. As soon as we stood to attempt our exodus, my brother busted out laughing, silencing everyone from the patrons to the cooks. There were no plasma TV's hanging on the walls back then, blaring updated information of the day minute-by-minute. There wasn't even a Philco TV set showing the *Best of Hee-Haw* hanging in the corner as a distraction. The jukebox blared country music only, every seat in the house was in the smoking section, and the traveling rumor mill was how information got around back in those days. My brother saw what we were about to do and he busted out laughing, being unable or unwilling to control himself. We immediately sat back down in our booth, ordered some more coffee and waited for the next opportunity to make a break for it. Ten minutes passed and we tried again. Once again, my brother busted out laughing at the prospect of our Dine and Dash maneuver, thwarting our efforts to fulfill the "Dash" part of our trip as the "Dine" part had reached its conclusion. Brian and I did what came natural: we calmly sat back down again and ordered more coffee. We could both have put out a house fire by the time we made our exit, if liquid caffeine converted to piss could douse a fire, and I was ready to kill my one and only brother. We tried four times to make our exit and he busted out laughing every single time. On the fifth time we just got up, walked toward the door, and when we got close we bolted like two fully dressed KKK members deposited magically center-court at a NBA All-Star game or a Little Wayne concert. We ran our asses off to the parking lot next door, where we had parked the car, jumped in and hauled ass. We never parked in the subject restaurant parking lot in case we got blocked in. My brother told me later that while he was busy laughing his skinny ass off at us, not a single person looked up. He said it was as if we were invisible to everyone there but him. Not a cook or waitress or even a patron noticed we had departed the establishment in great haste. After a few minutes, our waitress said out loud, "Did anybody see these two leave?"

My brother said it was the very first time he blew a half chewed edible object out of his nose trying to keep from laughing at the waitress' late delivered observation. He also realized he had better high tail it out of there, paying of course, in case he was fingered as an accomplice. The life of a straight arrow, thinking the observation of a crime was as bad as committing it.

My brother said it was the anticipation of witnessing our deed that caused him to laugh out loud rather than the actual deed itself. He said the casualness of our actions and how it looked as if we had done it millions of times hit him like a comedic ton of bricks. All I know is I was prepared to shank his ass with a dull butter knife before we left. He was laughing like a hyena when we passed him and he had obviously defrayed whatever attention that might have been directed at us onto him. I am sure the unsuspecting staff and patrons thought he might be clinically insane or maybe just on some sort of dope, normal for that time of night and the geographical location of the Casa de Waffle in question. It was extremely funny later on, but during the time of our attempted escape, only he was laughing. I had thought about punching him in his throat (rather than "jookin" him) while we were leaving as punishment, but I am sure it would have attracted the cops or at the very least placed the attention on us, which we obviously did not want. Plus, explaining to my parents how I had stabbed my brother in the neck at a Waffle House while running out on the bill might prove to be too large a mountain to climb at family gatherings. We never invited anyone else to participate as a casual observer again after that particular incident, and for good reason.

The next day Brian and I arose and headed towards Atlanta to enter a wing eating contest we deemed a free lunch. The contest was put on as a means of advertisement for an older established restaurant in the city of Atlanta near Little Five Points. The advertisement hit the radio airwaves via my favorite Rock and Roll station. When we arrived, there were numerous hopeful participants in attendance with the winner of said eating contest receiving 100 additional hot wings and two pitchers of beer. We could cover our food and beer all at once, and for free! The place was a low rent biker dive, evidenced by the high back stools having names engraved on bronze plaques designating what was obviously a very regular customer's seat. That or a drunken dude purchased a stool and wanted his name engraved on it, so the bar complied. Brian commented about how it was like an engraved invitation to drink beer, and I couldn't help but agree. Brian and I won the wing eating duel hands down and immediately became unpopular with the local stool jockeys and bikers that regularly attended the bar slash shit-hole. There were some real live ex-cons and Hell's Angel types present when we collected our winnings, and they were not happy with our "college boy looks and smart ass attitudes" as I heard one say. I was a big dude, but I am sure there were a couple a dudes present in there that had taken it the "hard way" while in prison, if you catch my drift. These guys were pissed at the world types, for either getting caught at whatever felony they committed causing them to be incarcerated, or just the fact that they had gotten their asses handed to them by a couple of college boys with smart ass attitudes in a wing eating contest. We were in their bar and we were obviously no longer welcome. It pissed Brian off to the point he said, "Screw 'em! We won and I am enjoying our wings and our pitchers of beer and they can all kiss my round hairy ass!"

Good old Brian. He would pick a booger out of a dead cat's nose and flick it at a cotton mouth rattlesnake and not think twice.

We both decided to just sit and slowly enjoy the spoils of our contest, and they could all metaphorically suck the peanuts out of our metaphysical dump. We laughed it up, eating and enjoying the cold Killian's Draft Beer we had been awarded as the much deserved spoils of our contest. I remember the beer brand because it had just been introduced and the distributor sponsored the contest. The beer was out of place in this bar as Pabst Blue Ribbon and Schlitz, preferably served warm and in a dirty glass, was the established swill of the regular patrons.

We were constantly shot dirty looks by the regulars as a "get the hell out of here" sign, meaning we were no longer welcomed in the shit-sewer bar they called home. It had a directly opposite effect on us both. Brian would eat a wing and loudly exclaim,

"Damn these are good hot wings and great free beer we won!"

It was pissin' off the locals to the point of possible homicide so they commenced to having a contest of their own. Now Brian and I were in a fraternity so we had observed and tried every possible way of drinking beer. These dudes were "funneling" beer at the bar meaning they had a clear rubber tube with a funnel that could hold at least a quart of beer. The object of the game is simply to drink or drown. You filled the funnel full of your favorite malted beverage, usually the cheap beer to start as you would spill half of it as an amateur, put the tube in your mouth and have an accomplice lift the funnel above your head and let gravity do what it does best. Most folks got beer showers as the contents of the funnel usually overtook the unknowing victim, choking them with the swift flow of carbonated liquid. It was funny to watch and we got our laughs in also watching the drunken bikers try to determine a winner.

After watching for a good twenty minutes, Brian said,

"I'm gonna go get in the contest and kick all their asses again!"

I warned him to just stay put as I was indeed the oldest and supposedly the more responsible of the two of us. My attempts were unsuccessful as Brian was a driven young man and when he made his mind up he could not be swayed until he was satisfied or chained down. I had come to learn this about him early on so I threw my complementary warning out and let it go. I got up and followed Brian to the area where the bikers were seated and playing their drinking game. He walked up to the edge of the circle they were sitting in and he said:

"The smart assed college boy has a joke."

Silence.

The entire crowd stopped what they were doing and gave Brian and me the look of death. Brian was buzzed and I feared his alligator mouth was about to write a check his tadpole ass couldn't cash. He continued, "You biker dudes will be telling this one to your prison buddies next week when you get busted for having too many tattoos."

"Oh shit," was all I could produce as a thought.

I could see in my mind's eye these guys going for whatever hidden gun or knife they must have been packing in case smart assed college boys needed to be killed for telling a bad joke.

"Tell the joke, asshole," the biggest one of the bunch said.

"Ya know what the difference is between a Hoover Vacuum Cleaner and a Harley Davidson Motorcycle?"

Every man has something he believes in. Some believe in having more beer, some believe in God, some believe in the Marine Corps. All of the aforementioned bikers in this story were loyal to Mr. Harley and Mr. Davidson, the inventors of a particular brand of American-made motorcycle that has a worldwide following with many followers considering the brand to be second to Jesus only. Truth be known, Jesus probably came in second or third to most of the gents in attendance that day and only if he rode a Harley. I saw their panties getting collectively wadded up at the mere mention of Harley-Davidson by this well dressed smart ass who had invaded their domain, won their wing eating contest and had taken their beer as a consolation prize. I could hear the headlines now.

"Two college boys with smart ass attitudes murdered and dismembered – film and complete story on Eleven Alive News tonight!"

Brian repeated himself, but this time louder.

"I said, DO YOU KNOW WHAT THE DIFFERENCE IS BETWEEN A HOOVER VACUUM CLEANER AND A HARLEY-DAVIDSON MOTORCYCLE…DAMMIT?!"

I could envision the closed casket funerals we were going to have and wondered, to myself, if any of my past girlfriends would attend. I guessed not.

More silence. This had better be a good one, damn it, Brian. His chest swelled in anticipation for the coup-de-gras, or the violent ass-whooping that may have followed it. To this day, I am unsure.

"The position of the dirt bag."

Silence… Oh Shit.

Seconds later, the entire circle of bikers busted out laughing so hard they could not breathe, choking and gagging, slapping knees and backs as each tried to catch their breath unsuccessfully. Brian's ass had dragged us kicking into the veritable cave of the giant grizzly bears and had somehow convinced the bears to share dinner with us. We had instantly become regulars in the time span of one joke, and the only thing left was to engrave a plaque and mount it on a barstool. We enjoyed the rest of the day with our biker friends, ending with the bartender taking a picture of the two of us with the bikers. That picture hung in the place until it closed years later for a condo complex to be built.

We got a serious chuckle from that story and Brian was still in charge of the story telling.

The train sped on.

Chapter · XVII

**It may be that your sole purpose in life is simply
to serve as a warning to others.
– Anonymous**

THE STEERING wheel of storytelling was still in Brian's grasp, and he continued with the Atlanta trip and it had been a doozey. We packed a week's worth of activities into a few memorable days. After leaving the wing eating contest biker-bar soiree, Brian and I decided we'd take in some of the sights up and down Peachtree Street, the main artery that bisected Atlanta. There were numerous places to go, from the Limelight to the Fabulous Fox Theater. We parked down the street from the Fox and were walking up Peachtree Street towards the lit up marquis that fronted the legendary theater. When we arrived at the front entrance, we spotted two girls that I knew and we began talking about the events that were scheduled to take place that evening. It was only 5:30 or so as the wing eating contest had taken place at 11:00 am and we stayed at our bar for a good five hours or so, getting primed for the events later that evening. Both of the girls were serious rock and roller types, attending every concert their budgets would allow and this day was no exception.

We decided to hang out with the girls, as they were connected (whatever that really means) and, as good looking women often did, they got recognized by the crew members, getting asked back stage to party with the band. The girls told us if they were able to get backstage they'd give us their tickets and we could catch a show for free. I was cool with that. Free concert and drinks with some good looking women. There were worse things I could think of for entertainment. We had learned that Keith Richard's band was the headliner. The band was called the Cockroaches and, although I liked the Stones, Keith Richards reminded me of an old fart that had already died and just forgotten to fall over. He was a great guitar player, evidenced by his long time participation in The Rolling Stones. I had seen the Stones once in the Omni before it was torn down, so seeing Mr. Richard's band for free was okay by me. Of course, Brian was game.

These girls were experienced groupies and knew just where to stand when equipment was being unloaded for the show by the roadies. These guys also had a second job: finding local hotties for the band to have a good time with that had a dulled sense of morality. It took a few minutes before my two friends were noticed and approached by the roadies to accept their invite to be backstage "helpers." We had two free tickets to the show, the girls handed over some pity cash for abandoning us, and they left us with two damn good seats.

We took our killer free seats four rows from the stage center (these girls knew somebody to get tickets this good) and Brian and I got the show of our lives. The Cockroaches were actually The Rolling Stones, and they were debuting their newest album, *Undercover*, and of course all the great hits from the boys from across the pond. It was a killer show and we had a heck of a great free time. After the show, we did not wait around for the girls, as we suspected they were busy earning their keep for getting backstage (good looking and willing, I assumed, and it was now time for them to compensate the band for the backstage privileges they had received).

Brian and I decided we'd head back towards my brother's house, post concert, and hit the hay. We stopped at a Denny's for a cup of purchased coffee (no D&D here) and as soon as I cleared the door, six of my buddies from High school hollered at me from the back of the restaurant. Brian and I walked back and sat at the table with my inebriated friends and it became a meet and greet for my buddies and Brian. My buddies had apparently been there for a good two hours, raising hell and ordering just about everything on the menu twice. Brian and I just ordered coffee as originally planned and our waitress, obviously annoyed at the length of time the boys had been seated, was pissy, tired, and ready to go home. I am sure my other friends had been the icing on a very crappy cake for her that evening. Brian and I could sense her impatience via her sarcastic, yet resigned, demeanor. We drank our one cup of Joe and left a generous tip on the table. We asked her for a bill so we could make a speedy exit and not be included the festivities the boys had already started. She brought the bill, seventy five cents, and I dropped a five on the table, as did Brian, using the guilt money our concert going honeys handed us before disappearing. Our waitress got a nine dollar tip for two cups of coffee and zero flack from the likes of Brian and me. She smiled at us and with tired eyes thanked us as we headed for the door.

Unbeknownst to us, the manager had called the local law as a precaution on the rambunctious gentlemen, in case anything out of the ordinary might have come up concerning the large bill that had been accumulated by the hoodlums I previously called friends. Brian and I stepped outside the front door and had gotten only a few steps away when all manner of Hell broke loose.

The no-good-worthless-sons-of-bitches were D&D-ing on the giant tab they had run up at the Denny's! How dare those criminals!

Next thing you know, blue lights went off all over the parking lot, and like the two dumb asses we were, we took off running. It looked like every cop in Atlanta was in attendance and anticipating free doughnuts with every criminal caught that evening. Brian and I were not guilty of a thing (at the Denny's, at least), but we ran just the same out of instinct. I guess it was all the past D&D events where we were actually culpable coming into play and at a very bad time. It may have been a natural reaction, based on the fact we were worn slap out, causing us to run when we didn't need to. I guess tired, guilty folk do that kind of a thing. It was stupid, I know, but at the time it seemed reasonable to the two of us. As we ran away, we both jumped down a big hill that led to the large hotel parking lot next door to the Denney's, all while being chased by two very fleet footed cops. I hollered to Brian to slide under the jacked up truck ahead and I slid next to him under the jacked up truck beside his. I pulled myself up into the suspension and hid there until the two cops ran past and I was satisfied we had made a clean get away. We slid out from under the trucks and wouldn't you know it, here runs a third cop, Barney Fife but with a gelatinous ass and looking like a four-hundred pound dark blue colored, polyester barrel of monkey spunk. I'm telling you this lawman was so fat, if he broke his leg sausage gravy would have poured out. On that day he was hero number one as he pulled his service revolver, probably for the first time, and told us to stop in our tracks. We complied because he had a gun, then he cuffed us and walked us back to his car, depositing us in the back seat to take us to the Atlanta City Jail for book-in. We explained that we had only ordered coffee, which was true, and he could ask the manager and the waitress for verification.

"You damn boys are guilty of something or you wouldn't have run from us, you no good slime balls" sounding like a line from Hawaii Five-0.

He didn't bother to check with the Denny's manager concerning our innocence. He had his boys and he was proud of it. I'm certain that after he delivered us he celebrated with a chocolate cake or a couple dozen cheese burgers. However he celebrated, I'm sure it involved bacon or frosting, and maybe both.

We were taken to a pink (and I mean pink as pink gets) jail cell full of drunken slobs, one of which had driven his family car onto Road Atlanta, during a race, and had caused a huge wreck for some of the on-track competitors. He had gotten sloshed on Boone's Farm Strawberry Hill wine and decided he'd show them "wine and cheese boys how to race a damn car" – his exact quote. It should be mentioned that Boone's Farm was the finest of the cheap swill wines, and the bottled strawberry equivalent of Kool-Aid and Vodka whose ingredients concluded with "Aged on the way here!" printed on the label. The story concerning the errant race track driver was verified by the news report the next day and I dared not tell my folks I had sat in jail next to Larry-O Andretti earlier that evening. Later, I distinctly remember my old man commenting on the rabble that populated the jails these days citing my former jail mate as an example. I just agreed and kept my pie-hole shut. Telling papa-san I had heard Mr. Jailhouse Andretti's confession story first hand would certainly do me no good.

Brian and I were booked in then transported via police van, smelling of hot moist ass and armpits, to a justice of the peace to be charged with theft of services, a misdemeanor crime which Brian and I were not guilty of that day. When we arrived at the Justice's office at his house (he had converted his garage to a damned court room as God is my witness) he proceeded to read the charges filed against all eight of us. I felt certain he also did taxidermy, cremations, transmission rebuilds and supervised the overthrowing of small countries for a nominal fee. He asked us what we were doing with our lives and I told him I was about to finish up at Troy University. Brian said he was attending Troy also and another friend of mine was presently attending Jacksonville State University. One of my high school buddies, Don, was also asked where he attended college and he said, "The University of Dittler Brothers"… his then current place of employment.

It was damn funny at the time and even the judge couldn't help but laugh at that statement, cracking us all up. He wasn't about to cut anyone present any slack at such an hour, mind you, but we all laughed just the same.

As fate would have it, the law required that the manager of the Denny's to come to the judge's makeshift courtroom and she brought the waitress to identify the guilty parties. When she saw Brian and me, our waitress stated we were the two best customers she had that evening and were not involved, in any way, in the criminal activity the others had been guilty of. She even had the two fives Brian and I had given her as a tip as evidence. The judge asked us why in the hell had we run away and we knew any answer was going to sound stupid so I, the diplomatic one, said:

"At this point, your honor, any answer I give will make us both sound like bigger morons than you and God already know we are."

On our way out the door, one of the dudes that were indeed guilty, named Tim had called his Mom to come rescue him. She was a protective and somewhat co-dependent parent of an embarrassing nature (the protective part I should say), and she came running to his aid. As she was walking in the makeshift courtroom and as she passed me she said, "What have you hoodlums gotten my Timmy into?!" It was more of an accusatory statement than a question of her son's guilt or innocence. Yes, she was one of those mothers with a perfect son who never did anything wrong and unbeknownst (big word alert) to her, he was a bigger criminal (relatively speaking of course) than she'd ever know. We all rode "Timmy" hard about his Mommy's accusatory statement for the rest of his life around us. He's moved on now and in an ironic twist of fate, became an FBI agent. Fitting I assume. I am proud of my old friend. He worked his way into a tough profession despite the D&D incident. I'm sure his mom blamed me and anyone else he might have known for her son's brief criminal history, at least the stuff he got caught doing.

The Denny's manager was kind enough to give Brian and me a ride back to the restaurant and man, let me tell you, she lectured us both like a seasoned pro. She told us in no uncertain terms; "I've been where you're going, you hear where I'm coming from?" was her exact quote, and proceeded to tell us about her own sons and all the trouble she had dealt with while they were growing up. She even offered to whip our asses with a belt right there in the parking lot just to help us along the way with the life lesson she was trying to teach us right then. We graciously declined and thanked her for the ride. It spelled the end of our Dine and Dash adventures for eternity and we'd figured we'd just been extended grace by the older experienced mother of six boys. We had received sage wisdom from the diminutive discipline expert on kid raising, and her wise words have been repeated numerous times by me to my own children on occasions involving maturity or the lack thereof. I have never forgotten her and am still grateful for her testimony to us both. Her words were like a corner stone for me, kinda like the one's the Mason's placed on the foundations of old buildings. Lesson learned.

On our way home, we stopped at an old trucker café named The Bluebird, an Atlanta landmark, for just for one last cup of coffee to rehash the evening's events and to get our story straight in case we had to lie our way out of whatever came next. When we arrived, it was a little before 7:00 a.m. and we were both beat like government mules. We ordered our hot coffee and creamed and sugared it to perfection, not making eye contact with any patrons in the small quiet breakfast restaurant where we decided to end our day, or begin it, as the case may have been. It was nice and quiet in the Bluebird for about five minutes when that silence was crushed. Through the double front door bursts a big dude lookin' pissed off and screaming for coffee and food. I will confess that I spilled my cup from jumping as my nerves were frazzled from the events leading up to that point and lack of sleep.

This guy was a ball of rage wrapped in a sun burnt, tattooed shell, screaming for his breakfast, complaining about everything from the consistency of the grits to the runny eggs, then the undercooked then overcooked bacon. The toast wasn't buttered enough and the damned jelly wasn't cold and what kind of shit-hole outfit they were running there and nobody said a word. I was too tired to confront the asshole and Brian knew we had dodged a bullet (or two) earlier so he kept his eyes on his coffee and his trap shut. The guy screamed for the bill and the cook said it was on the house, obviously trying to rid the establishment of the nasty element the crusty old fart had quickly become. He looked at the cook and said,

"It reminded me of my mother's cooking..." he said in the general direction of the cook. The cook briefly smiled when the ass-faced trucker finished his sentence, "...except I don't remember her takin' a shit in it before I ate it."

The trucker reluctantly threw fifty cents on the table as a tip, and grumbled something about the place paying him to eat the pig slop he had just choked down. When he cleared the door to go out to his big rig, you could hear a collective sigh from the patrons seated about the room. We heard his big rig's diesel engine crank and begin to clatter noisily as he shifted into gear and revved the massive motor to hasten his exit. When he drove past the door, his big-rig's engine screaming in protest, we all saw what must have made him such a nasty fellow. This gigantic, burly, tattooed, rough-as-a-night-in-jail dude was driving a giant pink truck with "KOTEX" written in six foot tall letters painted down the side. I guess we all figured out why he was so pissed off.

Everyone there busted out laughing and Brian and I received a fitting end to a very eventful weekend in Atlanta. Brian and I told the Kotex driver story to numerous people and they all enjoyed it. Brian even used the subject matter for an English 102 paper as his final exam. He only got a "B," as the professor stated in big red marker on the front of Brian's paper, "One weekend could not have held that much activity, so it could not have happened that way. The Rolling Stones part must have surely been fabricated." Brian produced a copy of his concert ticket, but all it said was "The Cockroaches."

Screw the guy, it happened. I was there and I could hardly believe it myself.

We were both laughing uncontrollably when we were interrupted by the enormous locomotive, jerking forward and aft, the cars banging in their moorings. It was a tell-tale sign that the train was slowing down.

Chapter · XVIII

"There seems to be no sign of intelligent life anywhere..."
– Captain James Tiberius Kirk; Star Ship Enterprise

THE TRAIN we had become such reluctant travelers upon began to slow down. We were not exactly sure where the train was located geographically, and it really didn't matter to us anyway. The primary objective, for me at least, was to exit the coal-driven beast as soon as circumstances allowed. I had philosophized (yep, it's a word too) that there were going to be some trade-offs concerning safety and a compromise or two to be made for a successful dismount of the single-minded ambassador of doom we were so stupidly situated upon. Here was the compromise; I would throw Brian off first and land on him, as I was the one that had to be pretty when I walked to get my diploma. I had not shared this particular revelation with Brian yet and probably would not until the actual time to jump came. This was akin to mutiny but I figured Brian would understand somehow as he would not have to walk for his diploma for a few more years. Save for Brian landing on his face, he'd have plenty of time to heal from the injuries he would definitely sustain when I landed on him after we jumped at such a high rate of speed. I just hoped we would not get maimed and discovered years later by some excavation crew scraping gravel or replacing train cross ties. I also hoped that if we indeed met our ends that day we'd not land together and decompose with our bones overlapping in some weird looking, homo love-lock. I wouldn't want anyone to think any worst of us than might already be suspected. Of course it would be years later and I would definitely not care at that point. How was this whole thing gonna play out short term was my only thought.

Of course, I also was thinking about the intelligence factor (or lack thereof) concerning this trip. It made me think of ranking some very stupid things I had done when I was a kid and I shared them with Brian. The first thing that popped into my head was when I placed my life and the life of my friend and next door neighbor, Mikey Langford, in my young hands for an unexpected ride in my dad's immaculate 1963 Riviera. I am sure it was the very first time I actually feared for my life and had brilliantly escaped certain death, both by vehicle and by father. I was six, maybe seven years old and my Dad was a sure enough car guy. He worked as a supervisor in the U.S. Post Office and he did OK for himself and his small family living in the West End area of metro Atlanta, Our residence was located on Greymont Drive, and it bisected Avon Avenue downhill from our humble abode, dropping off sharply after crossing Avon and continued to the back gate of Fort McPherson Army Base or "Ft. Mac" as we all called it, and beyond that to the rest of the known world. Crossing Avon Avenue was a guaranteed death sentence, so guaranteed by my mother, as she did not mince words concerning this rule and the punishment that would accompany such a violation. I guess kid funerals were expensive and she had better things to do with her and dad's money. It's important at this juncture to know that my dad loved cars (relevant to the rest of this particular story so hang in there) and I am certain it's where my love for all things automotive originated.

Dad owned a 1931 A-Model Ford with an "AAAOOOGA" horn, shiny jet black with cream colored spoke wire wheels. It was a head turner every time he drove it, which was often in the hot and humid summer times in the South. The A-model was his fix-er-up car and he did an awesome job with it. He also saved his hard earned dough and purchased a beautiful black 1963 Buick Riviera in spring of 1965. It was the envy of every dad on our street, as it was only two years old when my Dad purchased it, trading in a crappy Falcon and a cool fifteen hundred hard earned dollars for the luxury liner. Let me tell you, this car was loaded with every option; silver (yes, silver) leather, two-plus-two bucket seats with a console that ran from the front all the way to the rear, air conditioning that would chill a 6.5 ounce Coke in the bottle and just about anything else you placed in front of the six carefully positioned vents occupying the awesome dash panel that looked like what I thought the cockpit of a fighter jet or a space craft might. Ironically, it was a special ordered car by a Delta Airlines pilot named Don Jacobs, evidenced by the silver plaque mounted on the glove box door. It could outrun the word of God and radar, as it came with a 425 cubic-inch "nail-head" dual quad beast of a motor, with "465 Wildcat" (the 465 stood for the torque the motor produced) painted in red on the breather lid, and it would spin the wide white-wall tires at will. It had a console shifter, and back in the day there was no such thing as a locking steering wheel or any other significant safety features other than the ones that came with a hint of common sense. Safety features like keeping your damn kid and his best buddy out of it when it was parked facing downhill towards busy Avon Avenue. That probably sounds "transfer of blame-ish," I know, but I fully understood I was traveling deep into ass-whoopin' country simply by sitting in my Dad's car without his knowledge. My dad never left the keys in it but it was back when you could park your car on the street and nobody ever considered messing with it or anything else you parked or left in your yard. He had owned the Riviera for two years keeping it immaculate and I mean Marine Corps immaculate. A person could safely eat off any part of that car without worry. It was that clean.

Mikey and I had decided on one summer day we were to be *Lost in Space*, our favorite TV show other than *Star Trek*, the favorite of every kid in the known universe back then. Every young boy I knew loved *Star Trek*, and with the possible exception of the horny Captain James Tiberius Kirk's seemingly endless quest to mate with everything that wasn't nailed down or Klingon, it was a great show and our first drive on the outskirts of Sexville. This particular day we were *Lost in Space* and I was the Robot and Mikey was Will Robinson, boy genius and son to Captain John Robinson. Will Robinson had a knack for figuring out a way to get himself, the evil Dr. Smith, and Robot out of trouble inside of a fifty minute show, so I figured he must have been a genius. I had postulated (I heard that word get used by every space captain on TV) it best to not do the dad/son (My being Captain John Robinson and him being Will, boy genius) thing with my then best friend, so Robot would have to do for me as nobody wanted to be the evil Dr. Smith. We climbed into our black spacecraft manufactured by the Buick Motor Company, a division of General Motors, and went through pre-launch proceedings. She was a fine craft; I knew what she could do and was ready to take her out for a blast through the closest galaxy available. We had fashioned space helmets (which actually came in quite handy a few minutes later) from our football helmets, painted shiny black with gold Fleur-de-lis emblazoned on either side, left over from playing football for the Cascade Saints.

We had a smooth take off and all was going well for a few minutes when Mikey noted that Klingons were hot on our trail and we needed to make a quick escape. Mikey had committed a rather simple faux pas by combining two separate yet equally cool TV shows involving space travel, Star Trek and Lost in Space. It was an acceptable mistake, as everybody knew that Klingons (Star Trek bad guys) had a cloaking device and our sensors would not detect them until it was way too late. Plus, the Robinsons ship did not have photon torpedoes so we were goners if something did not happen fast as far as an escape was concerned. Besides, the USS Enterprise (Star Trek) was on a five year mission, to explore strange new worlds and boldly go where no man had gone before. The Robinsons, on the other hand, were just trying to get back home after the evil Dr. Smith stowed away and purposely screwed up the ship's flight computer. This action catapulted them, at light speed, to galactic parts unknown, delaying whatever consequences awaited nasty evil doctors back on Earth.

As a kid, I often wondered if the USS Enterprise ever crossed paths with the Robinson's vessel would Captain Kirk or Doctor Spock steer them in the right direction back towards Earth. Captain Kirk probably would have, but only if Daddy Robinson allowed him to make out with the older Robinson daughter first, I figured, as an even trade. I also knew if the Robinson's made it home, it was game over and end of the show as they'd no longer be "Lost in Space." Maybe after they figured out where they were, they could just ride around some, but, "Happy in Space" sounds like a kid's reading show on PBS and doesn't sound as dangerous as "Lost in Space" so I guessed they'd just stay lost and keep their jobs. There were only three channels back then in all of TV land and the

Robinson's crossing paths with the Star Trek boys seemed like a remote possibility to me back then. I mean, the galaxy could only be just *so* big.

Anyway, I hollered for Mikey to do something quick as mixing two space shows might disturb the space-time continuum (I heard that get said a lot so it seemed appropriate) and there'd be hell to pay if that ever occurred. Besides, the Klingon ship had to de-cloak in order to fire its weapons so I, as the Robot, figured we'd make it out somehow. In the excitement Mikey reached down and pulled the Buick's floor shifter from Park to Neutral, and the ship we were captains of that day was entering a strange new world. Our space craft was rolling towards Avon Avenue, and I was holding onto the steering wheel while standing up in the driver's seat, an offense that would introduce you to the other side of my dad's two sided belt, which I'm convinced he invented From experience, one side was for wearing with business suits in conjunction with my dad's mirror polished wing-tip sized thirteen shoes, the other side was for ass-whippin's. Remember, my dad was an old school U.S. Marine, and let me tell you this: he quit school because of recess. He did not play. Especially when he laid down the rules and you (I) broke them.

I was standing up in the front seat of my dad's pride and joy. I was indeed holding on to the steering wheel and driving it, steering it, all without his knowledge. Mikey and I realized we were about to travel to a place never visited by either of us at such a young age. I really needed Mikey to do the "Will Robinson, boy genius" thing as fast as he could but my greatest fears had come to pass…Mikey became an Earthling faster than Mr. Spock could mind-meld you into submission. I had been reduced to mixing space shows myself as panic quickly set in.

"Danger, Will Robinson, danger!!" was all this Robot could muster as my sweat filled hands were both glued securely to the steering wheel…

I was driving a car, or really aiming the craft more than driving, if you insist on correct nomenclature. The steering wheel was more for me to just hang on to rather than a device to aid in avoiding crashing into another vehicle. We had gotten up to a decent rate of speed when we crossed Avon Avenue and my young short life passed before my eyes as we threaded between the two cars coming from either direction. I remember the color of the woman's eyes in the car approaching from the driver's side, just so you'll know how close we actually were to one another. I know now that if any one of the three cars brought together by fate, *Lost in Space & Star Trek* and Masters Jimmy Hall and Mikey Langford, would have had an extra coat of factory applied enamel paint sprayed on their metal bodies we would have surely hit each other. It was by the thinnest of margins Mikey and I missed the two cars. Mikey and I injected ourselves into the lives of the two unsuspecting drivers so quickly that I'm certain neither driver had a chance to touch the brakes on their cars.

They were desperately trying to get home from a long day's work, whose end led up to our brief and potentially disastrous encounter by no fault of their own.

Mikey and I had successfully passed phase one of our survival tests and that was not getting killed crossing Avon Avenue. I understood my mom's reservation about crossing Avon Avenue now, but I am sure she meant walking and not driving, across it. Phase two was coming with a vengeance and that phase involved preventing my Dad's beautiful, cherished, immaculate, clean-as-a-fire-truck Buick Riviera from getting scratched. This would prove to be a most difficult task and the phase we failed miserably. The car was going a good thirty five miles per hour under only the power of gravity that day. Both momentum and gravity did their respective duties that day, and us two, young mavericks at best, were on a journey to what was ultimately a crash site. That inevitable fact meant we would have rather been doing anything else besides what we were doing at that moment.

When the Riviera left the ground and launched itself into the abyss that was the other side of Avon Avenue things got really interesting. I said earlier that we were wearing football helmets and that would prove to be to our great advantage and I will explain that part now. I am certain we were a good fifteen feet off the asphalt after we crossed "Don't Ever Let Me Catch You Crossing Avon Avenue" as I had come to know it. I genuinely thought the name of the road was "Don't Ever Let Me Catch You Crossing Avon Avenue," but the little green street signs were too small to hold all of that. I guessed my Mom knew the origins of the streets name because that's what she called it all the time. My initial thought was "Oh Crap! I've crossed Avon Avenue and I'm gonna get it now."

That is what I was thinking as the Buick gently floated airborne towards the landing strip awaiting beneath us. Mikey and I actually had a brief encounter with weightlessness enjoyed only by spacemen, the Robinsons, and most of the crew of the Starship Enterprise, with the possible exception of the guys that wore the Red suits as they always got killed. I envisioned parachutes being deployed (I really just liked saying deployed when I was a kid) but I couldn't find the button in time.

As a side note, I remember being a kid, taking a dump one time and telling my Mom, "You would not believe the two Logs I just deployed. Abe Lincoln could have added a wing onto his one room cabin with those two."

She was not impressed and wondered out loud who I might have heard such a rude and despicable thing from. Truth was, I'd heard my Dad say stuff considerably worse and regularly, but I couldn't use my Dad as an excuse. She was looking to cast blame upon someone besides me so I gave her Dickey McGrew. Dickey was the first guy we knew that cussed and had a Playboy collection, and we instantly liked him. Moms have ESP, so mine knew right away he was trouble. His mom, on the other hand, was a full-on hottie and the only mom to wear Go-Go boots and a mini skirt to our intramural football games. Oh the shame of it all. I was sure that catching her as a wife was like the dog that actually caught the car he was chasing. She, Raquel Welch and Anne Margaret were the original reason I became and still am a boob man and she populated many a young boy's dreams back then, namely mine. We used to call Dickey's mom the "Dairy Queen" and for good reason. She always looked like she was shoplifting two cantaloupes in her tight shirts. She loved me for some reason and would always hug me when she saw me. I really liked it as she always smashed my face into her rack and would not let go until I got dizzy from lack of oxygen. I figured if I were going to die this would be how I wanted to go out and certainly not driving my Dad's prized possession across Avon Avenue. I hoped my headstone would read:

HERE LIES MASTER JIMMY HALL

KILLED BY BOOB HUG SUFFOCATION

That sounded a whole lot better than,

HERE LIES MASTER JIMMY HALL,

JUSTIFIABLY KILLED BY HIS DAD

FOR WRECKING HIS SWEET ASSED BLACK 63 RIVIERA

WITH SILVER, YES SILVER, LEATHER INTERIOR.

Death by boob suffocation would look good on a tombstone and the getting killed by the dad thing took up way to much space. Dickey's mom was every young boys dream and every married man's wife's worst nightmare as she was a veritable Playboy bunny with kids that cussed and had Playboy books. I asked her to adopt me one time, thinking I could get away with cussin' and I figured a whipping from her must have been like a dream. She called my mom and told her about my plans and I think my mom agreed to the adoption itself, but also told her she would more than likely bring me back after a few days. I was willing to risk it if Dickey's Mom was willing.

I will return from my Boob Suffocation Death tangent now and tell you first that the flight in our makeshift spacecraft was wonderful but the landing was most unfortunate. Mikey and I slammed headfirst into the beautiful dash with such force that it left black and gold paint marks (The New Orleans Saints colors our helmets wore) on the steering wheel and the glove box we slammed up against during sudden deceleration. We smacked the ground with such force that when we finally stopped, we were both in the back seat, in the floor. I have no idea how we wound up there but it was my first introduction to chaos theory and one I'd not soon forget. I am sure that Mikey had "deployed" in his cut off blue jeans evidenced by the smell emanating from inside the formerly lovely pride and joy of George William Hall, Sr., USMC and United States Post Office supervisor. I, on the other hand, was a dead man.

I knew this after I climbed out of the driver's side window that busted out when we landed. When Mikey and I exited the formerly beautiful automobile, the full force of combining two separate space shows came to bear. I entered a vortex that I am sure was the beginning of the end of my young life as I knew it. To my amazement, neither one of the oncoming cars involved in our successful "Phase One" adventure even slowed down. They just kept on driving to whatever safe place they were headed. I was certain of one thing, I wanted to stow away with them, Evil Dr. Smith style, after I examined the crushed and battered former spaceship Mikey and I had called our own. I took five steps back and to my utter horror my Dad's car was indeed dead and I had killed it.

To begin with, the hood flew up bending it back over the roof of the car which I also noted was dented from the force of the hood smacking it. I also saw that the two doors would not open and they were seriously out of line. The two front fenders were elevated a good ten to twelve inches as evidenced by the two flat wide white wall tires having much more clearance than I remembered them having preflight. The front bumper was off the car and I could see it protruding from the underbelly of the car, twisted like a piece of used dental floss or a discarded pipe cleaner. The back bumper was pushed up so high, the trunk would more than likely not open it was so dented in. This car looked like something Picasso might have designed if his painting career hadn't worked out so well for him, a veritable modern art master piece.

The story continues…

Chapter · XIX

"Truth is beautiful, without doubt; but so are lies."
– Ralph Waldo Emerson

"The pure and simple truth is rarely pure and never simple."
– Oscar Wilde

AS MIKEY and I exited from our now destroyed former space ship and my Dad's most prized possession, I learned an instinctive maneuver that day and one I would later utilize numerous times to include the scaffold swinging incident and when confronted by the Police at front door of the Denny's years later during the D&D days Brian and I enjoyed together.

I ran.

Mikey Langford and I ran as far and as fast as we could away from our homes and up Avon Avenue. We were going to join the Peace Corps or something, anything that would keep us from facing the hell that would be my dad when he found out his car was trashed and I had done it. In reality, Mikey had pulled the shifter into neutral and I could have thrown his ass under the bus but I was just as guilty and he was my friend. After all, I had put my P. F. Flyers on the Silver, yes silver, leather seats, crossed Avon Avenue AND drove (we'll call it that) my Dad's car without knowledge or permission, so I was dead three ways right there. We ran all the way to Mitchell's Store, at the far end of Greymont Drive and the back gate of Ft. Mac, what seemed to be a mile or two but in reality were just over five eighths of a mile from my house. We did our usual; we walked around to the back of the store, grabbed six bottles each that had already been turned in for deposit, marched to the counter and collected our thirty five cents each, then walked out with a cold Coke and Chic-a-stix each in our young, juvenile delinquent hands. The drink and candy had enough sugar to make your hair stand on end and keep you from sleeping for a good two days, which I am sure I would need if I were to be a fugitive and on the run. I am sure Mr. Mitchell was wondering what two seven-year-olds donning football helmets might be up to, but I am sure he had other things to concern himself over, and we were paying customers…sort of. Our appearances never occurred to us as we could only focus on avoiding death, so we formulated a plan. We'd make the long walk down Campbellton Road, the street in front of Mitchell's store which was across the road from the back gate of Fort Mac, hang a left down Epworth Street, paralleling Greymont Drive three roads over, cross Avon Avenue once more and circle all the way back around to our houses down Lanvale Drive. That street stopped at Mikey's house on that corner and my house next to it, returning in the complete opposite direction from where the Rivieras untimely death had occurred. A seven-year-old mind had decided playing innocent was the only way I would ever see the light of day that summer, as punishment back in those days was having to stay indoors and this infraction might keep me indoors for a good year or better. It is funny how times change. Punishment these days is making a kid stay outdoors, indoors was a fate worse than death to my crowd of friends. I borrowed a page from *Hogan's Heroes* (a kid and adult favorite TV show from the sixties) and all the conniving antics they pulled on Commandant Clink and Shultz were going to finally pay off. Mikey and I had tunneled our way to freedom! And my folks were convinced that watching TV was a bad thing.

It took us a good forty five minutes to return to our houses the very long back way. When we rounded Lanvale Street, the street that circled into and eventually butted into Greymont Drive and Mikey's house, we noticed there were no kids out playing. We walked next door to my house, as innocent looking as a pair of newborn babies and what we beheld was what seeing a UFO for the first time must have been like. There were cop cars with lights flashing and folks from all over our neighborhood in attendance at the show. It looked like a flying saucer or the *Lost in Space* ship had landed on Avon Avenue (the TV one, not the one we had piloted earlier that day) and every kid and adult was in attendance to witness the mayhem that was the crash landing of our former spacecraft. I instructed Mikey to play dumb and not whisper a word to anyone anywhere as his mom and dad would have to pay up for the damages to my dad's car. Mikey was indeed the ships navigator and had pulled the shifter out of park causing the death and destruction to my dad's most prized material possession. He asked me if I thought it would work and all I knew was, it had to be better than the truth. I recall all the events of that day rushing back to me when I saw the movie *Animal House* and the scene after Boone, Otter, Pinto and Flounder (a pledge) took Flounder's brother's new four door Lincoln Continental on a road trip and killed it dead by drunkenly crashing it into everything and every car on the road after leaving the "Dexter Lake Club." The Lincoln was later to be resurrected as the Delta Tau Chi "EAT ME" mobile, owned by Flounder's older brother Fred. The upper class brothers instructed pledge Flounder to lie about its demise and they'd back him up. It went something like this:

"What'll I tell Fred!!??" Flounder asked.

"We'll tell him you were taking great care of the car. You parked it out back and in the morning…it was gone!!" says Eric Stratton, reassuringly.

"Will that work??" replies Flounder, in great distress, weeping.

"It's gotta work better than the truth," Stratton, says with confidence.

Mikey Langford and I grabbed a seat on our front steps and quietly watched the action from our elevated vantage point. I could see my dad, his arms raised in abject confusion, asking questions I am sure only I could competently answer concerning the fate of his car. I am sure he asked the police in attendance numerous questions they could not answer. He was asking in the direct, calm manner that always scared the shit out of me whenever he quizzed me concerning the comings and goings of any young man in need of guidance from a father who cared as much as he did. Next thing you know, my mom and Mikey's mom appear out of what seemed to be nowhere (Mom skills), and drilled us both new ones, individually and collectively, military style concerning our "where-bout's" during the destruction of my dad's most favored automobile. I am sure their actions originated out of the excitement concerning the events at hand and the adrenaline that accompanied it. The "Where in the hell have you two been?" factor played a small role in their concern also, I assumed. We wisely stashed our space/football helmets in my crawl space to conceal evidence and to prevent any outside chance of premature death or incarceration for us both. My mom grilled us, and then Mikey's mom took a turn. Then they grilled us separately and then switched us up and grilled us again, in an obvious attempt to extract the truth if there was any truth to be extracted that day. Neither one of us broke.

Mikey did slip up and confess to going to Mitchell's store, a crossing Avon Avenue infraction, so I got my ass busted by my mother. Three licks from her with a small belt and it never hurt, ever. Getting a whipping from her was an easy piece of time, so I just hollered a lot then she usually felt guilty and let up. She usually ended it with the "this hurts me far more than it hurts you" speech, a card most Moms played when confronted with having to whip a kid's ass. Truth was, it actually did hurt her more than it hurt me as she was a real wimp with the rod of correction. My mom couldn't whip her way out of a wet paper bag if her life depended on it but she could threaten your life like a pro. I would much rather have been tied to and dragged around behind her 1956 Bel-Air for punishment rather than be lectured by her for what seemed like days. She'd speak of the early grave we were digging for her with our disobedience, one shovel at a time, and crap like that, all intended to layer guilt upon us a like a carefully crafted double-decker *Dagwood* sandwich, usually served cold with a side of poor-poor-pitiful me soup. My brother, sister and myself knew she would live to lecture for at least one hundred plus years or better and would probably have to be gagged before we chucked her in the clay. My guess back then was if she died and was buried you could put your ear to a drinking glass above her grave and still hear the lectures she had not completed this side of the dirt. I'm not trying to be disrespectful or irreverent here, but I hope you have a clue to what I am saying here. I figured when parents had kids, they went to birthing classes first and then had required kid-lecturing classes second. I am a world class lecturer now myself. Just ask my three kids. It's genetic I guess. You inherit it from your own children.

I often wondered about whatever place my mom might end up in after her death, and I also wondered if God would allow me to be lectured by her if she and I both made it to heaven. If she did indeed get to lecture me there, I thought maybe I would rather go to "the bad place," kinda like in "The Adventures of Huckleberry Finn" when Huck told Aunt Polly he'd just soon go to hell rather than have to sit still and get lectured by her. For me (and Huck Finn too I guessed) the down side was that if the Devil was in charge of Hell and distributing eternal punishment, he might have my mom imported there to lecture me for eternity so I lost either way. I wasn't sure how God worked back then, but I was sure that he would not allow one person's heaven to be another person's hell, if you catch my drift. I figured I'd let God sort that out as I was as close to meeting Him, or the Devil as the case may be, as I had ever been in my young life based on the events transpiring right then. If Mikey squealed or I caved in from guilt concerning the previously unscratched car we had been occupying earlier that day, I was indeed going to meet God or Satan. It would definitely be down escalator for me that very day if the truth got out and I kicked the bucket right then. I figured it was better than having to confront my father, and an eternity of lectures by my mom, so I made peace with it.

When my dad concluded his business with the local authorities, he walked into our house with a face as red as cherry Kool-Aid. Only half mixed strong and blood red, when you just had gotten the sugar to dissolve after ten minutes of stirring, just before filling it up to the eyebrows on the Kool-Aid pitcher. He was pissed off after he had been told by the cops that a rash of crimes similar to this had taken place a few streets over from us and in Atlanta also. My dad was insured to the hilt as he believed it was better to have it and not need it than to need it and not have it when it came to proper insurance coverage.

Of course, he lectured me on never getting in the car ever without him present and of course to never put your shoes on the leather seats. It took two months to get that car fixed and he sent it back twice to General Motors for other items in need of fixing due to the accident. The insurance company had discovered that Buick and GM were having issues with transmissions slipping out of park and causing damage. My old man had his beloved Riviera fixed and never experienced a rate hike afterward as a result of my covert and still as of yet undiscovered cruise in his car. The insurance company and GM wanted to "total it out" but he asked either of them how hard it would be to locate a custom ordered Midnight Black with silver, yes silver, leather interior fully loaded with the same rare engine and dual four barrel carbs, train horn option that would wake the dead, cruise, power everything, including a ball scratcher as my Dad so lovingly put it. I always asked him where the ball scratcher button was, but he said if he told me he'd have to kill me, as ball scratching with anything other than one's writing hand below the age of eighteen might cause premature blindness. He wore glasses on occasion, so I guessed he'd hold down the mysterious scratch button until he needed the reading spectacles, avoiding blindness altogether.

The Riviera came back to us in pristine condition and my Dad loved that car as much as any man could love an inanimate object. He would probably own it today if my mom had not given it to a towing service for the towing bill generated when my dad was out of town on business and she had unexpectedly broken down. I think the move was strategic on her behalf as I figured she might someday ask for him to choose between the two of them and she was hedging her bets. Also, my dad had Triple A and they would handle anything car related and towing was included. This fact alone furthered my dad's theory that my mom had purposely wandered outside of the boundaries of safety my dad had carefully constructed with car insurance and Triple A. I thought he might divorce my mom over that incident and it still remains a sore topic forty plus years later. I distinctly remember my dad calling the towing service and arguing with them over a twenty dollar towing bill versus an extremely nice Buick Riviera as payment. The dudes at the towing service knew they had a jewel of a car in exchange for a minor service and never budged. It sat beside the towing company's building until many years later the company closed and the Riviera disappeared.

Ironically, I happened upon that same Riviera in a junk yard when I was in my thirties, and I asked the owner of the junkyard's son if I could buy it in an attempt to restore it and give it to my dad as a gift someday. The dude stated his dad had bought it new and he would never sell it. I marched him over to the car and showed him the old gas tickets in the console; still lovingly organized by my dad, the Marine, in the little folder he kept them in along with all the service records to accompany it. While I was looking through the console I spotted a small red button in the front of the console and for a brief moment thought I had located the much heralded ball scratcher button my dad had expounded upon so long ago. I figured I was over eighteen (way over) and I would not go blind at this point, and maybe I could just let it scratch until I also needed reading glasses, like my dad, but I digress. As I sat there in the driver's seat and pushed the red hot button of love, what I thought was the rarest option on any car ever made, I heard a muffled pop and to my amazement, the trunk popped open. My Dad…we were gonna have us a talk.

The owner's son insisted it was not my dad's car and refused to sell it even after I asked him to reach his hand down beside the back seat behind the driver and see if there was a silver Mustang Hot Wheel I deposited there and played with when I as a kid. Sure enough, it was there but the butthole didn't budge and I left empty handed, save for the Hot Wheel, leaving the receipts in case I ever crossed paths with my former spacecraft and my Dad's most prized inanimate object again. I never saw that car after that day and I have looked through many junkyards since then in hopes of finding, restoring and taking one last ride through a major or even a minor galaxy or two with my son. And let's not forget the red console button. It seemed like a story a man needed to pass on to his son as a sort of legacy. Maybe.

I am fifty-three now and I am certain my dad will someday read this account concerning his Riviera and its brush with fate. Screwing around with the time space continuum by two young boys flying a spaceship without a license proved to be a daunting task. I was glad Mikey Langford kept his mouth shut and I was sure I had saved his life by not telling. I also realize that I would just now be getting off restriction, forty six years later, if I had fessed up to the whole thing way back when. Live to tell the tale another day seemed to be the best rule of thumb.

It had to work better than the truth.

Sorry, Pop, I mean it.

Train brakes squealing meant one thing…time to exit this beast!

Chapter · XX

"Under certain circumstances, profanity provides a relief denied even to prayer."
– Mark Twain

OUR TRAIN ride looked like it might be coming to some sort of end as our vessel appeared to be slowing, based upon the squealing and jerking of the train, and the violent surging and speeding up while we tried to stand. Remaining seated with our butts planted firmly on the creosote coated wood seemed to be the best option available. Falling off the train and being cut in half might not be a fitting end to this story, much less being ground into meaty kibble chunks after rolling in the giant rocks lining the tracks. As I sat there a few more stupid things I had survived as a kid came to mind and I shared them with Brian. I think he was trying to wrap his brain around the dismount also and might have been waiting for me to come up with a brilliant idea "Will Robinson" style. I was fresh out of solutions save for throwing Brian off and landing on him. Hmmm…

I was certain Brian would be unwilling to let me land on him to break my fall. I just had to present my proposition in a way he'd totally understand, which actually meant I'd have to lie to him to get it to happen. That type of persuasion was something I reserved for those I didn't like much but used when self preservation was important, but never on a friend. I had learned the technique at an early age from my Mom. She needed someone to sit with her youngest daughter while she enjoyed the violence of military conflict played out on the big screen in all its Hollywood glory. It brought to mind a story from my youth and I shared it with Brian as our train was making its decision concerning our soon to come dismount.

As a kid I was exposed to a lot of motion pictures. My mom was a movie nut and loved war movies of every kind. I recall one day in the summer time going to watch a war movie titled *Tora! Tora! Tora!,* another movie where some stupid country tries to overtake the world and the United States goes in and kicks their asses. That day, my younger sister insisted she did not want to watch a war movie and my mom concurred, as long as one of her brothers "agreed" to go see a movie with her. Agreed meant she would tell me to do it and I'd like it or else. My older brother, by a scant one year and eight months, allowed that he needed to see as many war movies as possible for aiding in the maturing process. This amounted to a weak and transparent suck up maneuver he implemented, so I would be the victim of the girly movie and all the girly crap that accompanied it once again. My brother was a straight arrow, smart as a whip and could suck up to grown-ups faster than the speed of sound. If you held a Dairy Queen soft-serve vanilla cone out the window of your car traveling seventy miles per hour, it could not melt any quicker than it took my brother to win over an adult from scratch. I admired that trait and it was one I did not inherit either from him or my parents, so basically I was screwed. I was the middle kid and that meant, and I quote,

"You never follow the good example of your older brother and you're a bad influence on your younger sister."

Now how in the wide, wide world of sports was a kid to overcome that Mantra? I caught on quickly and worked my "middle kid" angles as best as I could, covertly and without getting murdered by my mom or dad. I'm sure the extermination of an unruly kid back in my younger days would have been considered a mercy killing by any court in the land. I was careful not to disturb the balance of the *force* back then, even before I was sure what the term meant, working my middle kid survival program to perfection.

The *middle* kid. These three words say volumes to those of us with the title. We are the adventurous ones. We are the ones who invented the term, "Hey man watch this," the famous last words of hundreds of thousands of redneck fools. Those who insisted on jumping off high places and landing on and in who knows what after drinking way too much liquid adult bravery enhancer. We were the drivers of automobiles at seven years old. Not to say we are all drunken, stupid ne'er-do-wells or future parolees from the prison system. No, we were Presidents of the United States of America like Abe Lincoln, Teddy Roosevelt and Woodrow Wilson. Well known comedians like Carson, Leno and Conan O'Brien. Peace keepers like Desmond Tutu, MLK, Jr. and the Dalai Lama. Rich dudes like Trump and Warren Buffet and actors like Bob Hope and Richard Burton. We were also young men on the way to being fraternity men, college graduates, train riders and adventurers. So much more than any old first or third kid could ever be. After all, if my brother failed it would be easy to blame it on the middle kid…me. If my younger sister skinned her knee and I was in another state, it could somehow be tracked back to the middle kid…me. We were the comedic, peace keeping, presidential, future rich guy thespians and we had to go watch *Mary Poppins* with our little sister because my brother was a professional ass kissing suck up. And I hated it. It was like a curse had befallen me for some cosmic reason beyond my control, payback for the as of yet undiscovered crashing of my dad's Riviera thing maybe.

I had unexpectedly crossed paths with my buddy Dickey McGrew and another great friend of mine, Cary Chandler, in the lobby before the girly movie started. Let me say this again, I was being forced to see Mary Poppins with my kid sister. My friends were going to see *Night of the Living Dead,* or some cool movie involving dismemberment and consumption of body parts by mindless zombies. They asked me what I was going to see and I think I said *Clubbing Baby Seals, part III; the Reckoning* or something manly sounding that day, lying my young skinny ass off. Having to admit to sitting through two hours of a movie my own mom wouldn't even agree to watch with the only other female living under our roof was a bad idea. Admitting to watching that movie, even if forced to by a parent, was akin to being photographed in the Winnie the Pooh Pajamas your Grandma gave you (included with the 30 pair of underwear and tube socks) for a Christmas present, then having the picture circulated around the school without your knowledge. I was certain that Dickey and Cary were enjoying the flesh eating movie, cussing up a storm and reading Playboy magazines, all paid for by Dickey's big hootered momma. Me? I was watching Julie Andrews float around with an umbrella babysitting a bunch of Cockney brats while hanging out with Mary Tyler Moore's husband. She was a brazen hussy, just like Suzy the Floozy, as far as I was concerned. Of course I had no idea who Suzy was then but my *Mary Poppins* movie experience made her easy to identify when I did meet her years later in college.

Damn it.

I was an amateur cusser back then, utilizing the Biblical cuss words like "damn," "hell," and "ass." These were the basics my Dad used and every time he did, my mom would scream "George!!" as a weak but necessary form of moral protest. My mom, on the other hand, could make a drunken sailor blush, especially when she drove a car. I realized that everyone going slower than her was a dumb-ass and every one going faster than her was stupid shit-head. I figured all the folks going faster and slower than her must have been middle kids too, like me. I'm certain my mother must have at least thought of me in those terms, stupid shit-head and dumb-ass I mean. She was human and I was after all the middle kid.

Mom did help get me started as far as introducing the secret language known as cussing went. As my knowledge of the English language grew beyond the Biblical "damn, hell, ass" realm, I expanded my repertoire by using combinations. "Damn it" and "damn you" were simple. Hell was expanded by "Hell no" and "Hell yes." Adding "Oh" to the front of the aforementioned combinations helped to express attitudes concerning any situation. "Oh Hell No!" was a definite keeper as much as "Oh Hell Yes" was. Ass, on the other hand was the biggie. Dumb ass, smart ass, lard ass, fat ass, ass hole, ass hat, ass face, ass gripper, ass licker, you name it and we connected the word ass to it. The ubiquitous and timely addition of the word shit was the proverbial clincher, and opened up a whole new world of cussing to all of the seven year olds I hung out with. Shit head, shit face, shit ass, shit stick, shit lips, shit licker, shit sniffer, shit eater, and let's not forget the reversals like dip shit, stupid shit and dumb shit (a slight breech of etiquette, but acceptable just the same as they both described a lack of intelligence on some level). Dickey McGrew brought the word shit to us and it was considered a gift among us non-unionized amateur cussers. It would be our first introductions to non-Biblical swear words with many more to follow as the young cuss master Dickey found us worthy. Dickey could have entered the cussing Olympics and won Gold, nurtured by years of tutelage under the instruction of his father, the Bella Karoli of cussing, at his side. Summer and Winter Gold medals, I am sure, hung proudly over the fireplace in the family room at the McGrew compound, surrounded by black-and-white photos of the elder McGrew coaching Dickey on Gold medal winning combinations. The only thing missing for Dickey was his picture on the front of a Wheaties box, his numerous medals hanging around his neck, and his best shit-eating grin proudly on display. Dickey McGrew could have given seminars on cussing and surely made millions, drawing thousands of kids from the metro Atlanta area.

I was confronted by Dickey and Cary immediately after the cool *dead people eating living people thus making more hungry dead people* movie they had enjoyed. I had seen a friggin' (a much more advanced yet understated "Italian" cuss word) *Mary Poppins* movie with my younger sister and I was in full damage control mode. Steering my naturally chatty little sister away from my buddies proved to be a difficult task. I had to keep her at a distance so she didn't mistakenly flap her gums giving away my unwanted *Mary Poppins* movie-going trauma. I knew that as kids, we all wanted to fly and the whole *Mary Poppins* thing gave me an idea concerning air travel and one I would share with all my buddies interested in airborne adventures via umbrella. I had extrapolated, from having to suffer through *Mary Poppins* the movie, that Ms. Poppins was on to something. In my estimation she was a pioneer in flight akin to the Wright brothers, except she never crashed or even had her dress fly up. My dad had a great big golf umbrella and a ladder, and I had a roof that was a good eighteen feet off the ground. I was sure that I could talk at least one of my friends into giving it a whirl, utilizing my best middle kid strategy.

I had convinced Tad Pruitt, a blonde-haired hellion and the youngest of seven brothers, to give it a shot and he quickly decided he was up for the challenge. Tad was a dude that always had something to prove, and let me tell you that sucker could fight. The first time I was introduced to how cold concrete felt on my back was complements of Master Tad Pruitt. I learned a big lesson the day I pissed him off and I remember it well. It was sunny day and my six friends and I were playing on a tire swing that swung over a large nasty pool of funk we considered the gateway to some filthy wetland-down-under in the woods between our neighborhood and the back side of the junior high near Brown High school, our final educational destination if we'd all have stayed in our neighborhood past 1968. The pool stank most of the time, so we considered it an act of bravery when someone swung out far enough to nearly reach the other side. We had the tire swing rigged with a secondary rope tied midway up the rope the tire hung on. Tad had climbed up and tied the second rope, climbing the tree first and then walking the branch it hung on. Tad then shimmied halfway down the hanging rope to tie the secondary rope. Young Master Pruitt suggested we could get better, higher swings if we pulled the rope after whomever was piloting the tire got going good, and boy he was right. Tad decided he would attempt to jump off the tire swing landing on the other side of the pool of ooze (which probably was the cess-pool for the schools, truth be known) if we got him swinging high enough. Tad had the balls and we could provide him with the platform and momentum to give it a try. He got some serious swings in when he attempted to make the jump, a proverbial Evel Knievel of the tire swing if you will. With the possible exception of not having a parachute or a net to land in or on, it should have gone off without a hitch. Tad's only safety net if he didn't make the jump would be a pool of smelly fart water he swung carelessly and defiantly over. As far as we knew, he risked being eaten by whatever Loch Ness type creature might be living or at least visiting under the smooth-as-glass surface. The slick surface was disturbed only by the intermittent bubbles emanating from the center of the lake of fire we were certain the Devil himself had dug. Four of us got Tad swinging so high I was sure the take off would go smoothly and the flight would also be spectacular. Poor planning meant the landing might be seriously similar to Mr. Knievel's greatly documented poor landing at Caesar's Palace in Las Vegas. It was the first time I ever saw what a leg getting broke in slow motion looked like and I did not want to go there. Google it, you'll see what I mean.

Tad had the height, and the guts, and when he reduced his flight countdown to "Three...Two...One... JUMP!" was when yours truly (me) got introduced to Tad's ability to fist-fight. Just before he said "JUMP," I jerked on the rope ever so slightly and Tad went head over heels flipping, as his balance and momentum were thrown off ever so slightly, sending him headlong into the dookie-juice pool bubbling menacingly beneath him. It was like witnessing an unintentional swimming pool belly flop by Sonny Liston or Muhammad Ali but in slow motion. I use former boxer's names to describe Tad's hilarious failed stunt for good reason. When we all ran back to the playground behind our school and awaited Tad's return from the deep sea adventures I had helped him achieve. He indeed showed up pissed off and ready to whip someone's ass. That ass he sought happened to be the one attached to me. I'm not sure why he chose me that day, maybe because I was laughing, but I was indeed introduced to what a thorough ass whipping felt like.

Note to young self: don't piss off Tad Pruitt again.

My revenge for the dookie water ass-whippin' I received would come later in the form of the *"Mary Poppins* Incident" as my buddies would call it afterward. We had doubled-dared and even triple-dared Tad to take the golf umbrella, climb the ladder to my roof in my back yard and jump. He was hesitant—as I'm sure he had multiple opportunities to know what cold concrete felt like on his back too. Tad's knowledge was produced from fighting all of his bigger brothers, all blonde, all insane and all having the ability to fight like game roosters. I personally saw hundreds of great fights in Tad's back yard between all of his brothers and also saw Tad get his ass kicked numerous times by the other six Pruitt's. The Pruitt boys fought each other over anything and everything, and they fought dirty. Mrs. Pruitt, Tad's Mom, would usually get the garden hose after the boys when they fought, spraying them in the face to distract them before she rapped them on the head with her knuckles. Tad's Mom was meaner than a rattlesnake, and a woman I wouldn't even make eye contact with because I was certain she was Medusa's first cousin. Getting your butt kicked that much and Tad's position at the bottom of the proverbial butt kicking totem-pole made him sharper and considerably scrappier than the average kid of our day. I guess gettin your own ass handed to you on a semi-regular basis does that to a kid.

There were seven of my friends in attendance on jump day, the three Jimmy's, Jimmy Hall (me), Jimmy Pair and Jimmy Crumbly, also in attendance was Charlie Wells, Dickey McGrew, Harold Duval and Cary Chandler. All were present to see Tad do the *Poppins* off my roof and get a taste of my revenge served up ice cold. If you notice I said seven of my friends were in attendance. I purposely did not count Tad as a friend after the ass whipping incident. I slowly set my revenge trap by befriending Tad post butt-kick. Back in my younger days and usually after a fight, you and your opponent became good friends. This fact was a small but important part of my revenge fueled master plan. Of course, I lied and told Tad I had successfully made the umbrella aided leap numerous times without incident, knowing he never backed down from a challenge. My other buddies had all been bullied by Tad and his six blonde-haired, demon-seed brothers at one time or another, so this was a sort of blanket revenge for us all. Tad hustled up the ladder I placed on the side of my house, in the back yard, and out of sight. I carefully positioned the climbing device so my mom could not see the activities from the kitchen sink window she so often populated during the day. I did not want an adult to step in and screw up the plans we had carefully concocted as a leveling of our field. I suggested to Tad that he get a running start so he could clear the bushes lining the side of my house, my buddies quietly agreeing in case Tad wanted to hand out an ass-whippin or two after his crash landing. In fact, the bushes would have been useful as a landing pit but I would then have had to explain to my dad why his perfectly trimmed boxwoods were crushed flat. My dad was still in denial about his crashed Black Riviera with the silver, yes silver, leather interior, so I did not want to risk pissing him off by crushing the foliage he lovingly kept perfect. If you got a grown up started, there was no telling where they might wind up, and crashed Riviera land was the place I was the most vulnerable and had the least effective troops.

Before Tad jumped, he said that this must have been like *Mary Poppins* flying with her umbrella and of course none of us, especially me, owned up to knowing what in the Hell he was talking about. I knew exactly what Tad was talking about and I, with Mary's influence, was about to make a positive experience out of a negative experience by convincing Tad to do the jump. For a brief moment I considered telling him not to jump but decided against it, my revenge bone (spelled PRIDE) still sore from getting the crap kicked out of it by Tad. Tad got a good ten step running start before he jumped off my roof, umbrella deployed, wide eyed and blonde hair fluttering in the wind. There I stood with what must have resembled a devilish grin smeared across my young and only recently healed face. The previously mentioned ass-whipping Tad laid on me a few weeks earlier that summer for disturbing his flight across cess-pool pond and subsequent turd water bath landing still lingered on my face and in my soul. Tad was renamed "Larry Poppins" that day as his flight was flawless. His umbrella caught perfect air and his jump was near perfect with the possible exception of him landing on Charlie Wells, breaking Charlie's leg in the process. I'm sure Tad would have broken a body part if not for Charlie acting as a landing pit of sorts. I could not figure out why Charlie didn't move when Tad jumped. I guess he was just dumbfounded by the whole thing, as Charlie was our nerd friend who always made straight A's. Charlie was the kid that built the three stage rocket kits you launched on the playground, ending with the popping of parachutes and gentle landings. I could only guess the jump must have appealed, if ever so briefly, to Charlie's desire to be a spaceman. Witnessing Tad's weightless flight, before he landed on him, must have mesmerized Charlie to the point of paralysis. It was the first time I saw any bones get broken in person, and poor old Charlie hollered like he had eaten a bag full of honey bees. He was really howling it up good when all the adults quickly showed up and Evel Knievel had nothing on Charlie that day in the area of leg breaking. The biggest difference between Charlie and Mr. Knievel was Charlie never left the ground, or even muttered "hey man, watch this" to get his leg broke.

Our revenge came later after Tad's dad got wind of his flight and subsequent landing on Charlie's leg. Tad's father was in the construction business and had a great sense of right and wrong and he exercised that sense in this matter. Tad broke Charlie's leg doing something stupid so Tad did all of Charlie's chores until his leg healed up. He cut grass, took out the trash, washed cars, trimmed bushes, you name it and Tad did it for Charlie. Tad's cold concrete lesson was a summer of someone else's chores, on top of his.

That would teach him for whipping my ass.

As I mulled the satisfaction of conveying the story over to Brian as we both laughed, our train ride appeared to be possibly coming to a conclusion as we slowed down to what I thought to be survival speed. We had been traveling at seventy plus miles per hour for two and a half hours so half that seemed like a good jump speed. Brian and I swiftly planned our dismount…

Chapter · XXI

*"Intelligence is like owning a four-wheel drive truck.
It allows you to get stuck in more remote places."*
– Garrison Keillor

FEWER THINGS in life bring more pain than knowing you have to do something you do not want to do. That's how this train thing and our exit were going to go down and Brian and I both knew it. The prospect of breaking legs and arms just wasn't on my "to do" list in life. A reminder of this magnitude was kinda like getting a tattoo when you were drunker than Cooter Brown (I figure Mr. Brown must have been a drunken SOB to get such notoriety), then waking up to find a tattooed likeness of the Tasmanian Devil prominently displayed in living color on your upper arm, calf or any other body part for that matter. Having a tattoo on a major extremity would prove to be hard to hide after the fact, especially if you had not intended initially to get one, but seemed like a much better way to have a reminder of a time when common sense did not prevail and the prize was a broken limb. My point is, a tattoo was less painful long term reminder of a youthful misstep than a permanent limp or an appendage that bent in directions not originally intended when God designed the human body on the sixth day. Our options were limited. We were on a speeding train and needed to get off and there was not a tattoo artist in sight. Brian and I left our Crown Royal at the frat house, and we could have made good use of the bravery that consuming a lot of liquor in a short amount of time provided. It apparently worked for Mr. Leroy Bubba "Cooter" Brown (not his real name mind you but I am sure he was an Alabama Native), and it would have worked for us if available. Our dismount was a serious "must do" and completely necessary if we didn't want to become temporary Canadian citizens, where Brian and I thought our train was destined. As far as a graduation ceremony was concerned, I was ready to just settle for a Xerox copy of my diploma and done deal. Forget the pomp and circumstance, hand me my paper followed by a slap on the back and let's call it a day. Unfortunately, that was not the way things were intended to play out for Brian and I that particular sunny, breezy day back in the end of spring 1984. It just couldn't be simple. It was the Disco music of my day and it had to be dealt with.

Now Disco music (if you could indeed call that noise music) was considered, to me at least, to be to be the darkest days in American music and I was not alone in my assessment. I did enjoy rock and roll, funk music, and of course Motown's musical offerings. I most likely sound like an old fart, but rap music makes me want to be a better man. Hell must have rap music piped in twenty-four hours a day for eternity. Forget Lakes of Fire and weeping and gnashing of teeth, just deposit me into Hell's version of Detroit, Michigan and play Snoop Dogg or P. Diddy non-stop. Ask anyone living in Detroit and they will tell you. Build a giant wall around it and blast rap music (or polka) all day and see how many prisoners get rehabilitated and how expeditiously it happens.

In my teenage years, I was a fan of Earth, Wind and Fire, a great Funk band of the 70's. I had gotten to know a girl while I was working at Six Flags over Georgia and she appreciated the Earth, Wind and Fire boys' music as much as I did. I had always heard that they threw a great concert and had a show that would put a three ring circus to shame. She called me one day and told me that they were coming to the Omni, a since demolished yet awesome concert and hockey venue in the heart of my beloved Atlanta, and she had tickets on the first row floor, so I was game. We had no idea what we were "in for" when the day of the concert arrived. We usually parked at the Hightower MARTA Station off I-20, the first feeder station on the East-West line for Atlanta's growing rapid transit system. When we parked the car and entered the Hightower MARTA Station it looked like a National Pimp Convention was being held. I had no idea what might be going on, if indeed all the pimps in the United States of America had convened, but I didn't ask questions as all present seemed to be in a very good mood.

We found ourselves a seat on the MARTA Train and headed west towards Atlanta and ultimately the Omni International Hotel and Convention Center where the concert in question was to be held. Our train made four additional stops along the way all in the parts of town most white folks fled in the late 60's. "White flight," as it was called, was a Southern cultural phenomenon. The Civil Rights movement was not going well, agitators on both sides of the issues made living in the city a nightmare, so most white people perceived flight to the rural areas to be the only solution back then. History will judge the rightness or wrongness of both sides but I felt a sense of great division that still lingers to this day. Seems to me that racism is big money business to a chosen few, both white and black, and why kill the cash cow if it continues to produce milk. Keeping racial tensions at bay means that someone connected to the government is going to get paid to either regulate or mediate it. In other words, somebody's going to get paid. Running away seemed to be the best solution to me when things got tight so in some ways, I guess white people ran away too, but for different reasons than I did. My decision to leave was made for me, as I was attached to whatever home my parents decided to live in, wherever it might be located. I do know that my family was the last white folk out and we brought the flag with us and that was the late sixties. It was now the late 70's and not much had changed along those lines. Saying more, good or bad, would require more words than I have space to offer here and would be best explained by someone far smarter and more culturally aware (meaning they make money off it) than I am.

When we arrived at the Omni, it was as intimidating a sight as these eyes had ever beheld, before or since. My date and I were both wearing blue jeans, I in tennis shoes (Nike had just been invented so Chuck Taylor's or P. F. Flyers were as Tennis and Basketball as it got then) and a Led Zeppelin tee-shirt I was gifted as proof of attendance at a specific Zeppelin concert when I was 14 years old with my then best friend, Kenny. I would say that's a story for another day but I might forget it and it bears telling so I'll do that now. Hey, it's my story and you're reading it so you'll like it or you get your money back, but not your time. At this point, you've swum halfway across this river so deciding to quit and swim back kinda defeats the "swimming all the way across" theory now doesn't it?

When I was 14 I had this friend, Kenny, and he was a true rock and roller from way back. His brother, Gordon, had been at Woodstock when it was not such a big deal to say you had actually been there, and generally no one gave a giant crap as the hippy movement wasn't as revered a form of rebellion back then as it seems to be now. Gordon was real stoner, as he smoked weed, drank and did just about whatever he pleased as a means of suppressing the ill effects the Vietnam War had upon his whole being as a human. He was a cool guy, never pushed weed on either of us and always encouraged us not to drink, smoke, do drugs of any sort or ever start. He always said,

"It's like jumping off a high building or jumping out of a plane, man…except you keep falling and sometimes you hit the ground and sometimes you just keep falling."

He threatened to throw a "Cold Concrete on your back" (Tad Pruitt style) ass whipping on us both if he ever got wind of it happening. In all fairness, he was a stand up guy in my estimation. Gordon, via my friendship with Kenny, introduced me to Hendrix, Zeppelin, The Doors, Clapton and numerous other bands that, back in the days of my youth, our parents warned us about. It's amazing listening to that music now and seeing how harmless it all was. Back then listening to rock and roll was the proverbial grease on the slippery slope to some unknown, but greatly warned of, special division of hell as far as most parents were concerned. Now you hear it in elevators and as background music in grocery stores. The funny thing was I listened to it to piss my folks off and boy did it work. Rebellion 101, grow your hair long and listen to Rock & Roll.

Kenny was a guy I met while playing middle school football and he was the guy that could shave in the fourth grade. Every dude I have ever known, regardless of where they went to school, knew someone like that and Kenny was the dude that, for me, filled that slot perfectly. His older brother, Gordon the Stoner, drove the coolest 1966 Chevelle Super Sport with a 396 cubic inch 375 horse motor. It had a Rock Crusher four speed (if you have to ask, don't ask; just nod and keep on reading) with a factory 4:11 posi rear axle that he purchased with his sign-up bonus before formally pledging allegiance to the U.S. Army and entering the hell that was the Vietnam War. He joined the Army on his birthday (he didn't want to get drafted for some reason) knowing he was considered white trash for not going to college and first in line to go anyway. Gordon left in June 1968, did his one year in country and afterward stayed up north to be involved the Hippy movement and Woodstock. He then returned back to Douglasville in 1970 and was never the same.

The Cortez Silver Chevelle was only two years old when he purchased it and he hardly ever drove it, but owned the road when he did. He also had a cool 1969 Mustang fastback with an automatic he'd let Kenny drive at fourteen years old. Yep, he drove at fourteen years old and he looked not one day under twenty-one. Kenny had hair so thick growing on his back if he fell asleep face down on the floor you'd swear he was a bear skin rug, so passing for a twenty-one-year-old was breeze. I sometimes wondered if he was some sort of undercover cop working for the FBI. He looked old enough to drive and he'd regularly buy his brother's smokes and beer and never once get ID'd at any of the local stores Kenny frequented in support of his brothers mind numbing habits.

Gordon was a huge Zeppelin fan and the blimp boys had planned a stop at the Omni during the transition between *Houses of the Holy* and *Physical Graffiti,* so Gordon immediately purchased his tickets and was kind enough to purchase Kenny and me two tickets to boot. All we had to do for payment was to, and I quote, *"Never betray Rock and Roll, man."*

His exact words, so we had agreed in fact to remain as loyal as we possibly could. I was game for the concert, but getting my parents to agree to let me go see Led Zeppelin was an exceptionally large mountain of deception to climb at 14. I was not a card carrying member of the Lying Liars from Liarville clan, but I was an apprentice (I did have a secret decoder ring) as was every kid I knew, with the possible exception of my brother and any of his friends, the suck-up squad. Going to see Led Zeppelin was a mountain as high as Everest in stature and it was all I needed to traverse to get the chance to see Bobby Plant sing the blues, Rock and Roll style, with 20,000 of my soon to be closest future best friends. My mom and dad liked my friend Kenny well enough, which proved to be somewhat of a curiosity to me as they didn't seem to like any of my friends back then. I guess he and my dad could talk intelligently over how efficiently Gillette razors could shave versus a Norelco electric razor or how good shaving cream in a can provided superior shaving lubrication as opposed to regular bar soap. I didn't have a horse in that particular race, as I was a good year from having to shave anything. My middle kid scheming was in full swing and would require me to bring all of my previously learned skills to bare if I were to ever see the inside of the Omni and "Mr." Led Zeppelin himself. I had Kenny to thank for making that wish a reality and I never lifted a thumb nor had to tell a stretcher (also known as a lie) to my folks.

Kenny had concocted a brilliant idea and that was that he and I were going to an overnight Church Camp lock-in and would they mind if I went with him? My only guess was my parents must have thought I might be in need of some sort of redemption, so it seemed like a great idea to them. "To thine own self be true," was the way the saying goes and I was fine with myself back then. The only requirement for "GO" was for my dad to speak to his dad and all was green-lighted for lift off. Kenny gave my dad his brother Gordon's personal phone number Gordon paid for and had hooked up in his room only. Back in the day, having two phone lines in your house was uncommon, kinda like having a swimming pool in your back yard, or having two pairs of tennis shoes at one time. Two pair of tennis shoes, a pool, or two phone lines was akin to being considered wealthy. Gordon could imitate his dad perfectly and he could switch from Stoner to Ward Cleaver (that's Beaver Cleaver's dad from *Leave it to Beaver* to those of you who've been asleep for the past fifty years) in less than two seconds.

I was navigating uncharted waters for the first time. I had never utilized others to pull the wool over my folk's eyes. If discovered, I had years of lecturing to look forward to and just maybe an ass whippin' thrown in for good measure. It was a risk I was willing to take.

Chapter · XXII

"Life is Hard. Being Stupid makes life harder."
– John Wayne

KENNY'S BROTHER, Gordon, would answer the phone stoner style so when he realized it was my dad on the line, he'd ask for him to hang on for a second while he got his and Kenny's "dad" on the line. Gordon missed his calling, I tell ya. That dude could act better than Charlton Heston as Moses himself. Mr. Heston had nothing on Gordon back then, at least as far as imitating an authority figure went. If there were stoner Oscar Awards to be given out, Gordon was a hands-down best actor winner. I could only assume it was something he learned in the jungles of Cambodia as a means of survival. I first appreciated his skills and even recognized its advantages, but later realized it was a coping mechanism of sorts for Gordon. He was one scary dude when his skies darkened and I realized how cool Kenny was as a brother to Gordon during those times. Kenny was Gordon's gatekeeper of sorts and Kenny proved to be his connection with reality.

Gordon did, as I said, buy tickets to see Led Zeppelin in concert and Kenny and I agreed to never "betray Rock and Roll" as our only means of repayment. I know now Kenny earned his concert tickets, and then some, as he was saddled with a big responsibility, babysitting Gordon's idiosyncrasies at the young age of 14. I was a hitchhiker of Kenny's good fortune and we both were going to catch a ride with Gordon to go see the show. The pre-game scenario had been set as I was going to church camp and my parents were likely better off for not exactly knowing the full truth. We were going to *"The Houses of the Holy"* and Robert Plant, Jimmy Page, John Bonham and John Paul Jones were preaching that evening and I was expecting revival.

I was not disappointed.

As it turned out, Gordon backed out of attending the concert at the last minute and he gave us his extra two tickets to scalp before the show. I guess he was going to visit some of the "dark places" Kenny described to me and he did not want to be outdoors that day. I wondered, out loud, how in the world Kenny and I were going to magically make the seventeen mile trip to the High Tower MARTA station (the same one I would later visit on Pimp day-but I'll return to that in a minute) without the advantage of having Gordon drive us there. My Mom was using her broom (think about it for a second- it'll come to you) so we could not use it as our aircraft that day so, as far as I was concerned, we were screwed. Well, in rides Stoner Gordon on his proverbial White Horse and to once again prove his complete coolness. He did it in a manner so profound it cemented his "Coolness" with me permanently. He threw Kenny the keys to his sweet 1969 Mustang and said "It's got a full tank of gas, see you when you get back…scalp my tickets and be sure to buy me two tee-shirts so I can lie about being there." Gordon gave me one of the two shirts and that was the very shirt I was wearing on Earth Wind and Fire day mentioned earlier on in this story and concluded (It does happen I swear) later.

The show was spectacular with the possible exception of the Atlanta Cops delaying the show to bust as many marijuana smokers as humanly possible during the intermission. They hauled out so many people that Kenny and I moved down to considerably better seats than the ones we started out with. It was a shift akin to moving from the shithouse to the penthouse, and Gordon got his money's worth after we told him of the events that took place that evening. Although Gordon had not attended, he could still tell the lie and wear the tee-shirt. As far as I was concerned, he was there. I could only guess the cops either ran out of handcuffs or places to incarcerate the hundreds of dope smokers that day. I assumed the officers just gave up after being overwhelmed by the sheer number of guilty concert goers, so they called it quits. Truth was they could have probably just chained up all the doors to the entire place as the only two dudes not stoned out of their gourds were Kenny and me.

After the legal festivities concluded and "The Man" was satisfied, the show continued. Zeppelin had millions of loyal fans and I could see why. When you laid down your hard earned scratch for them, they threw down a good four hour show for you. They played every song I knew, all of *Led Zeppelin Four* from the front to the back, most of *Led Zeppelin* (the first album) and all of *Led Zeppelin Two* and *Three*. It occurred to me the roundtable discussions that must have been held by Led Zeppelin's members and the management team they utilized when considering the names of their first four albums and how difficult it must have been for them. They also played songs off *Physical Graffiti* and a few from *Houses of the Holy,* quite the amazing a show for a fan of my stature. I had indeed been to church camp that evening, so I could look my folks in the eye and say it was a life changing event and I was sure that God had shown up. In high school, a few years later, Kenny got into the Disco era and left his Rock and Roll roots behind, thus betraying his pledge to Gordon. I, on the other hand, remained true. Gordon's request to "never betray" still rings in my ear, even now.

Back at the Earth, Wind and Fire concert, Cecelia, my date, was a brunette and beautiful. She was from Dunwoody, a high brow section of Atlanta and her mom had her life planned out for her before she had a chance to live it herself. She and I had become very close in our two years at Six Flags over Georgia amusement park, "The Flags," as we called it, a place where two thousand grossly underpaid high school and college students went to party every summer under the guise of having a job. It was the lowest paying and highest reward job I ever had, as what it lacked in pay it more than made up for in good looking chicks. Cecelia and I worked in trams, the buggies that picked up and transported hundreds of thousands of paying customers from the massive parking lots to the front and rear gates. Patrons paid enormous amounts of money to stand in long lines and sometimes ride roller coasters. Charge guests a lot to get in while underpaying your employees was a recipe for huge profits. It was the pot of gold at the end of some corporate rainbow and I was a contributor at least in some strange, indirect, underpaid way. I delivered the cash-rich fun seekers to the massive park's front and back doors where Warner Brothers cartoon characters picked the pockets of its patrons one overpriced hot-dog, slice of pizza and soft drink at a time.

Working trams was considered a great job and one the Six Flags organization took very seriously. Serious in that they only picked the most gorgeous girls and reasonably good looking guys (I was picked to be a part of it, so that's my summation) to present the best example of Southern wholesomeness as humanly possible.

"You never get a second chance to make a first impression!!" I remember the perky orientation worker saying when I agreed to work at slave labor rates with gorgeous tanned young women. I wondered if that applied to perky orientation people so sickly sweet I wanted to upchuck when I heard them speak. Yorking up my lunch on her polished pair of high-heeled Spectators (it's a black and white high heeled woman's shoe—for the fashionably declined) would leave an impression she'd never forget all right. It might even get me moved to pumping out port-a-johns or selling overpriced rubber dog shit and fake vomit in one of the numerous inside the park stores, both a green suit job (explained in a second), so I swallowed my dislike of her style and just smiled and nodded.

Trams people worked outside the park, and that meant you never mixed with the other park workers who slung hash, swept up stuff and controlled lines of overheated people looking to get the kind of thrills most of the employees found in smoking a doobie. Tram folk all had great tans as we were always in the sun (farmers' tans but what the hell) and all the girls were hotter than the asphalt we stood on eight hours a day. Working outside the park made all the tram people very protective of the their own, and made most inside the park workers think Trammers were assholes due to the different job title and wicked suntan. We had special uniforms, bright white with blue accents making the suntans a stark contrast. "Insiders" wore drab nondescript uniforms in colors designed to help workers blend in with the landscape. I say all that so you'll get an idea of how attractive Cecelia actually was. She had long chestnut brown hair, the most blue-green eyes I have ever seen and she was built like an as of yet discovered playmate and every young man's fantasy. She was a huge sports fan, liked cars, and could drink beer with the best of them. If she weren't so good looking I would have sworn she was a dude that converted to the other side. I met her dad once and he liked me instantly, but her mom insisted I was from a bad side of town which was anywhere in metro Atlanta other than Dunwoody. Cecelia attended Woodward Academy, a rich kid private school on the South side of Atlanta near Hartsfield International Airport. That made sense, as Dunwoody was as north as north gets and one might have even been accused of being a Yankee it was so far north. I took her to her junior prom at the protest of her mom, but her dad and I got along swimmingly. He loved college football and I was a serious college prospect then, being recruited heavily by his alma-mater, the University of Tennessee. If you know Tennessee fans, you know how rabid they tend to be and he was no exception. He wore orange underwear as a sign of loyalty to his beloved Tennessee Volunteers. It's strange I know but try me out on this fact, ask a true Tennessee fan where his "Orange is" and see what I mean. Trying to describe a Tennessee fan's loyalty is like trying to explain women or nuclear fusion…just harder, so I'll stop there and return to the Omni, and the Earth, Wind and Fire festivities.

When Cecelia and I walked up the long steps to the Omni from the bowels of Atlanta to where the MARTA Train ran, all we could see for what seemed to be miles were costumes and outfits beyond my ability to describe. I said earlier it looked like pimp-fest and it was that times twenty-five thousand. There were tuxedos of every color other than basic black. Sequined dresses cut up to "there" and plunging necklines so low it revealed nearly everything a woman had to offer, with the possible exception of her modesty. Giant brimmed hats, more capes than a comic book convention, shiny alligator shoes and what must have been the remains of hundreds of exotic birds, as every woman had a feathery boa around her neck and some of the dudes did too. Liberace would have had to completely rethink his wardrobe if he saw the styles on display that day. The rhinestone mines had been drained and there was enough polyester present to make the Monsanto Corporation's stock to split and up its production. Somewhere, Tony Manaro (John Travolta's character on Saturday Night Fever) followers were exceptionally proud. Cecelia and I were a modern day Lewis and Clark going into strange lands never before explored by white people. She and I thought we were quite literally the only two white folk in attendance that day and we stuck out like a pair of sore thumbs.

Cecelia asked me if I thought it might be a good idea if we just left, sold our tickets and stuck to albums or eight-track tapes as the sole way we'd enjoy the rhythmic funk styling's of the gentlemen known as Earth, Wind and Fire. I said "Oh Hell No!" (Thank you, Dickey McGrew). We entered the large hall like Tarzan and Jane and saw the show of a lifetime. Cecelia's mom worked for a dude named Alex Cooley, an Atlanta concert promoter and all around good guy as long as he got a taste of the gate and concessions. Cecelia's mom had given us front row seats to the most amazing laser and light show these eyes had ever seen and it was a show we'd both never forget. I was used to my "white boy" bands coming out on stage, picking up the instruments of their trade, and giving me what I thought was my money's worth. The Earth, Wind and Fire concert was a social event, as evidenced by the way folks were dressed, and the show was like you may have heard a Black Church Revival might go with "hoopin' and hollerin" and lots of singing and dancing. The "white bread" concerts I had been attending were like Presbyterian Bingo night at the local retirement village when compared to the raw energy we witnessed at the Omni that evening.

Obviously, Cecelia and I weren't dressed up like the other eighteen to twenty plus thousand ticket buyers and got many a sideways stare from the majority of the other attendees, which was until we walked down and sat front row center. We magically became a perceived force to be reckoned with as we were assumed to be either connected or rich (both of which befitted her, neither of which applied to me) or both. I was glad to just not get knifed or robbed, as Grady Hospital was the prime landing spot for the unconscious injured in Atlanta and the Gateway to Hell as far as healthcare was concerned.

Those were transitional years for Atlanta, and the South as a whole, and my date and I had unknowingly risked life and limb (or so we thought) to see Earth Wind and Fire live. As it turned out, we became pioneers of sorts as everyone in attendance knew us as "Tarzan and Jane" as we were called by all the awesome people we met at the show. Folks on the return ride on the train recognized us and greeted us without hassle. I spoke jive fluently since I grew up in the West End, one of the roughest neighborhoods in Metro Atlanta after I moved away. Seeing Earth, Wind and Fire in concert caused me to expect more out of my concert dollar and more out of church, when I attended. Of the hundreds of concerts I attended over the years, Led Zepplin and Earth Wind and Fire remain the two that I'll never forget.

Try making that connection sometime.

The jumping negotiations were about to begin and Brian and I braced ourselves for death or worse....

Chapter · XXIII

*"I told the doctor I broke my leg in two places.
He told me to quit going to those places."*
– Henny Youngman

THE TIME had finally come. Our train ride was coming to an end whether we wanted it to or not. Brian and I decided we were going to make the jump and face the consequences of the landing later. Later was to come faster than I can describe here as the actual exit, landing, and aftermath would be within seconds of each other. I heard it said one time of high-wire walker Karl Wallenda's fall in San Juan, Puerto Rico in 1978, the fall didn't hurt, and the flight wasn't so bad, but the landing was awful. Now I will say we were certainly not up 150 feet above the tracks and it wasn't like we actually had to jump, mind you. It was that *I* needed to jump and get my ass back to Troy, and pronto, for my graduation ceremony. That show was to take place in less than five days from right then come Hell or high water, with me or without. After five years of Charlie Bradshaw's terroristic dominion over every aspect of my life, plus my frat stuff and the additional hell I had invited upon myself with Coach Bradshaw because of the frat stuff, I'd had enough and was ready to "exit, stage right" to quote Snagglepuss the Tiger. I had indeed met my wife, I did not know that for sure then but I had met her just the same, and she was to be in attendance for the graduation festivities. I will attempt to adequately describe her briefly but using too many words to describe the indescribable is a fool's folly.

Becky is the girl of my dreams. She's different than any woman I have ever laid eyes on and she beats 'em all, hands down, in every department. I was a senior in high school the first time I laid eyes upon her and she was but a sophomore. I remember exactly what she was wearing on that life-changing day and I was dumbfounded by her beauty, and still am to this day twenty-nine-plus years later. Green eyes that parades and national holidays have been started over and wars have been fought because of. The most beautiful, silky brown hair I have ever seen. Her figure was like Salma Hayak's in her prime, fully visible in the dance scene in *From Dusk till Dawn*, so rent it and you'll see what I mean. The best part was she was fully unaware of all of her physical attributes and she has the sweetest Southern belle personality a man like me could ever hope for. She was as smart as a freshly minted jammed finger, as in, "damn that's smarts!" (Work with me here) and I had fallen for her the second I laid eyes on her. She had only gotten more completely awesome over the five years (any sooner and I'd have blown it) since I had seen her last and that is a complete understatement.

Captivating.

It was the end of my senior year at Troy, fall quarter just before Thanksgiving (actually the day before) and I had just gotten home from taking my finals and was completely worn out. My former long-time hometown best friend (former in that it's funny how time can make some friendships like tires…they just wear out) knew I was coming home and came by to convince me to go visit the newest redneck bar to come to Douglasville. I refused numerous times but finally relented, just to shut him up, and that was to my great good fortune. I had admired Becky from afar for the rest of my senior year in high school, but I was just too intimidated by her beauty to even make intelligent conversation with her, a rarity for this middle kid. I had asked her to let me sign her yearbook in hopes of writing something she might find funny and memorable, as I was going to move on to another life that did not include seeing her every day. I had signed my football scholarship with Troy University by then, so my life was planned out at least for the next four years, and that was OK by me. At the time I was dating the prettiest, well second prettiest, girl in the school but my heart was broken, smashed, crushed and stomped flat for her. Here I go explaining something that you don't give a rat's ass about so I'll conclude by telling you that I met her that night, five years after I had graduated from high school on the side walk going to said redneck bar and immediately asked her out on a date. She said yes and we were married sixteen months later.

It should be mentioned that when I asked to her to marry me informally, I requested that she retrieve her yearbook from my senior year and turn to page 82 (My football number my senior year) and read to me what was written there five years earlier. It said, and I quote, "…I Love you and Marry me," which was the only thing I could think of to get her to possibly remember me and she had no idea how serious I was. She maintained I wrote that in every yearbook (That would be female's yearbooks mind you) that year but as God is my witness, I only wrote it in hers. A whole lot of stuff happened between that time, including Brian meeting her (actually just seeing her) and telling me, "*Jimbo, if you don't marry her you are a full-on dumb ass*," to the actual wedding itself. The poor girl sealed her fate with an "I do" and the rest is history. I think twenty-nine plus years later, she agrees with the "sealed her fate" part, but what's a dude to do, ya know? I've lived relatively happily ever after, but you'll have to ask her about her "ever afters." Twenty-nine years of marriage. It's been seven (maybe) of the happiest years of her life and at least eighteen of mine.

Ruth Bell Graham, Evangelist Billy Graham's wife, was asked one time by a reporter,

"Have you ever considered divorce?"

"*No*" she answered, "*but I have considered murder.*"

I don't know for sure, but I can only guess at how many times Becky might have been standing over me in my sleep and her with a large black cast iron skillet in her hands, ready to knock me coo-coo because of what a pain in the ass I am. I guess it's just the normal ebb and flow of marriage, minus the cast iron skillet part. I run the risk here of making her sound like a real stinker but in reality she's a kind, gentle soul and I'm like a snorting bull in her well organized china shop. There is not another person walking this planet that evokes as much passion, both homicidal and romantic, as my wife does for me. That girl pisses me off where all others fail and she can go from zero to full-on bitch in less than one wrongly inflected word emanating from my lips. I say all that but I must also say she, and only she, owns the keys to my kingdom. It's called love, and I'm a full on disease-ridden lover of my wife's infectious ways. "But she's like a maze, where all of the walls are continually changed," according to John Mayer. And me, well, I am patient with puzzles.

Alright, enough already with the lovey-dovey stuff and let's get back to death and possible destruction of our legs, arms, and every other part that might not land on something softer than a rock.

Here's how it went down.

Brian and I had to decide how to exit the train and decide quickly. That was the easy part, as jumping was the only option presented to us. I had estimated our rate of speed by counting seconds off and timing the mile markers as they passed. The tell-tale jerking and lunging of the train was a definite sign that something was happening and it was something we'd have to take advantage of quickly. Our sloop was slowing down, due to the train entering a town (we hoped at least) and bowing down to the train gods before speeding back up to make the trip through whatever community we had piggyback ridden ourselves into. As the train slowed down and we were able to stand without trouble it became easier to negotiate how we might make the transition from healthy young men to possible quadriplegics or worse. Death from jumping was a distinct possibility. Remember the whole getting found years later, just bones and ripped up clothes, all tangled up in some mysterious, untrue, gay pretzel lock? I remembered, and considered it then. I was the elder statesman and the brain-trust between the two of us, so it was like I was actually thinking for us both.

It was like the blind leading the insane or something far worse. I could say the completely wrong thing back then, but say it with conviction and Brian would have followed me into a gunfight with just a vinyl comb in his jacket pocket if I'd asked him. He was that kind of a friend to me. I think if Brian knew my cool demeanor was covering up an intimidated, big ole white boy, he'd probably screamed for his mom right then and there. I had never done anything like this before and made plans to never ever do it again.

One thing was for sure, I could check off riding a train hobo style across town from my life's bucket list. I could also add jumping off a speeding locomotive 190 plus miles (I was guesstimating) from my point of origin to my bucket list too, then check it off if my arms still worked. Maybe I'd get a companion dog to do it for me as a present, when I became crippled and unable to feed myself from the jump and subsequent landing. I feared that every other bucket list item I would ever want to do might have to be done from some sort of rolling device, like a wheelchair, with my ass planted in it or on it permanently. I guess the very worst thing that might happen would be to have lightning strike at the very second we jumped, striking us both and melting us together in some sort of abstract punishment from *The Twilight Zone,* the one reserved for stupid people.

You get the picture of how a mind works when confronted with such shit and Brian and I were facing with the aforementioned prospects in real time. I tell you man, when you make life and death decisions while speeding on the back of a train, important things (like living) tend to have greater clarity, and stuff that used to piss you off takes on significantly less space between one's ears. It was a life lesson I never forgot and the event mellowed me out considerably. I did survive the ordeal, evidenced by my ability to type this story so that truth should be self evident. By my calculations, rough though they were, I estimated us to be traveling at approximately forty to forty-five miles per hour. The tracks were straight, which meant we could tell if another train might be coming and could plan accordingly. You could feel the train actually relax as it slowed, so we quickly negotiated our exit. It came down to one basic and undeniable conclusion: jump, clear the rocks, and live. We had to decide either to jump forward, with the train's movement or run towards the back of the train, against its movement. The latter move made the actual jump slower but it meant we'd land backwards and whack our heads on the ground, hardened by years of tar, diesel fuel and creosote soaking into the dirt, making it as hard as Chinese arithmetic.

We briefly considered the possibility of *diving* off but that would definitely lead to a cracked noggin, meaning death at worst and concussive amnesia at best. Now that would be humorous, both of us diving and getting knocked silly, only to wake up not knowing each other, who we were and what the hell we were doing out in the middle of nowhere. The only reason to consider diving was to try and prevent breaking a leg. But a good set of legs with a brain on the outside, sunning itself, made it a poor option so we passed. Last choice available to us was to run and just leap off the train and roll when we hit the ground. I knew we could not possibly land on our feet and decelerate under our own power. Running definitely won out as clearing the rip-rap rocks lining the tracks, freshly cultivated from Satan's rock quarry, was a serious consideration and very necessary in order to be able to walk out of this unfortunate scenario sans limp. The only down side was dealing with the added speed from running forward but it was a trade off we'd have to live with. *Hopefully* live with.

So the stage was set. We were going to jump and roll, forward not backward, with a running start so as to clear the devil rocks and still have a chance at walking. We debated the final scenario for a good fifteen minutes, the equivalent of eight and one quarter miles at thirty-five miles per hour and I knew every minute meant more walking and farther to travel, maybe busted up walking to boot, so we gave each other the knowing look that said "see you on the other side" and let her rip…almost. Brian stopped me and asked,

"Jim. If I live and you die, will you be pissed off at me if I just never tell anyone about this whole thing?"

"Nah, I'll be dead and it won't matter anyway," I said with a grin.

He laughed too and was laughing when we started running….

"ONE, TWO, THREE, JUMP!!"

Chapter · XXIV

NOTHING QUITE feels like the summer wind blowing through your hair at forty-five miles per hour.

Nothing.

I realized I was riding on the back of a giant white unicorn through some small town where a festival was being held as a celebration to the many uses of the coconut. I realized also I was the Master of Ceremonies and mayor of the small village, lined by snow capped mountains all topped with cherries and spaghetti, with rivers of carrot juice flowing down from in between the peaks. The rivers were populated by green spacemen riding on inner tubes of various colors while the banks were lined with fish watching the proceedings with scuba gear on.

I gave a rousing speech, attempting to bring a combination book printer and Texas style Chili manufacturer, to the town of Lardassius, Arkansas, population 1,253. I wasn't sure if my speech was effective or successful as the prospects told me they would "get back to me." Meanwhile, my wife, a drug smuggler of sorts, muled in high fructose corn syrup hidden inside the carcasses of burnt out airplane tires for use in manufacturing vinyl siding for mobile homes. She was recruiting new "mules" at the school for wayward Shakespearian actors she founded and financed with her mule money. She was also being investigated by the FBI for being a co-conspirator in the Volcano Retirement Village real estate fiasco atop Mount Blowhard. Her and I were going to have to have a talk, and soon.

I'm not describing some hippy-era acid trip gone bad, but that's how hard I got my bell rung when I landed. It's amazing what your brain will do when jiggled too hard, much less slammed into, as a result of jumping from a fast moving object and decelerating too quickly. I figured the sudden head trauma was like taking pieces of dreams and reality along with my thoughts and imagination and dumping it into a blender and hitting puree. Then, forcing my brain sort it all out was like two blind dudes playing Scrabble. I just hoped my landing didn't leave a scar either mental, physical, or both. Survival was first.

The sun was shining very brightly that beautiful day and the smell of burnt rubber permeated my nasal membranes. I laid there wondering if I was in some sort of heaven, paradise, or purgatory, as I often wondered who got it right as far as religion was concerned. I was being very optimistic thinking I was in the general vicinity of even a concept of some special location, divine or otherwise, after the last five years of my life. It felt like I was floating and it was not such a bad thing thinking I might be dead or at least on the way there. I guessed hell could have a sun and lots of burning stuff also, if the pictures and the movies I had seen were any indication of the topographical landscape of Satan's neighborhood. Maybe it was Lucifer's own personal way of making it extra bad on me before things got hot and the eternal coal shoveling began.

I read a joke about hell one time and it went sorta like this. A man and a woman get to Hell, and Satan himself allows them to preview some of the types of punishment they'd get to spend eternity involved in and then they get to choose for themselves, post-preview. The first room had burning walls and screaming people listening to rap music or polka non-stop somewhere in Detroit. The next room had people being beaten with a fiery, razor blade sharp whip while itemizing deductions for the Devil's IRS. The third room had lots of people standing knee deep in a pool, drinking coffee and smoking cigarettes, laughing it up and smiles all around.

"We'll take room number three, Mr. Satan," they gladly exclaimed.

"Are you sure?" Lucifer asked sternly. "It's for eternity, so choose wisely."

"Room three is for us" they both eagerly replied.

The two were in the room for only a few minutes when one of the Devil's supervisors walked in and said, "Alright, coffee break is over! Time to get back to standing on your heads."

OK, it's a crappy joke but you have got to know how hard I thumped my skull after the landing.

I had completely forgotten where I was and what I was doing when the heat of the ground permeated quickly through my tee-shirt and my spine. The sensation forced my brain to remind me of the fact that I was laying on my back resting upon something hot, uneven, and rather smelly. Smelly as in it had the odor of burnt motor oil and sweaty armpits combined with a sour milk glaze; heady, with a slight pecan aftertaste. I had heard you'd smell burnt rubber when you have a concussion, but I wasn't so lucky. I had a mouth and nose full of nasty train dirt. I was coming to, after the jump, and I realized where I was and what I had been doing for the past three hours. I heard Brian say,

"Jimbo, you alive, man?"

I knew at the very least he was able to speak and I was able to hear. That was a good sign, as I figured breaking one's back or neck might cause your hearing to go south. Brian's words also aided me in remembering my own name, which really sounded strange at the time. Listen, I had done a lot of stupid stuff in my life, but never had I ever jumped from a speeding locomotive, so this was a whole new unexplored territory for me, and I assumed Brian too. I'd only been his friend for two years plus this train ride so he may have very well jumped off a train before. I turned my head to see Brian lying a few feet from me, his hands over his head while lying on his back. He was examining and popping his knuckles in a steady hollow sounding cadence, like counting each digits presence and performance with each loud pop. He was also rubbing the pebbles and dirt coated in black tar off his arms while simultaneously blocking the bright Alabama sun. I could see him manipulating his wrists and elbows to make sure they still operated properly so at the very least he did not have above a C-5 spinal cord injury. I had gone to the chiropractor a time or two when I was younger and learned what parts of your body might work depending on how high or low you snapped your spine in an accident. I learned this while looking at a poster used as decoration in one of the small rooms where my chiropractor plied his trade. I'd study the intricacies of the human skeleton while I waited. I had, quite possibly, the most famous chiropractor in the history of chiropractic medicine as my doctor.

I was briefly associated with the most prodigious chiropractor in these United States of America, Dr. Sid Williams, founder of Life Chiropractic College in Marietta, Georgia. His son, our quarterback my senior year in high school and Dr. Sid's namesake, was someone who I considered to be a good friend. He and I had become friends my senior year of high school football as I was also a tight end on offense and his favorite target on third and short (keep reading, you non-football types). I had suffered a neck injury at one point and Dr. Sid came down to the sidelines to administer an "emergency adjustment" for me as a means of helping me get back into the game.

Dr. Sid was a textbook opportunist and had the looks of a Cro-Magnon man and an American Indian, with coal black hair. He wore tailored suits, and a generous supply of Native American jewelry usually rounded out any outfit he might be wearing regardless of the occasion. He was a full time showman, salesman extraordinaire and former tight end at Georgia Institute of Technology, and from what I could tell a damned good one at that. Dr. Sid was a man of great stature, meaning he was a big dude, and spoke with a kind of confidence that one might use when trying to sell something people might not buy unless otherwise forced. It was an uncanny skill, but one he mastered and had down to a science.

When I first met Sid, Jr. he was damaged goods, psychologically speaking, as his father pushed and cajoled him on everything he attempted and nothing seemed to be good enough. Sid, Jr. was a quarterback, and a damn good one in my opinion, but never quite made the grade in his father's eyes. It was a real shame in my estimation as Sid Jr. had serious skills at the position his father had chosen for him.

Dr. Sid had taken a liking to me for some reason and had invited me to vacation with the Williams clan in Daytona Beach, Florida. It was the summer before my senior year was to begin and that was where I fell from grace with Dr. Sid over two pain relievers and one glass of water. Dr. Sid woke at 5:00 am every morning and woke Sid, Jr. up shortly thereafter and as I was a guest, I woke up too. The deal was that I and Sid, Jr. would have to throw and catch 500 passes a day while on vacation to keep young Sid sharp. I realized why I had been favored by Dr. Sid after the fourth day because he'd sit and count each pass, rejecting the ones he did not approve of. So the deal was we'd exchange 500 passes that met Dr. Sid's watchful, sometimes approving eye and it usually took three to four hours to accomplish that goal. My arms were so tired by the fourth day I would have needed help to wipe my own ass, if only I could have first picked up a fork to eat with, thus setting the digestive process in motion. I was looking forward to getting back to my standing in the hot parking lot at Six Flags eight hours a day job as a break from this action.

One day Sid, Jr. and I threw what must have been 1200 passes to meet the allotted 500 quota set by Dr. Sid and I must say it was like being in an oven standing on Daytona Beach for those six long hours. It could not have been less than 102 degrees when we completed our chores that morning and Sid, Jr. developed a headache of apocalyptic proportions. Dr. Sid, being the control freak he was, immediately got his portable adjustment device and went to work on Sid, Jr. in attempts to alleviate his intracranial malady. After two solid hours of twisting and cracking his neck and manipulating his back, I suggested that maybe two Tylenol and a glass of water might have worked quicker. Silence fell over the room and I had instantly become the unwelcomed heretic. I had achieved most unfavored guest status at that point, as medicine of any sort was considered contraband and never to be utilized in the human body for vertebral subluxation. It was a good thing we were leaving the next day or I am sure that Dr. Sid would have either made me walk home or purchased me a ticket on a Greyhound bus just so we weren't breathing the same air in the same room any longer.

Brian called out to me again, "Hey dickhead, you still alive?"

My brain told me to answer and after a few seconds I did.

"I'm alive, ass face (Thank you again Dickey McGrew)."

Our collective senses of humor were apparently still intact. I slowly began to move my parts and to my great surprise nothing was broken or twisted in a different direction than originally intended by my maker. Brian was sitting up by now and he was looking around at the landscape adjusting to our new and unusual surroundings. I was also sitting up thinking, *I'm actually alive!* And damn glad of it. We were about eight feet apart and looked each other in the eye, squinting from the bright sun, knowing we had dodged a bullet of sorts and we both just grinned knowing we had luckily side-stepped traction, surgery or death. I looked left and saw that we had indeed cleared Satan's gravel by just a few feet but we must have rolled when we landed and found ourselves incredibly close to the tracks where it peeled off at a fork, unseen by us pre-flight. The train we were riding had completely disappeared from view which was a strange thing. We could see a full half mile down the tracks, in both directions, while riding the train but could not see the end or the beginning of it in either direction. Our former train was a hum-dinger with four giant engines at the front and two in the middle, indicative of a train with a massive amount of cars and extremely heavy loads. We could not even hear it making noise telling me we had been knocked silly or completely out for a good twenty minutes or so. We were just looking around, assessing the current terrain. Next thing you know, a loud whistle blows, standing my hair on its end. It was a train whistle designed to warn folks on the tracks to get the hell off as death was approaching. It (the whistle) could also have been used to raise the dead if so needed. It scared the proverbial shit out of us both and caused us to jump up with great speed and run in an attempt to get as far away as fast as possible. We quickly learned that neither of our legs was broken as instinct took over and we hauled ass as fast as we could to get out of the way of the screaming locomotive.

Then reality hit. As we were running, we both stumbled and tripped, not over each other or the tracks mind you, but over our clothes. Mine did not fit as good as I remembered them fitting and I soon figured out why. I looked over at Brian and he was holding his pants up with both hands while running like a hobbled, three-legged plow horse. He was running in an attempt to avoid any item hanging off the outside of the oncoming train from knocking his block off. At the last minute we both basically dove out of the way into what appeared to be a nice grassy area that hid a pile of gravel (not the devil kind, but gravel just the same) so the second landing we made that day was also painful but successful. After we brushed ourselves off and again checked ourselves for wounds from the dive into the grassy gravel, I took notice of Brian and how he looked. I was so taken aback that all I could do was laugh, and I mean belly laugh, at his general appearance.

Brian was covered in what I thought was black soot similar to the kind emanating from the smoke stacks of a coal factory, birthing energy then belching out its polluted afterbirth. He was full blackface and looked like one of the black and white movie characters you would see in some long ago Vaudeville show, as seen on a documentary via public television, with his cobalt blue and stark white eyes and white teeth contrasting against the pitch covering his face from hairline to chin. The soot covered his arms from shoulder to hand and any other part not protected by a barrier, cotton or otherwise. He was a sight to behold and something reserved for the cover of a National Geographic magazine. He laughed at me also, as I apparently looked the same. We had done it finally, we had taken on the full persona of a hobo, and I was going to graduate from college in a scant few days. I had ridden a train to God only knows where on a whim, a calculated whim but a whim just the same, and had successfully exited the vehicle without broken bones.

My dad told me one time,

"Son, there are no one-sided coins in this world…consider the consequences of your actions as the payment for the pleasure you might receive from said actions."

That sage advice came into full, crystal clear focus for me then. I now had to face the other side of the coin and that was getting back to my future wife and parents and graduation ceremony. Simple enough. Wait for a train and ride back.

Wrong.

When Brian stood up and we weren't running or avoiding death, I saw a sight that still makes me laugh every time I think about it. It was Brian's ass, both cheeks, hanging out in the breeze. The unfortunate part was I felt a slight breeze in my ass area also. I told Brian when I was able to speak,

"Dude, your ass is hanging out of the back of your britches!"

I laughed so hard I nearly fainted. Next thing you know, Brian says,

"Dude, your ass is hanging out too and your shirt looks like it got hung in the dryer door and tore it all to "Hell and back, Texas."

We both walked over to a non-grassy area and accessed our clothing situation. It quite literally looked like a stick of dynamite had been shoved in each of our pairs of blue jeans and exploded. The ass of Brian's pants and boxer shorts were completely blown out and resembled (the pants mind you) a sort of blown gasket on a very large engine when you considered the black tar and creosote ground into the material. The knees of his britches were ripped open and one of the legs was nearly ripped from waist to knee. His tee shirt was also smeared with black soot and tar balls from the rough landing we had experienced a short while back. I'm not sure why either one of us cared that much, but it might have equated to nervous small talk when having to examine you best friend's lack of proper clothing. I had blown the ass out of my pants too, but not as severely as Brian. My ass was showing, mind you, but just one cheek peeking out from a small tear in my skivvies and not in full-moon phase like Brian's was at that moment. My shirt was ripped, knees blown out of my blue jeans too, and I was covered in soot and tar-coated dirt same as my partner in crime and flight. My right shoe had the toe blown open, like my toes had made a failed attempt to escape from the canvas prison they resided in. My right sock was ripped also, looking like insulation between the inner wall and outer barrier, my toes protruding.

If it weren't so damned funny I might have thought it was a lie, except I was there with my best friend in the entire world. We were living the other side of the coin, as my Dad had so wisely put it. Brian and I had little choice in the matter of clothing and less choice on how to fix the clothing issues we both faced. Brian had to remove and adjust his pants and boxer shorts to cover up his shiny white ass. He took off his pants and spun his boxers around backwards, as a crude but effective means of covering up. I had to do the same but I was a *tighty-whitey* man and the ass wasn't blown out so bad on my britches but required removal for inspection just the same. I found a piece of wire on the side of the track and Brian used it to hold the butt of his pants back together. Well actually just hold them up, since his belt busted from the force from the landing. The front of my jeans had also ripped at the zipper for some reason so I just un-tucked my shirt to cover it up. Problem solved. I had a white ring around the bottom of my shirt from where it had been tucked into my jeans and Brian said I looked like some artsy-fartsy clothing designer, that it drew one's eye away from the awful outfit I was wearing designed by the events of the day.

So there it was. We had successfully jumped from the train and lived to tell the tale. We sat and started hammering out a plan to get us back to Troy and my graduation ceremony. Brian pointed out that it would be a travesty for me not to attend my graduation ceremony, causing him to miss the opportunity to scream and holler when my name was called. I was motivated not only by the desire to get home and see my future lovely wife and my family, but also wanted to take a shower and eat bargain rib-eye steaks again. I also wanted to drink excessive amounts of Crown Royal a few more times before the graduation ceremony. That event would shuttle in my maturity and the beginning of my new life.

We had some serious traveling to do. We both looked like we had survived a nuclear explosion and lived to tell the tale. Black faced and ripped clothing, blown out shoes and asses hanging out, but alive damn it! It was the time of my life and I was living it one minute at a time. The plan for our return was basic and all it required of us was to go back in the direction we came from.

So we started walking....

Chapter · XXV

*"Nothing flatters me more than to have it assumed that I could write prose-
unless it be to have it assumed
that I once pitched a baseball with distinction."
– Robert Frost*

IT WAS going to be a very long trip back home for Brian and I, and we both knew it. When our trip started it was as innocent as a drop of water in a large ocean but had become a tsunami of sorts in just three-and-a-half short hours. I could explain the previous statement by saying Brian and I had originally intended just to take a ride across Troy, maybe eight to ten miles. We knew enough people, locals and students, and it was a friendly small college town so getting a hitch-hike ride back to our frat house and all the comforts therein was a no-brainer. The return trip across Troy, in what we assumed would be a simple jump off maneuver, had ended up as a 190 plus mile odyssey from our point of origination to the geographical grab bag we found ourselves in at that moment. I repeat the particulars of this scenario over and over so you'll understand the significance of our situation. It was a great trip and offered a unique stage for Brian and I to reflect on the years we had constructed our friendship from strangers to brothers. Each situation shared and survived equaled a brick that would serve as a foundation of sorts upon which we built our lifelong friendship. I'm sure some of the stories you've read here seem like something out of a college frat movie and I am sure many of you have similar stories you could share. The difference is I am writing mine down and you are reading them.

Brian and I looked like we had been incubated in and then launched rectally from a coal mine when we started our journey back. It was a comical sight and I laugh out loud about it still. I call it my *tourettes* laughter, and I am usually rendered speechless when trying to offer an explanation of my outburst. It's amazing how an event is imprinted on your psyche with such force it can sometimes be like you just did it. Maybe it's a symptom of whacking your melon so hard it imprints on your brain when your mind resets its reality after the trauma. Kind of like a bird coming out of its shell and imprinting on the first things it sees. Nah, that's bullshit, this was just so funny it never left the part of my brain that dispenses humor. I will say that when Brian and I left the frat house on our journey and we exited so quickly we'd even forgotten our wallets. There were no cell phones back then so that wasn't even a consideration. We didn't even have a dime for a pay phone call or money for a bus ride, both of which we'd not soon find in the remote terrain we were standing in.

We were in what we deemed to be the middle of nowhere and neither one of us could even see a transmission line for phones or electricity telling us the remoteness of our exit point. The only evidence of civilization, besides our individual ability to walk erect and communicate in the same language, as opposed to grunting, was the train tracks that we stood upon. If not for the tracks I would not been at all surprised if Native Americans or Bigfoot himself might have strolled out of the woods. As it stood, save for a decent Elvis sighting or UFO abduction, this story was barely shy of a trip to the local nuthouse for the teller. As hard as our landing had been, I would not have been surprised if Elvis had showed up flying a UFO offering us a ride home. Plus the thought of being Bigfoot's bitch or his dinner had no appeal to me so getting out of there became priority number one.

We started walking and pondered how this event would be told over the years to come. I told Brian that regardless of how we explained our desire to ride a train, the event would be interrupted with a statement of how dangerous or illegal it was. It's telling would undeniably be met with resistance in the form of a "what the hell were the two of you thinking" or something along those lines. Brian told me, without a doubt, this would definitely be something he'd omit from his resumé when time came to choose a profession upon which to build his future financial success. I wholeheartedly but reluctantly agreed.

As we sat pondering our next move, I reminded Brian that it was his turn to share a story.

He told me of a story about a teacher he had when he was in the fourth grade who had somehow garnered the ability to predict a child of nine years' future means of employment. He told me on one particular day his teacher had each student fill out a questionnaire and be prepared to hand the assignment in to her the next day as the foundation upon which to build her predictions. He stated clearly that the questions were not difficult and he was the first person done on the day the teacher handed the assignment out, but she insisted each student take the paper home and ponder the questions overnight. When the time came to assess the futures of each child, she instructed each candidate to first sit up straight and she'd render each verdict out loud, and from her desk. She read each one as if she had been invited to a view of each child's future by God himself or by some crystal ball she had purchased in exchange for her mortal soul. Brian said he was not what she considered one of her favorites and I considered that to be a good thing, as I had lived with a world class suck up and I considered myself a veritable expert on the breed. If Brian were indeed one of those suck up people, I would not be telling this story now. I have a suck up radar and can spot one almost immediately.

Brian's teacher read each summation carefully beginning with the girls. I'm not sure of the individual names of the student's in question so for clarity's sake I'll just use recognizable Anglo-Saxon names from my youth.

"Cindy" the teacher said with great anticipation, "You are going to be a great doctor."

Confident smiles from the happy child.

"Jenna, you are going to be a world famous Musician."

"Jessica, you are going to be the first female Astronaut," until each girl had her future predicted.

Then the boy's turns came and each young man waited with great anticipation as his future was decided.

"Scottie, you are going to be an accomplished and respected builder."

"Jimmy, you are going to be the CEO of a large corporation."

"Mike, you are going to be a Congressman (That's way back when that was a compliment)."

And so on and so forth until she had doled out the professions of each child present with the exception of Brian. Brian sat there waiting anxiously for his future to be predicted by the seer of success his teacher made herself out to be. Brian said she was reaching for the class math book, obviously finished with the exercise at hand and moving on to the next, when he raised his hand.

"Mrs. Crabgrass?" Brian asked.

"Yes Brian, what is it?" she asked with annoyance in her voice.

"Mrs. Crabgrass, you told everyone what they were going to do in the future but you forgot mine."

His teacher reached into some strange lower file on the side of her desk obviously annoyed by whatever the crystal ball she owned told her concerning Brian's future employment. The regular file she held each child's future in was sitting in plain view on the top her desk so Brian assumed she had kept his in a special place reserved for the future President of the United States or the man that would invent the cure for cancer.

"Oh, let's see, Brian, Brian Horst, hmm… let's see here…uh, yes Brian Horst…" she said as she nervously shuffled through her special secret file reserved for, what Brian thought at least, the student that was headed to the top.

"Oh yeah, Brian Horst…" she began, "*You're going to drive a Bread truck.*"

"I showed her. I'm a fourth year sophomore in College and stuck out in the middle of nowhere," Brian said with his special sarcastic brand of humor that had "kiss my ass, bitch" intertwined throughout each word. "Time of my life…" he added, his blue eyes and white teeth shining in a grin framed in black face.

If the story of his future, as predicted by a sour apple fourth grade teacher, weren't so damn funny I thought I would go find her and kick her right in the knee. What a completely crappy thing do to a kid. Brian had an incredibly brilliant ability to deliver a great story and keep you off balance as to the outcome. For a split second I believed he was proud of the fact he wasn't a bread truck driver but reserved the right to choose the occupation if necessary. My only question for him was,

"Why a damn bread truck? Why not a milk truck or wrecker driver or just a driver, of some sort, not directly involving baked goods?"

We figured his teacher must have been scared of bread truck drivers when she was a child or maybe she just didn't like bread. If she didn't like bread, then as far as I was concerned she was un-American. Get Senator McCarthy on the horn, we got us a pinko-commie in our midst. I have a hard time trusting someone that will not eat a sandwich or toast. We decided to get moving after that one.

Brian and I had been walking for about thirty minutes talking the whole way, not a human being in sight, and settled on a set cadence in order to make quick work of the task at hand. We were talking politics or the invention of car air-fresheners when we heard a noise emanating faintly from the woods to our left. It began as a rustle of sorts and then a faint guttural noise accompanied the rustling in a manner that spelled numbers. Whatever was in such a hurry had the advantage of company as the sound grew like a choir of sorts. There was one exception, the song being sung sounded like dogs upset over their kibbles being taken away for chewing up a shoe, or humping the leg of one's mother-in-law when she came over for a visit.

I was right about one thing, it was a noise a dog would make if he were pissed off all right, and these dogs were indeed pissed off about something. Brian and I stood watching from a distance in anticipation of seeing a Mutual of Omaha's *Wild Kingdom* moment with a wild pack of dogs chasing a deer, cheetah style. Then catching and subduing it making an itinerate smorgasbord of rare cooked venison steak or whatever kind of red meat the chased critter in question might have been made of. We stood watching as the distance between us and the upset carnivorous critters diminished quickly, when it occurred to me that Brian and I might be on their menu that evening. It became obvious the pack of dogs or wolves or cheetahs wanted us to have us over for dinner, and not in a good way.

I had never seen a Cheetah catch an Impala out on the Serengeti ending in a nice game of cards or letters exchanged (pen pal style) between the two of them afterwards. Somebody's ass was getting eaten after the sprint ended. The event was always caught in slow motion and in living color by the filming crew led by Jim, the guy that usually dove in the pit of wild anacondas or distracted the massive stampeding elephants while the narrator, Marlin Perkins, sat at some remote vantage point. I had learned something very important whilst (fancy word alert) watching the wild animal shows that usually came on after the cartoons delivered on Sunday mornings just before *Gospel Singing Jubilee*. The lesson was you do not want to be Jim or the Impala or whatever was getting chased, ultimately ending up in the chaser's belly. I was also on a high protein diet, but I liked my meat cooked medium and shoplifted whenever necessary. On that day, Brian and I was the Jim *and* the Impala, as both of us realized that we were going to be on the menu if caught. I wanted so badly to be the narrator sitting in some remote room overlooking the festivities. It was 1984 and somewhere people were sitting in air-conditioned comfort watching HBO or MTV, fully unaware that Brian and I were being chased by a pack of wild dogs in the middle of nowhere. We were running as fast as our clothes and our scrambled brains would allow us, to a point still undetermined at the time. Twenty years from now, a cave filled with the bones of humans eaten by wild packs of dogs would be discovered and our fates would have been discovered. I hoped if that was the way we'd end up, it rated at least a B-movie or documentary starring us. I had heard of some cultures eating dog meat, so I guess a turn-about is fair play, for the dogs at least.

I could hear the dogs getting closer and as we ran I realized we were just expelling energy best reserved for a good dog fight. Well, in a human versus dog fight, if you wanted to get technical. Plus, the Marquis of Queensberry Boxing rules would definitely not apply in this situation. I hollered to Brian about where in the hell we might be running to and he said he was following me. It was yet again another case of the blind leading the insane, so I stopped running out of fatigue and turned to face my pursuers.

Two College Boys with Smartass Attitudes Found in Blackface and Exploded Clothing, Eaten by Lycanthropes in the Alabama Outback

That would be the headline of the newspapers when and if Brian and I were ever found, post creosote covered dude buffet. I thought about the scenario at hand and in a moment of clarity realized we were not in a civilized area. We were where the dogs lived, and that fact meant we were fair game for the planned feast. The sun was still bright and our vision was not impeded by anything other than the tall grass the werewolves ran in while pursuing two college boys deposited on the wrong side of dog town. Brian and I might as well have been on the plains of some remote third-world country being pursued by the most photogenic local fleet-of-foot man-eaters available. No one was going to witness the soon coming festivities but us two, as up-close and personal as it could possible get.

For a brief second of survival driven weakness, I realized I only had to outrun Brian to survive. We were family, and I might have to explain what happened to his Mom if the outcome was poor and only I survived. Brian's mom was a sharp woman. If I lived only because I had outrun the carnivorous beasts first, and Brian second, she'd get the truth out of me faster than any secret government truth serum could, so I passed on the thought.

We decided, or had our decision made for us by tired legs beaten by a forty-five mile per hour jump, to stand our ground. There was not a thing in sight we could climb to render ourselves unreachable to our foes. When we turned, I instinctively stooped to pick up a rock as mechanism of defense. If my ass was getting chewed up at least one of the dogs was going to be having abstract dog thoughts after I cold-cocked the ever lovin' shit out of him (or her) before I became permanent dog chow. Brian also picked up one of the devil's rocks and cocked his arm for launch at whatever upset critter that might show itself to us. I stood like Tom Seaver ready to throw a fast ball to end the game in a blaze of Hall-of-Fame style glory.

I was the more athletic of the two of us based solely on my years of continuous sports and conditioning, so I hoped I would do the game proud when called to pitch. It sounded like the dogs were right on top of us when we heard what sounded like music from some angelic choir. It wasn't singing mind you but the sound of a speeding locomotive sent by God himself. The dogs cleared the grass, saw the two of us, and immediately started to run in our direction. The canines were on the other side of the tracks and Brian and I positioned ourselves as far on the opposite side of the tracks as possible. It was a means of buying time until the train made it to us, creating a natural diesel driven barrier between ourselves and our furry friends. As the pack of four or five dogs ran, the train blew its whistle as a warning and the dogs slowed to see what the noise was and where it originated from. The lead dog had made its mind up that he was going to taste one or both of us that day and that decision would prove to be what amounted to its undoing. Fido (my name for the bitch) could have crossed the tracks quickly and Brian and I would have had to deal with just one dog, upping our odds of not getting chewed on, and increasing our chances of survival.

I am not sure if it was a survival instinct when Brian made his throw in the direction of the rabid dog. When the leader made his run for what he assumed was his dinner (us) he forgot that he was attempting to outrun a speeding train in order to accomplish his mission. When it came to eating and reproducing, what I assumed all wild dogs focused the bulk of their attention upon, a train rarely factored in any dog's equation. Screwing and eating red meat was an existence envied by most of the two legged dogs I knew and hung around with, so, on some strange level, I felt Fido's pain.

The beast ran and as he ran he tapered his path towards the tracks in preparation of crossing over toward us. The train was about 150 yards north of our location heading south toward us at a good seventy miles per hour. I knew this because I had become an expert of sorts while riding a few hours earlier. Just before the alpha dog was going to cross I felt a *Whoosh!* of wind and an object pass so close to my ear it briefly drowned out the loud noise of the approaching train. I was looking straight into the red eyes of the hungry dog hell bent on biting one or both of us as we stood on our side of the tracks. The whoosh I heard was the rock Brian had picked up, about the size of a baseball, and threw at the hungry mutt. I was sure the dog never knew what hit him as Brian's bottom of the ninth with bases loaded and a full house perfect pitch hit the dog right between his eyes. "*Steeerike Three…you're out!*!" I heard in the part of my brain that dispensed justice.

The dog reacted in a manner befitting any dog that had been beaned by a two pound rock between the eyes and in full stride. Brian had introduced Fido to Sir Isaac Newton and ole Ike won. "For every action there is an equal and opposite reaction," became a painful lesson for that dog that day and one he'd only get to learn once. Fido stumbled and fell just as he made his way onto the train tracks and he probably had no idea what hit him (from behind at least) when the train struck him on the north side of his southbound self. The train was introducing Fido to Mr. Newton's laws of motion twice in one day and in the most intimate of ways. Fido went spinning and tumbling on the same side of the tracks his other hungry friends were running on and just before he landed, I saw the other dogs catching up to him. Brian and I stood shocked, initially by the accuracy of his throw and secondarily due to the fact we were just plain tired. We stood still for the five minutes it took for the train to completely pass us by. When it did, we saw what being the lead dog must have been like and the disadvantages of being said dog. Alpha dog was lying injured and bleeding while the other dogs circled him, also growling, I guess in anticipation of eeking out some sort of underdog revenge on what appeared to be upper management. I could only assume the other dogs' smelled blood as they tore into the alpha dog with a primeval bloodlust. It was a personal life-long lesson in upper management and the numerous hazards encompassed by deciding to lead people, and dogs too I figured. I have found in most cases there wasn't a discernible difference between the two, with the possible exception of the dog giving you the courtesy of growling at you to your face before sinking its teeth into you.

I was proud of Brian. The dude had single handedly saved us from getting our asses chewed off by a pack of rabid dogs. He had thrown a perfect strike with a two pound rock all the while facing the adversity of an oncoming train. All this he accomplished under pressure, with the ass blown out of his jeans and in blackface in the middle of nowhere. As we quietly walked away, the new alpha dog was being decided upon and the old alpha dog was enjoying his retirement party complements of his hungry canine buddies and Newtonian physics. I guess it goes without saying, but better Fido's ass than ours.

So, Mrs. Crabgrass, wherever you are, here's Jim Hall saying,

"Let's see, Brian, Brian Horst, oh…someday you are going to be an itinerate pitcher, saver of lost souls, and the only person to ever be inducted into the Baseball Hall of Fame in Cooperstown for throwing a perfect strike with a rock."

"If you ain't the lead dog, the scenery never changes."

Lewis Grizzard

Chapter · XXVI

B RIAN AND I dispensed repeated high fives accompanied with equal amounts of hoots and hollers for a good twenty minutes after we put a mile between us and the unexpected feast the other non-management dogs were enjoying. I probably told Brian he was "the man" a hundred or so times after the perfect, between the eyes strike on our ravenous pursuer. He had accomplished the aforementioned feat under the most pressure a human being might find themselves facing while not engaged in battle. All of my "bravery" on the playing field had not amounted to a hill of shit in comparison. Way back in the beginning of time, when God set the wind in motion and decided where the water would stop and the beach would start, he created a granite formation. Thousands of years later that granite would be mined, ground up, purchased in bulk by the host railroad company whose train had deposited us at our current location, lining some obscure piece of train track in the proverbial middle of backwoods nowhere Alabama. On its appointed day, the piece of gravel would be picked up by one Brian Keith Horst and used to fend off the devil himself in the form of a rabid feral dog. His amazing accuracy might have very well saved our lives. I was ready to stand and fight the dogs to the death, but Brian had the will to live and shoplift steak another day. I was beholden to him and prepared for him to parlay that fact into something huge as far as payback was concerned. What the terms of the payback were, I did not know, but it existed just the same and trailed behind us like a bean dinner fart. I felt that it had become somewhat of an act of providence that I would indeed graduate in the next few days. I knew that if we were to matriculate in the same place any longer, Brian would have expected some sort of restitution for saving our asses. Hell, I would have.

We walked and talked of the previous event for a good three to four hours as we slowly, meticulously and hungrily made our way back to Troy and what was to be our temporary home for only a short while longer. I had always sworn I would live and die in Georgia and my five year sabbatical in L.A. was soon to end. Brian asked me how we might utilize this trip to our collective benefit and I told him I had no idea. I was at a total loss on how to give heed to the kind of stupidity it must have taken to even consider this scenario a success. My own thoughts reinforced the fact that it would not be beneficial in any way to tell any adults, friends or even future prospective employers about the events that occurred over the last few hours. There would be no good way to explain this story other than to question the doers of the deed and their collective lack of judgment. I will confess it was a great time, in retrospect, and was extremely defining in nature for us both.

I have seen so many friendships dissolve due to separation and geography and I am sure it is in God's great design for life and survival of marriages that some friendships wear out. I was fortunate in that my and Brian's friendship did not, due to the fact we lived so far apart for all the years after I graduated from Troy. I could not imagine now Brian being my neighbor over all the years of struggle and success. Our shared odyssey was an event so fantastic and far-fetched it would be unbelievable to the hearers and one that I am sure might have gotten old quickly when repeated at barbeques and friendly gatherings that inevitably accompany the ebb and flow of life.

I must say now that I probably owe my life to Brian, and now you know that too.

Brian and I had decided to make a run for it and set a faster pace back to Troy. He and I had figured out how to adjust our clothing, or what was left of it, so as to make the running part of our trip a little less of an effort. We weren't running pledge course speed, but we had calculated we were still a good 165 miles from our home, beds, and high brow shop-lifted grub we had grown accustomed to. We had agreed, in fact, that this portion of our trip was Biblical payback of sorts for the nefarious activities Brian and I had been engaged in. Brian and I accepted this punishment like men and trudged onward in our torn clothing and blackface, figuring fate, fueled by poor judgment, was having its way with the two of us.

While we ran we speculated on the fact we probably scared the wild pack of dogs with our looks alone and maybe they were more afraid of us than us of them…maybe. Of course we could only express our fear with bravado and rocks and at the very least it had worked for us the one and only time we needed it too. The well timed train didn't hurt our efforts either. It was a lot to take in and more than we could process that day, but while considering it we also agreed we'd better make quick time if we wanted to see a bed and a hot shower again. We also agreed that avoiding any more dog packs would be a good thing, as I was sure that lightning would not strike twice in one day. Not the dog pack part mind you, which was totally possible because of where we were, but Brian throwing a clutch pitch to save our lives twice in one day.

As we ran and talked, Brian asked me if there was any event that might compare to this one for me. I did have one football story yet to tell. Brian eagerly awaited the tale, as they usually spelled my rage against the machine that was Coach Charlie Bradshaw. It was my senior year playing football under his watchful, disapproving scrutiny. I recall in earnest how Coach Bradshaw treated seniors on his squad, as he usually extended a modicum of dignity to the survivors of his extreme physical boot camp known as "The Drill" to those of us who made it through. I actually looked forward to getting a little respect from him, but I would be wrong in that assessment as waiting for that day to come would be akin to waiting for hell to freeze over.

My first game as a senior was against University of Tennessee at Chattanooga, a division one school that was a powerhouse in its division coming off a National Championship season the year before and predicted to be a repeat winner my last year involved in the sport. I had garnered numerous pre-season awards and accolades but none from my own coach as far as an All-Conference or All-American bid was concerned. Nomination by one's own coach was essential for any post-season rewards and none would come from mine for me. I guess I was getting my reward for not kissing his ass and playing along with the BS he dished out. I know you might think it is sour grapes on my part, but I must convey to you the severity of our program. I said before that when I met with a few other college football players, even they knew of what a hard-ass Coach Bradshaw was. It was a legendary feat if you survived "the Drill" and I did survive with my sanity intact and no butt-breath from ass-kissing. Some dudes could play that game. I could not. I never gave Bradshaw the bird or spoke poorly of his ancestry (at least not out loud), but much could be said by silence and that was my tactic. I broke my thumb in game one time and taped it to my hand only to break it worse later on in the same game. After the butt chewing I received from Doc the chicken killer, Coach Bradshaw actually half-heartedly complimented me on my fortitude in one of our numerous meetings held after every performance on the gridiron displayed in living color in front of the entire team Sundays after the games.

"How's your broken thumb feel, Jim Hall?"

I pondered a good response.

I said, "Feels like a broken thumb, Coach Bradshaw"

Silence.

"That's not the God damn answer I was looking for, hoss."

"Feels great, coach," was all I could muster. Shit, I couldn't win for losing with that crotchety old bastard. Bradshaw could put up a Christian front for most everybody, but for the sake of truthfulness and the force with which he led, I use his exact words here.

When we arrived at the University of Tennessee at Chattanooga, unloading our gear and entering the enormous field house, I was asked by Coach Bradshaw to meet with him and my position coach, Jim Tompkins (who was one of the finest men I have ever been coached by) for last-minute strategy purposes. I thought I might get invited to ride the pine for some strange and still, as-of-yet unknown infraction, like smiling at practice or encouraging my teammates like most good soldiers did when at war. I was walked around some corner, away from my teammates and out of earshot of the other coaches when

Bradshaw's orders came down. It was simple and would not be questioned and went as follows.

"I want you to play left defensive tackle this game."

I was a nose guard and I was surprised, as we were molded into the position we played from the first day we put our pads on the first day we practiced the college game. What he asked was like driving a right hand drive car in some far-away land that utilized terms like meters and liters instead miles and gallons. It was so unusual even Coach Tompkins threw up a protest of sorts, only to be shot down by Coach God. I had no choice but agree as I needed a ride back home to Troy and it seemed the only way I was getting there was to obey his orders. I never took any of it too seriously, as it was just life back then and I was living it. I still could not figure out why Bradshaw would break his own golden rule and move a player into a position he was not familiar with, placing the entire team in jeopardy since we used a scheme too complicated to explain here. Our defensive system was hammered into our heads and bodies over years of heated, protracted wars known as scrimmages, filled with disapproval and reminders of imperfection at every turn.

I shrugged to myself and just said, "Sure, Coach," and let it go.

It was when we took the field for warm ups I figured out what must have accounted for the last minute change.

His name was Mike Vernon (I'm changing his name out of respect for him). He was a repeat All-American for three years running and at six-foot-nine, stood a whole head above most of his teammates. He was the biggest player playing in college football that year weighing in at a modest 360 pounds, unheard of back in 1983. I could see by the drills he was fleet of foot and was considered a sure NFL draftee by every available outlet that speculated on football players back then. I was not sure he was the reason for the last minute position change, but I had a feeling either Bradshaw wanted me to be completely humiliated by "Mount Vernon" as the gentleman on the loudspeaker repeatedly called him or if he was moving me out of necessity, or both. Now, I was no sissy at six-foot-four and 275 pounds of steel, determination and downright stubbornness, molded by years of workouts and practices that would make the hardest men give up. I figured I would give it my best shot and let the chips fall where they may, as the saying went.

When we met at the fifty yard line for the coin toss, I must say that Mr. Vernon looked considerably taller than six nine. It's amazing how much taller five inches makes a dude look when wearing sixty-five pounds of equipment designed to protect you from the likes of someone his size. They won the toss and decided to receive the kickoff, placing myself at my new position right away. It was not going to take very long to see how Coach Bradshaw's experiment was going to turn out. There were only four of us on the field, two for them and two for us (myself being one) and when we stepped up to shake hands and lie about being good sports, the standard drill in football, I looked Mt. Vernon in the eyes and said,

"You are one big dude."

He laughed to himself and asked me who his "victim" was for this game, meaning who was he was specifically going to humiliate in front of his home crowd. I told him I guessed we'd find out shortly.

One thing I did know for sure, I was certain I was the candidate.

Chapter · XXVII

"Where are you going?" Hamish asked.
"I'm going to pick a fight."
— William Wallace, as played by Mel Gibson in Braveheart

WE KICKED off and dropped the UTC player on his own ten yard line. When we ran onto the field and I lined up at left defensive tackle, it only took a few seconds to see that Mr. Vernon and I were going to become intimate friends for the next four quarters of our lives. When he walked up to the line, we locked eyes and he said and I quote,

"I hope you have life insurance."

First play from scrimmage, Big Mike Vernon introduced me to the weight of a 360 pound dude, with another sixty-five pounds of equipment strapped on, resting patiently on top of my whole being as I laid there unable to move. He caught me under my chin and rolled me over on my back like I had never played the college game before in my life. Meanwhile, UTC ran an 80 yard romp down to our ten yard line giving them only ten yards to go to score. Not eighteen seconds had elapsed from the clock and my uniform was filthy. I was already beaten like I owed Mr. Vernon a lot of money I couldn't immediately repay. Of course, I wasn't expecting any special treatment since I would have extended the same courtesy to him (the resting of my big ass on him instead of the vice-versa part) if our roles had been reversed. As I got up off the ground and jogged down the field to what awaited me there, I came to the stark realization that this was but the first quarter of play, only eighteen seconds had elapsed, and I was really, really tired. Pain and humiliation was on the menu that day and Mt. Vernon could deliver both with a vengeance that might make most men cry and run away. As I jogged down the field next to Mt. Vernon he heckled me as to what else might be in store for me the rest of that day. I was certain that a large part of Mt. Vernon's intimidation game, besides the fact that he was a friggin monster, was to run his mouth about the ass whippin' he was gonna lay on you. I just looked at him and sang WAR's song "Why can't we be friends?" (c'mon, you remember that song…"Why can't we be friends?"), eliciting a good laugh from him as we made our way back to the task at hand and our joint destiny.

When I reached the fifty yard line Coach Bradshaw called a time-out and hollered for me to join him on the sidelines for a quick chit-chat. Coach Tompkins, my position coach, moved to join us and Coach Bradshaw shooed him away like one might shoo a fly off the rim of a tall glass of cold sweet tea. It was just he and I (and the entire stadium full of folks) watching and wondering what might be the subject of our conversation that warm, humid Saturday night in Football-land. Our conversation went something like this.

"Well, Jimbo, looks like we have a decision to make right here, right now."

I agreed but he asked that I not speak and just listen. I knew his third person speech was coming.

"I'm in a situation here son and I am in need of a solution. What I have is a big ole corn-fed boy that outweighs my biggest man by 100 pounds and he (me) just got run over like a kitten that strayed out onto the interstate. Now I know that you and I have not seen eye to eye on much in the last four years, but I'm the coach and I make the god damned decisions around here. I consider you my best defensive lineman and one of the best natural talents I have ever coached. Now that's in forty years of coaching...including Kentucky and Alabama." (I knew he was doing the "pump up" at this point, there was NO way I was any of the things he just described...he made sure I knew that truth long before I was standing right there, right then.)

As Coach Bradshaw continued orating about my talents, I looked around to see if he might have been talking to someone else. He never handed out compliments, much less the one's he directed at me right then. He continued,

"You also have a decision to make Jim Hall and it's this: Is this day going to be the best day of your college football career or the very worst? It's as simple a question as that and one you have to ask yourself right now. This will be a day you'll reflect on all the remaining days of your life and wonder if you could have dug deeper and met the challenge you face today or rolled over and played dead. You might face challenges a lot bigger and on a different type of playing field than the one you find yourself on right now, but right now I have a challenge for you. Are you ready son?"

"Yes, sir." was all I could say, I didn't have a "No" in me.

"Yes, sir" was all I had. I was hurting physically and was looking for anything non-habit forming to ease my pain and all I had right then was a motivational speech from an old man that had treated me like an enemy at best and a thief at worse. I had faced Mt. Vernon only once and got used as a combination mattress/doormat of sorts just a few minutes earlier, so I was up for anything short of a small pistol shoved down my jock strap or maybe a brick to lay upside his head, Jessie Clyde Wallace Jr, III style. I locked eyes with him and never broke stare when he said,

"I have a plan (insert strategically placed pause right here). It's obvious they are going to score on us this play but here's the deal," he said with a certain authority appointed by

God himself and the Athletic Department of Troy University. "When you line up across from Mr. Vernon, the moment he touches his fingers to the ground I want you to knock the ever loving shit out of him, regardless if you are off-sides or not. I want you to roll him over or run him backwards enough to piss him off at you. We'll draw a penalty for half the distance to the goal line but that's fine. The next play, when he walks up to the line and drops his arms on his elbows, I want you to hit him with a Alabama haymaker right across his big assed head and run him over on his back. We'll get another penalty half the distance but that's fine too, now the third time's the charm Jim, "He'll step up to the line thinking you're gonna do it again, which you are, just this time when he walks up to the line the second he looks down to align himself you plow his big ass like a cornfield and I mean run him over on his back and just lay there."

I stood there with a grin on my face not believing what I had just heard.

"You should own him by then and he's gonna be jumpy waiting for you to knock the shit out of him again" he finished. "The fourth time he walks up to the line jump at him like you are going to plow him again but be careful as he'll probably be ready to fight you at that point. I'd suggest caution then, if you initiate the exchange you might get heaved from the game and we don't want that."

The last thing he said as I was walking away to join my teammates was, "Jimbo, if you don't whip this guy's ass you'll never play another down on this team again." I didn't acknowledge his words as I jogged away, but I damn well heard them as loud as if he'd announced it over the visitors P.A. system.

And there it was. The gauntlet had been thrown down. Psychology 101, build 'em up then tear 'em back down. Fear based productivity at its most basic and primeval best. I either best this giant right now or I ride the pine in shame for the rest of the season, and as far as he was concerned, my life.

I ran the forty yards slowly, contemplating the gravity of the conversation I was party to just a few seconds earlier, as the entire stadium watched me going to what they must have thought was my certain doom. I ran relatively close to the UTC huddle and their entire team stood and looked at me as I ran. Some had blood in their eyes, some pity, and a few just laughed and pointed.

Mt. Vernon called out to me,

"You and your coach discussing who will get the money from the insurance we talked about earlier?"

Me being the natural smartass I am just said,

"Naw, man, we were just talking about how much hair your girlfriend has on her back."

He instantly went from smiling to scowling in less than a split second. I had one thought: *If this doesn't work I am a dead man.*

When I reached our huddle, my teammates all stared at me and asked, "What in the Hell was that all about?"

I just snickered and told them all, "If I tell you I will have to kill you all. You guys need to just play along and watch the show Coach Bradshaw and I have cooked up for you this evening"

They all just looked at me smiling and looked at each other smiling and I told them, "You guys be ready to fight if necessary."

That might surprise you but it shouldn't. I played ball with some of the toughest dudes I have ever met in my life, bled the same blood in the same mud with them and would fight for them till the death if necessary. Plus the added fact that not one of them had the balls to take on Bradshaw with so much as a sideways glance made me the lone elder statesman in that huddle.

As The University of Tennessee at Chattanooga "Mocs," as they were called, broke the huddle Mr. Michael T. Vernon ran up to the line with his lips pursed, eyes narrowed, looking at me, obviously not humored by my knowledge of his girlfriend's back hair situation. The rest of his teammates meandered up to the line confidently, all staring at me, and the man that lined up next to Mr. Vernon pointed at me and said,

"We're running right over you, 63."

I looked at him and said, "That's *Mr. 63* to you, pussy (an insult wherever you played ball, especially when you were a senior)."

The UTC boys had not yet fully made it up to the line when Mt. Vernon touched the ground with his fingers and I executed Coach Bradshaw's first order, plowing his ass into the ground. Coach thought he might be ready to fight after the third or fourth time hitting him but he missed that one by three plays. Mt. Vernon was cussing me like a red-headed step child when I unsuspectingly hit him, rolling him over on his back and went limp on him like he did me on the first real play from scrimmage. I will say that both teams stood in disbelief at the sight they had witnessed as the referees broke us apart both of us shoving each other as we separated, us both commenting about how many legs our mothers walked on.

"I got something for yo ass, mutha-fucka" he shouted at me as he said something along the lines of "this is my house."

I was certain I did not see his name emblazoned on a giant sign outside of the field house or the entrance to the stadium so I reminded him of that fact also. That pissed him off further and that was a beautiful thing. I was indeed charged with an off-sides penalty but he was charged with unsportsmanlike conduct for cussing. My off-sides penalty was a half-the-distance infraction amounting to two and a half yards but the unsportsmanlike conduct penalty he received was a fifteen yarder and loss of down. When the penalties were finally sorted out, it backed them up twelve and a half yards and really pissed ole Mt. Vernon off, but good. He was breathing hard and determined to get my white ass in a way that could not have been pleasant. After that remark, I think I recall telling him that he probably didn't prefer girls with hairy backs after all but preferred men with hairy backs which shut him up. I hollered for his teammates to watch him next time they hit the showers, especially those with hairy backs. I was digging the hole as deep as I could get it, and I was hoping he didn't carry a pistol or have access to a brick either. I had entered a proverbial no man's land of insults and shit-talk and the game wasn't even started good. Hell, the only two dirty uniforms on the field were Mt. Vernon's and mine and we were technically still on the first down from scrimmage. It was all part of the plan laid out by Coach Bradshaw, except I added the shit-talk part myself for creativity purposes.

I then executed the second phase of Coach Bradshaw's plan and that was when Mt. Vernon walked up to the line of scrimmage and dropped his elbows on his knees I plowed his ass again rolling him over on his back, us both face to face, him cussing me like a drunken sailor on leave. I stayed on him a little longer than I should have but I enjoyed it. I also used that opportunity to use him "to get up on" as my fellow African-American teammates called it, inflicting as much elbow, knee, hands to the face, ribs and any other tender body part as possible while trying to get off of an opponent. Mt. Vernon came up swinging again, prompting another off-side for me and another unsportsmanlike conduct penalty for him. We backed them up another ten yards, five yards against us for my off sides penalty but fifteen for his unsportsman like conduct infraction, and attempted the second play from scrimmage for the third time that day.

On the third attempt at the second play of the game, Mt. Vernon was jumpy, snorting like a Brahma bull. As soon as he touched his hand to the ground, I delivered the Alabama Haymaker special ordered by my head coach; right across the head of the current All-American Senior and future National Football Leaguer doing time with the Minnesota Vikings and the San Diego Chargers for seven years after our gridiron meeting took place. When I laid him out the fourth time, a melee broke out on the field akin to a riot, except everyone wore protective gear while the gang scrap took place. Both of our squads had had enough, and the fight was on. It took a few minutes to get our two teams separated and the second play from scrimmage had not even taken place yet. I am sure it must have been some screwy record of sorts, two college teams on the field, seven penalties, three of which were unsportsmanlike conduct. Add in a huge fight, one play for eighty yards on the first play of the game and twenty-seven minutes had elapsed in regular time but only eighteen seconds had ticked off the game clock. Mr. Vernon and I received numerous warnings from the referees about ejection possibilities if anything else occurred between us that were not aligned with the execution and conclusion of the game at hand.

Coach Bradshaw was brilliant that day in his calculations concerning Mt. Vernon. It rattled his cage so hard that I owned him for the rest of the game. He was totally ineffective for the remaining three quarters plus fourteen minutes and forty-two seconds of the game. I punched and clawed at him every chance I had, knowing if he breathed a word in retaliation he'd get ejected from the game and possibly screw up his chances post-season. I put an ass whipping on him so bad he took himself out of the game in the fourth quarter and the UTC coach inserted a true freshman in his place. Of course, this poor newbie thought I was the giant killer as no one had owned Mt. Vernon, ever, so handling his freshman ass was a piece of cake. I will confess that at the end of the game I was so spent I practically had to crawl off the field, happy the ordeal had finally reached its conclusion. I was spent both emotionally and physically, but I kept it to myself.

When the game ended we did not prevail, but also were not saddened by the loss as Coach Bradshaw actually praised us in our efforts that day. It was indeed a loss, but we had made a terrific showing against a much bigger (at least at my position), higher ranked and supposedly stronger team. Those facts caused every future opponent we faced to fear us from that day forward. I could hardly walk afterward, tired and half stupid from the events that had transpired that day, and mistakenly found myself in the tunnel leading back to the locker rooms surrounded by a mass of UTC players post-game. I figured they were going to kill me on the spot. I was wrong in my assessment and was met with pats on the back from the opposing squad and even the UTC head coach told me it was the best performance he had ever seen from a guy giving up 100 pounds and almost five inches to an opposing player and his very best. I guess the best part, for me at least, was after we all had showered and dressed and I was attempting to crawl back (Ok, I was shaky legged walking) to the bus for the long ride back to Troy. I had loaded my bags under the bus and when I turned to make my entry to the carriage I was face to face with Mr. Mike Vernon himself, all six feet, nine inches of him, and he said something to me I had not heard in all the years I played under Coach Bradshaw.

"You are one tough ass white boy" he said, "and the best player I have ever played against in my career." I was impressed by his gravitas and gentle nature.

I apologized for the hairy girlfriend thing and he knew it was just shit-talk that goes on in every game between players. He even praised me for that too. We shook hands and I wished him well, even saw him play in the pros a time or two. The Chattanooga Times Free Press placed him on Tennessee-Chattanooga's All-Century Football Team, and in 2005 he was elected to the university's Athletic Hall of Fame. He was indeed a player as evidenced by his accolades, but on that day I gave him a game to ponder for the rest of his days and one I have drawn on as a source of inner strength when faced with difficult tasks, injuries, and the general manor in which life likes to kick a person in the ass from time to time. I'm thankful for that day and thankful to Coach Bradshaw for making me have to stretch my abilities farther than I thought they could go.

I was late getting to the field house the next day to watch films as I was beat like an old government mule pulling a heavy load. I have never been so tired and beaten as I was that day and I missed something that I was told by my teammates I thought I'd never hear, and didn't, due to my one and only tardy. I had never been late to any meetings, ever. Not before and not ever since. I was late that day for the first time in four years and Coach Bradshaw praised my performance up one side and down the other, as I was told. He was finishing when I walking in late just in time to get my ass chewed out by him for being late.

The UTC Coach mentioned my performance in the Chattanooga Paper that week and I was nominated for Gulf South Conference Player of the Week by him, but Bradshaw made sure that honor never had my name attached to it. I guess I shouldn't have been tardy.

Brian loved that one and asked me if I had any others…I did.

Chapter · XXVIII

BRIAN AND I had continued to walk and run for hours, not thinking about stopping for a rest. While we ran we talked, and the talking helped pass the time and shorten the long distances we needed to travel in order to get ourselves back to some sort of civilization. We only stopped to take a piss and Brian humored me by looking for a tree to hide behind to do his business. It wasn't like anyone might see him in the dense backwoods country we moved through and I certainly wasn't interested. I'd seen enough of his white ass after we landed, post jump, so I was good for life.

Taking a good ole stand-up man-piss is not an issue for men regardless of the time and situation he might find himself in. The great outdoors is a man's latrine, as I heard it so aptly put by numerous women folk over the years, and that is a truth and gift not lost on most men. Men had to go to war and shoot people, so it seems to me a little thing like pissing outdoors whenever necessary is a decent trade-off. Women get to have babies, not an advantage in my book, and a man who might question a woman's bravery after witnessing a birth of a child is a genuine, class A ass-hat (thanks again, Dickey) as far as I am concerned. Any man that volunteers to swallow a basketball and slowly inflate it as the months pass, then attempt to pass that sucker between his legs nine months later is a fool and out of touch with reality. Hell, hand me a rifle and a helmet and aim me towards the battlefield and we'll call us even. If men had the babies every other day would be a national holiday and every street in America would be named after a dude. Women make babies exclusively and most do so at the expense of the youthful figure they once had prior to conception. I'm not sure how this went from pissin' outdoors to women having babies but I confess, I am glad to be a dude. I am glad to be able to piss anywhere anytime, jump off speeding trains, eat shoplifted meats and drink unpasteurized beer, risking life and limb in the pursuit of all things American, including going to war if necessary.

I think the USA could use that particular tirade to recruit future soldiers for battle. Give any guy with a few ounces of smarts the choice between having a baby and going to war, and I am sure every future conflict that might ever get started would end quickly due to the enormous amount of dudes avoiding childbirth. That's excluding Broadway, and the entire city of San Francisco, of course.

Brian really liked the football story about the giant football guy and he asked me to continue talking about some of the crap we got into while traveling to far away exotic places, like when my football team made the trip every other year to Southern Louisiana (we didn't get out much, so work with me here). Hammond, Louisiana in particular, home to Southeastern Louisiana State University Lions and the "coon-asses," as we called them; Cajun young men drug out of the swamps to play football. Football gave them something to do besides shoot folk for trespassing in their hometown swamplands and make ammo. It was 1980 and we were traveling by charter bus to play the SLSU Lions in their stadium, built in eighteen days way back in 1937 as local lore and printed word had it. The stadium was probably originally constructed as a backwoods arena for killing animals or stray humans that wandered off the highway. Innocent travelers looking for a crawfish boil or a fish-camp serving spicy coon-ass food and Dixie death beer in the long neck bottle as a "washer down" might find themselves trouble there. I didn't know any of this for sure but I had this eerie feeling when we visited to engage them in a football game that something similar to the previously described activities did indeed happen.

Playing football in the swamp (not the University of Florida "SWAMP" mind you, but a real damn swamp) meant you watched your back whenever you got in your opponents front yard. Usually, the coon-ass fans were frisked for knives and small arms before games began, other than the ones in clear view. If one was not found, one was issued on the spot. This was rough country and we had come off swapping ass-kickin's, with the Lions winning in 1978, 45–7, with a record setting seven punts blocked and five returned for touchdowns. The Lions threw in one plain ole interception run back for a touchdown and a field goal scored to finish us off with time running out just to make sure it took. I think Troy accidentally scored, just to make it interesting, saving us the embarrassment of a complete annihilation and a shut-out. The game amounted to a mercy killing of sorts and would not soon be forgotten by one Charlie Bradshaw, head coach from Hell, on temporary assignment and stationed in Troy, Alabama by the Devil himself or at least one of his vice presidents.

We returned fire the next year and put a revenge type ass-whip on them at Troy in 1979 winning a fight riddled game 24-0 with Coach Bradshaw driving down the field with time running out just to return the favor extended to us the year before. Anytime we engaged them, regardless of the location, it was what amounted to a scheduled gang fight where a football game eventually broke out. The Lions were coon-ass dirty in every aspect of the game and I mean that with as little respect as I can convey. We did not play them on TV, so victory was for pride and pride alone meaning we clawed, scratched, kicked, elbowed, kneed, poked and prodded as much as possible. We utilized any underhanded technique available to us, including a few we made up, providing a new way of eliminating an opposing coon-ass player by whatever means necessary. This included any combination of the questionable methods mentioned earlier, but certainly not leaving out the old tried and true methods of delivering pain, like cleating a dude in the satchel or good old fashioned biting and eye poking. Coach Bradshaw insisted that we utilize our best sportsmanlike conduct at all times regardless of the opponent, save one. That rule was suspended when we played the dirty assed sons-of-bitches known as the "coon-asses" for those of us that ever had to fight it out with them on the football field. Playing the Lions at their home field also meant you faced the formidable coon-assed fans that were just as much a challenge as the team they screamed for.

Our offensive and defensive schemes were endlessly pounded into our heads and bodies via numerous repetitive drills, executed over and over for months at a time until a modest amount of perfection was achieved. I will tell you that we were damn good at the drills we were taught and the execution of the drill became second nature to us all. We were prepared both mentally and physically, as evidenced by our repeat winning seasons. Coach Bradshaw's number one psychological ploy was to always made you feel like you just weren't quite good enough but "you'd do in a pinch," meaning you were a starter, and it also meant you were tougher than the average football player regardless of the divisional differences. I knew it was all part of "The Drill." It was the subliminal, psychological, fear-driven part that utilized scare tactics and the passive-aggressive but ever looming possibility of losing your starting position and/or scholarship method. It was as integral a part of Bradshaw's game as your football helmet or your jockstrap. If any team were to succeed in victory, all mental and physical factors converged on the field of play. The old man created football players and winning seasons as efficiently as Crayola made crayons or Colonel Sanders produced fried chicken by the bucket-full. It was his sole purpose in life and he was damn good at it.

When our bus pulled into the stadium, I was sure I spotted a massive hog being gutted while strung up in a tree. For all I knew it might have been some voodoo style human sacrifice executed before every home game. It was situated at the edge of the parking lot next to a large boiling cauldron of God only knew what. I also noticed the stadium had three different types of access: by car, school bus and homemade, hollowed-out canoe. There was a swamp that oozed up at the very back edge of the parking lot and I saw families with muzzle loaders and coon-skin hats unload by the canoe full. They all sported camouflaged or flannel shirts (all Sunday-go-to-meeting quality, I am sure) and most came floating up with the entire family paddling for good measure. Most of their kids pledged their individual loyalties to a favored farm implement manufacturer (like John Deere or Case) on a filthy, one size fits all ball cap more than likely handed down as a family heirloom. They all wore insulated, sleeveless vests and chewed some sort of home-made kiddy tobacco used as a ramp-up to the hard stuff, like Red Man chew or Big Chief plug in the foil pouch.

The little ones eventually graduated to Skoal or Copenhagen, manufactured by Louisiana's own U.S. Smokeless Tobacco Company before hitting double-digits in age. Heck, every coon-ass kid wanted to be making "milk shakes," slang for the foam topped spit cups from dipping snuff or any type of chewing tobacco, filled to the brim with the funky spittle, produced then expectorated post chew. The only hold back was that each kid had to be in at least in the third grade before he went smokeless. Most of the kids in attendance thought Copenhagen, the city, was named after Copenhagen the snuff, doubling as an abstract geography lesson. I'm just kidding of course, it was actually the fourth grade before you could dip snuff, but that was only if you were a girl. I might sound like I'm being a little rough on the folks from Louisiana, but I can assure you it's only in preparation for the events that I am about to reveal.

When we got close to the field house, which I thought probably doubled as a cattle barn, our chartered bus got peppered with beer bottles and kindling wood from the various pre-game tailgate parties that had been going on for a good three days prior to the scheduled game. We were pummeled with boots, empty ammo shells, car parts, toys and anything else that wasn't bolted down. I also noted the overwhelming number of vehicles sporting four-wheel-drive set-ups, all with at least two shotguns hanging in the back window. I could only guess the charter bus company we hired had a hazardous duty bus with NATO 4 windows built to withstand up to a .50 caliber bullet and a full stick of dynamite from underneath. This was coon-ass country and anything could happen for the fun of it and that included mass manslaughter.

"Dem Bwaas dun gone and pawked dey bus whea we stowed our dinomite and it jus wenn off! How we gwannta knew dat?" I could hear a Cajun say.

We usually had between ten and fifteen Alabama State Troopers as ride-alongs on our trip just for safety purposes when we made that particular trip. They all drove heavy service vehicles with steel screen in the windows just in case of close incursions with the local gentry. I usually sat in the very back of the bus, hooligan style, and was generally the last guy to exit. On this trip I learned it was never a good idea to allow your teammates to get too far ahead of you as you might get swallowed up in the hundreds of opposing fans. They'd all stand quietly, shoulder to shoulder, watching you through a full week's worth of beard growth. They all wore baseball hats with heavy equipment logo's, pulled down low on the brow so all you could see was the whites of their eyes, and that was just the women folk. I tell you, these people would stand and stare at you as you grabbed your gear from the belly of the bus. The majority of them had pistols or knives strapped to homemade belts, crafted of some sort of snake or lizard skin. These critters were caught or trapped by endless generations of family members skilled in the trade. And you could bet your ass that somewhere on their person was the "Stars and Bars" of Dixie. These people were "under the radar" types, by my assessment, hiding from the federal authorities for terroristic threats made concerning the death of the eight track tape or leaded gas. These fans would look at you and grunt, doing that disgusted snicker thing designed to intimidate you in some form or fashion.

The crowd of swamp folk would part like the Red Sea when we approached, creating a human tunnel to wherever we tried to go and closed as we passed. This reinforced the primary reason I didn't want to get separated from the crowd I came with. I made the mistake of allowing myself to fall behind my group the first time I visited the wasteland on the bayou known lovingly as Strawberry Stadium. I got behind the wall of folks that closed around our team and as soon as I said "excuse me," as a reasonable and courteous means of asking for passage, I was met with blank stares and numerous partial sets of teeth in my face that looked and smelled like they had not seen the business end of a toothbrush ever. A full set of teeth in that crowd amounted to at least eight to nine people, as dental hygiene was not a top priority with this crowd.

These were low-brow folks that considered violence a means of entertainment and education, and had limited contact with the outside world. Most were still amazed that Jell-O gelatin didn't melt when you took it out of the refrigerator and wondered if the Devil had invented it. These folk argued about the knock down power of a .44 Magnum versus a .30-06 rifle and threatened to prove their point on each other if necessary. I hated elbowing women and children just to get through the crowd, as manners hadn't worked, but a man had to do what he had to do to survive. I had never seen so many uni-brows in my life on the men, women and even the small children. Musta been the net result of unchecked inbreeding.

I made it to the field house in one piece, thankful that the only exercise these folks did to keep in shape was shoot critters and drink home-made moonshine. This had to be the only state in the union where the women routinely outweighed the men two to one and could usually fight better to boot. I imagined foreplay between married couples around there might be settled with arm wrestling matches or shoulder punches after a few cases of cold Dixie's and a large chew of tobacco to make the buzz sustainable and complete. I guess by now you get the socioeconomic make-up of the crowd in attendance that day so I'll move on.

The entry gate at the front of the stadium had a last minute "bus-load or a dump-truck load" price for folks coming into the stadium in bulk, inside of ten minutes before kick-off. It was all quite a scene to behold and one I closely observed, placing it forever in my internal warning file for future reference's sake. I wanted to make sure I never broke down within twenty miles of here.

I just had to throw that last one in.

Chapter · XXIX

WHEN WE got suited up and made our way to the stadium for warm-ups, we were met again by the same tunnel of humans who separated only for the Alabama State Troopers. "Our" cops had hands on pistols and heads on a swivel (remember that one, don't you?). I watched one of the troopers carefully, and I don't think he blinked for ten straight minutes.

This Go-around, the coon-assed Lions' fans weren't silent as they were pre-game meaning the moonshine must have kicked in. It was a mob scene similar to what a shortage of free government butter and cheese day might be like at the local National Guard Armory. Our walk was the polar opposite of the types of walks teams took at their home field these days, with fans reaching out and touching the gridiron stars and exchanging proud nods with the loving home crowd. This inbred and inebriated bunch, on the other hand, was cussing and screaming at us loud enough to raise the dead. You'd have thought we were virtual Northern aggressors in the flesh, brought back from some past life to invade, and burn their homes and farms. It was an effective means of intimidation, if you allowed it to be, and I hoped it was not a foretelling of events to come from this deranged bunch of clod-hoppers. After we completed our pregame warm up drills to the stares of the shoulder-to-shoulder locals lining the end zone and the fences closest to us, we huddled up on the ten yard line. It was a distance necessary to get far enough away from the noisy mob as possible. We could barely hear ourselves think, much less allow the coaches the opportunity to share much rehearsed words of wisdom with us.

The best advice I heard that day was from Coach Bradshaw, telling us to be very careful not to tackle one of our opponents on their sidelines. Sliding into the five yard, no man's land area just in front of their bench populated by second and third stringers trained in the dark arts of stomp and kick, could prove costly to us. We had watched films from a prior year's contest when this very event occurred and witnessed the Lions' sideline opening up like a man-eating plant. This allowed the Troy Trojan player to successfully tackle the opposing player, only to then be swallowed then vomited from the mob with a pair of broken ribs. I took notice of how quickly the opposing ranks opened then closed around the poor dude. He was then swarmed by the helmeted players whose sole purpose was to inflict as much physical damage as possible, as quickly as possible. Any football player deposited into the destructive abyss known as the Lions' sidelines will tell you it was survival of the fittest. The coon-ass boys swallowed their prey hungrily then spit him out like poor Jonah being vomited out on the shores of Nineveh. Being in the belly of the whale (sent by God for Jonah's use as a taxi for the Old Testament conscientious objector) was like being in your own mothers loving arms compared to that sideline prison yard. It looked like the Lions players were River Dancing, kicking and stomping the poor soul who found himself trapped in the cage of humans. Bradshaw stated emphatically, if you found yourself in that situation to scramble to your feet then kick and punch your way out as quickly as you could, thus avoiding injuries not gained on the field of play. Our team practiced "getting up off the ground quickly when in a crowd" drills the week before the game as a preventive measure. I guess the only thing we didn't practice that week was how to effectively disarm a knife wielding football player or how to make an incendiary device from sweat, ground up fingernails and white, powdered field chalk. The practice week prior to our game was like a boot camp unto itself. Hand-to-hand combat tactics were incorporated into our normal five hour heated practices and it was as if we were being prepared to squelch a prison uprising.

When we reached our sidelines, I was surprised to find that the benches sat only a few feet away from the first row of stadium seats. This design allowed the opposing team's fans to be right in the middle of our game planning and practically in our game uniforms. This area was packed with the enemy's fans shouting and harassing every move we made and any attempt to retaliate was akin to pissing on the rebel flag itself. Two redneck Coon-asses were standing directly behind me and loudly exclaimed,

"Didn't we block six kick-offs and run 'em back for touchdowns the last time we played these asshole city boys?"

I was quite amazed by the correct sentence structure and proper noun-verb usage by the inbred looking gator-humpers. Of course, you couldn't block a kick off and run it back for a touchdown, at least not in organized football. And as far as the "city-boys" comment was concerned, I was from Atlanta, and directions to Troy was as follows; drive to the middle of nowhere and hang a left then you'd be right in the middle of Troy, Alabama. I guess to these dudes, *city boy* meant you had all your teeth and both eyes still in your head. The game films we saw from 1978's 45–7 ass whipping revealed that blocking a kick-off and returning it for a touchdown was the only way the Lions didn't score on Troy that year. I made a mental note, based on the blocked kick-off remark, that we had either two very intelligent comedians on our hands at best, or some serious dumb-asses at the worst, neither of which gave me comfort. I started to turn and look over my shoulder at the deliverers of the smart-assed remarks when I recalled Bradshaw's lesson number two: not to engage any person in the stands regardless of what might be thrown at you, either verbally or physically, over the short distance separating us from them. I remember asking one of our players where the Troy cheerleaders were and being told matter-of-factly, "Dude, they refused to come for their own safety."

I wish I could make words to describe the auditory experience one gained from sitting on that particular sideline during a game. It was quite incredible as I was cussed equally by old ladies, old men and little boys who could string together and deliver profanity better than a New Jersey wise guy. I just sat and laughed to myself, absorbing the electric fear emanating from my teammates, both black and white. Regardless of physical size and class rank, the experience made for an exceptionally level playing field emotionally that day. If you survived this chaotic event and prevailed on the field, victory amounted to a double-edged sword. You had to make an escape from the hell hole that was Strawberry Stadium and its dull and dirty occupants, most of whose last names had an "X" in it. I mean they spelled "GO LIONS" "GEAUX LIONS," for Pete's sake, and not even the French would claim them.

It had started raining in the first quarter, lightly at first, then turning into a gully washer just short of a hurricane, with gale force winds blowing branches and leaves from the buffer trees onto the field of play. The adverse weather conditions did not cause one single fan to leave that evening. I guessed it was going to be raining wherever they were that day so right there was as good a place as any to be wet. The screaming and hollering continued, interrupted by the tossing of popcorn buckets, empty beer cans, cups full of watered down Big K cola, more than likely the only place in the country you could get K-Mart store brand cola on tap. I observed that caramel-colored fizzy drinks sold in half gallon sized, flimsy paper containers at the stadium were the primary projectile of choice. When the thirst quenching moonshine mixer (for anyone over the age of seven) got rained in or watered down, it was hurled onto our side lines. I remember looking at our team captain and snickering at the popcorn glued to the back of his jersey by some sticky drink or tobacco spit. Getting clocked up-side the head by a large, watered-down cup of Big-K Cola mixed with moonshine and tobacco spit made you jump when it hit you broadside. It made your eyes water too, not from the cold but from the contents. You could not read nor make out the numbers on the backs of our uniforms from the mud and candy wrappers glued to our backs. You had to laugh at the sight of it, and it continued until the end of play. We all stood a good four to five inches taller by game's end from standing on the mountain of trash hurled at us from the stands.

I enjoyed seeing all of our coaches scared shitless from the intimidation being rained down upon us by the people attending the show. I hovered close to the State Patrolmen as the clock counted down, keeping my eye on his service revolver, *guesstimating* how many movements it might take me to grab his pistol and level it at a coon-ass if necessary. It was that bad, I'm serious.

All of that was sideshow, here is my real story. Along about the second quarter of play, I heard a little sweet voice off in the distance saying softly,

"Hey, sixty-three…" (My jersey number) quietly, as if from a distance, barely catching my attention.

The voice must have come from the only angel in attendance that day. The sweet sounding words repeated every thirty seconds or so when I sat on the bench, between defensive series, wafting down from the opponents grand stands. The words from the angelic voice fluttered like butterfly wings, in between the cussing and lightning strikes and was only interrupted by halftime. Coach Bradshaw calmly reminded us that winning was why we were there and to not, under any circumstances, engage any person in the stands in any way, shape, or form. He also instructed us to not meet at the center of the field post-game to engage the Lions in hearty rounds of "Good game" and handshakes. Regardless of the outcome, a fight would most likely break out and somebody might get shanked…or worse. These boys liked to fight when they won, and more so when they lost, proven by the last three meetings between our teams. Every time we played them some sort of fight ensued post game and without fail. Where we were geographically meant a home town advantage for our hosts, and they had their inebriated fans handy for skirmishes involving victorious unwelcomed visitors.

On October 10, 1980 we prevailed on the field of play 24-10 and escaped with our lives intact. We exited quickly, minus a few large bags of footballs and medical supplies, left as a sort of sacrifice or distraction expediting our escape. We didn't give a rat's ass about the loot we left behind as we exited the arena in a shower of beer bottles, most of them full, crashing against the sides of the bus while leaving the swamp. I witnessed our opponent's fans throwing stuff at our Alabama State Troopers escorts also, not caring about the amount of weaponry carried by officers of the law. I'm sure the Cajuns were trained at a young age to know the lack of jurisdiction the Alabama State Troopers held in any Louisiana Parish, probably the only legal issue most of the coon-asses cared about. I'd never traveled ninety miles per hour in a charter bus before but that day I did gladly. We were all spent, not just from the contest, but from the immense pressure the coon-ass fans put on display that evening. I must say I salute the fortitude and loyalty shown by them all that evening. It was a maelstrom of epic proportions, and their fan base didn't budge one inch. Our home crowd usually wilted if the temperature got above seventy five degrees and sunny. These folks were hard-core fans and I appreciated them, save for the skinned hog in the parking lot and the kids that could cuss better than most adults, chew tobacco, and eat a hotdog at the same time.

And last but not least, the sweet young lady who continuously called to me like some angelic harpy or freshly hatched hummingbird just learning to fly, discovering the sweet sound of its vibrating wings, like some tiny stringed instrument fashioned by some sweet old man experienced in the art of violin making. She chanted to me,

"Hayyy, sixxxty three…sixty thray, sixty threee," shortening the time between the times she'd call to me so sweetly. "Sixty three, 63, 63, 63, 63, 63, 63, siiiixxxty thhhhrrreee, 63, 63, 63, 63, sixxxxty three."

She continued, not eliciting as much as a glance from me. I had decided she'd not succeed at getting to me as I could hear her moving down closer from high up in the stands. Her voice smaller then gradually growing like an orchestra on some long drawn out aria, quietly building up to an awesome finale, ending with pounding kettle drums and crashing symbols resulting in emotional tears for the hearers. I would not be annoyed while listening to her sing my jersey number so many times. I thought she might be mentally challenged, with her mind locking on my jersey number as a lone way to reach the outside world, piercing it in millisecond views of normalcy for the duration of the spoken number "63."

"63-63-63-63-63-63-63-63-63-63-63-63-63-63-63-63-63-63-63-63-63,"she droned on and on and on for two whole quarters, plus the half quarter when I first noticed her chanting, all while being within in earshot of her between series, resting my butt on the concession stand fodder covered bench.

It had reached the closing minutes of the fourth quarter with maybe less than two minutes left in regulation play that I made my mistake. I finally turned around to make eye contact with the young girl wishing to engage me for an autograph or possibly my jersey in exchange for a cold Coca-Cola, Mean Joe Green style.

She was finally right on the fence calling my number to the back of my helmet…"Haaaaayyyyy SIXXXXTTTYY THRRREEEEE!!!" she said louder but still just as angelic as the first fourteen thousand times she had said it, her southern drawl making the three words sound like they had ten vowels instead of four.

I turned to look at her and said, "Yes, sweetheart?"

"My daddy asked me to tell you something" she sweetly proclaimed.

"And what is that my dear?" I asked innocently, anticipating a compliment relayed from her father, who might be a visionary among the heathens, recognizing my awesome football skills regardless of whose team I might have pledged my loyalties.

"He told me to come down here and tell you that you suck and to fuck off."

I was speechless. It was the first time that day I was actually SCARED.

We walked and talked for hours not seeing anything or anyone. It was great. Brian had a story for me...

Chapter · XXX

We have an old saying in Delta House: don't get mad, get even."
– Brother D-Day, Animal House

BY THEN, Brian and I had been walking for a good nine to ten straight hours. We just kept on telling stories and reminiscing about our two years as friends, dispensing stories from our separate youth and our joint adulthood (whew, that's a stretcher I guess) or pre-adulthood if you wanted to get technical. Brian and I had roughly calculated that we wound up just southwest of Cullman, Alabama, home to the then Grand Wizard of the Ku Klux Klan back in the early eighties. If you can imagine stepping back in time to the Jim Crow thirties and forties, Cullman was that kind of time machine, where minorities (and city boys in blackface) were not welcome. So we wisely gave the entire town and its occupants a very wide berth as we traveled. We were extremely hungry by then and could have eaten the ass end out of a sleeping goat. We figured starving was considerably better than trying to explain our looks, our situation, and our lack of any sort of identification to the local authorities or roaming vigilante squads driving pick-up trucks without mufflers. Getting caught there might get you no phone call, no civil rights, but maybe a few uncivil lefts along with a few jabs, upper-cuts and kick or two. You might also get a job making big rocks into small rocks as a means of convincing you to never pass through their fine town again. We debated on stopping by a store on the outskirts of town but thought better of it. It was made crystal clear that anyone not white had better have their asses out of Cullman by sunset, so we passed on making that thought into a reality. Brian and I were filthy, both covered by train dirt and creosote. I feared the local authorities would believe we were mocking their rules, both written and unwritten, by appearing in blackface like some ironic act of defiance and stupidity.

"Die-versity" in Cullman back in that day meant you were going to embalming school to be a funeral home director or possibly a taxidermist. Taxidermy was a starter gig to get you prepared for the big time, meaning you could "chuck 'em in the clay" and get paid for it.

If you could do a good job stuffing deer heads and you were lucky, you'd eventually get your shot at "layin' folks out," as I heard it called at a funeral I attended in the backwoods of North Carolina. I first heard the term used when I was on an extended visit to my beloved grandmother's house one summer when I was but a young lad. The biggest difference was, in the North Carolina funeral I attended, the deceased would "lie in state" in the home they resided in and then had to be buried within three days. Embalming was an unnecessary expense in that particular part of the world and rarely used back then. You had to get 'em in the ground before the seventy-two hours was up or they'd quite literally get smelly from decomposition settin in. Putting one in their final resting place smelling like an aged chuck roast or a dead cat sitting in the sun too long meant someone had to sit near the grave with a shotgun to run off the North Carolina black bears that populated the area looking for a free smorgasbord, even if it meant digging it up get at it.

Now, I was "citified" but I did not question the customs and culture of the hillbillies populating the beautiful hill country known as the Great Smokey Mountains. All I knew was they could make some righteous banana puddin', and a whole lot of it, for funerals and church functions. I didn't know the dude who had given his all for the feast I was enjoying, but I was sure glad my grandmother knew him well enough for us to get the invite. I got to eat "nanner puddin" and see a shore-nuff dead guy all in one day. It was weird seeing my first dead dude, but it was mellowed out by excess pudding consumption. It was definitely a Huck Finn/Tom Sawyer kinda day, and one I'm sure none of my back-home buddies enjoyed that summer.

The other "dead folk" tradition around those parts was for country folk to bring lots of casseroles made from vegetables picked fresh from the garden and fried chicken so fresh that I was certain the chicken in question had been thinking about "crossing the road" a few hours before. The chickens in question were beheaded with either a knife or "Doc" style, plucked and gutted, then battered and introduced to a hot oil swimming pool for seven minutes on one side and eight minutes on the other (of course, you went longer if you were teaching the breast meat how to swim, say eight to nine minutes on both sides). I myself am a thigh man, little brown meat and a little white meat, and 100% good. I figured if Colonel Sanders picked the thigh as his favorite piece of chicken meat (and that dude could make some fried chicken), who was I to argue? I will confess though, if the Colonel had the fried chicken recipes of the old ladies who fried the funeral chicken, he'd be a four-star General instead of just a Colonel. I guess Four-Star General Sander's Kentucky Fried Chicken just didn't have the same ring to it. The Colonel somehow worked it out to his benefit and profited from it just the same. I guess wearing a white riverboat gamblers outfit with a black string tie helped him sell his brand of fried chicken better than a military uniform, so the lower rank helped him considerably.

I suggested to Brian that we both just put our blinders on and keep walking ourselves past of the city of Cullman, avoiding any and all trouble that might accompany any extended visit by us to the clannish town. Cullman, I am sure, was considered beloved to its residents but I think I'd have taken my chances living in Detroit or New York.

Brian and I had put a good seven and a half hours of walking distance between us and Cullman and I figured the next logical stop was Birmingham. When we were riding the train we never actually traveled through the big city parts of the town. The trains usually hugged the outskirts of the towns where the industrial districts and warehouses were located, fed by the trains, disbursing the bulk goods via semi trucks to the consumer market. It was one system that had not changed much since the modern era of the train had been ushered in during the civil war times. Brian and I felt like we were keeping up a long-time hobo tradition, at least as far as riding a railcar as a means of (unintended) intrastate travel was concerned. We just had to work on perfecting our dismount a little more and we'd be the kings of the track. We had to walk another good 159 miles to get back to Troy by my estimation, and we'd see the sun rise and set at least once, maybe twice more before that feat was accomplished. This was straight walking, mind you, no sleep and only stopping to take a leak and sit for a few minutes. I asked Brian to share a story as I'd been the dominant narrator of sorts and I was eager for him to lay one out for me. I suggested that he not mention food, as our bellies were screaming for mercy and any avoidance of the subject would prove beneficial to us both. He agreed. He reminded me of the time he and I (we made up the entire pledge class the year we pledged), and the road trip we took to nearby Auburn University. We were invited to visit the Pi Kappa Phi chapter located there and to be the personal guests of the Auburn Pi Kapp brotherhood at the annual party they held every year during football season. The Troy Pi Kapps had a huge party every spring and we invited the Auburn contingency as our guests, treated them like royalty feeding them and getting sloshed on Oobeedo. We'd also introduce them to some of the lovely Troy girls with the previously described "relaxed moral attitude." It was our first formal (note that I said formal) invite to another campus and one Brian and I were really stoked about. The prospect of meeting some of the same type girls we had introduced our Auburn counterparts to didn't hurt either. As far as I knew, the girls were probably all cousins anyhow (we used to joke that everyone originating from Alabama were somehow related) so it was all good as far as the two of us were concerned.

We planned our trip quickly, meaning we didn't even discuss logistics until about ten minutes before we departed; standard fare for us both. We could both be ready to travel around the world in less than fifteen minutes if called upon. That fact meant traveling up to Auburn didn't require much more than a thought, gas money and a "let's hit the road" to happen. We were going to get lit-up and spend the night with somebody. We didn't know who, but we were staying the night just the same, even if that meant we'd just stay up all night partying. We'd done it a few hundred times before and we were young, so this was a piece of cake, time-wise, and we welcomed the most hardcore all-nighters to any challenge. We had a standing unwritten rule to not fall asleep in a strange place in a strange land, as this was college and most everybody I knew was in some stage of broke monetarily. You were either headed towards being broke or you were just plain broke with no middle ground to meander in. Strangers might interpret your sleeping as an invite to rifle through your wallet, extracting whatever monetary instrument you might have there, including credit cards, cash and driver's licenses (you could sell them to an under aged college student to aid in gaining access to the local bars). I know it sounds harsh, but we didn't make up the rules. They were there, long established before we arrived, and we abided by them.

Brian and I were like Lone Ranger and Tonto of the Troy Pi Kapp brotherhood and usually caught a good bit of shit about being loners. Most of the grief we caught revolved around not including or at least inviting the other brothers into our activities. Allowing them the first right of refusal seemed to be what was asked for but I would usually ignore the whiners and do my thing. I could have not cared less about babysitting somebody's drunk, passed out carcass, especially one who had been laying a wooden paddle across my ass as a means of expressing their superiority over me a few months earlier. After five years of Bradshaw's boot camp, anything the brothers attempted to throw at me as intimidation made me laugh. The older brothers, meaning those that had been initiated before us, encouraged Brian and me to become close friends during the pledge phase and we did. To us that meant we could depend on each other and anyone else could kiss our asses. I really liked my fraternity for the most part and the majority of the dudes in it. But there is always an asshole in every crowd and I usually didn't like to mingle with assholes so I left it at that. I figured anyone who couldn't be friends with me had exceptionally bad taste, as I could be friends with just about anybody, with the possible exception of an asshole. That might sound a little "ass-holish" in and of itself, but I'd also learned this about assholes; if you walk into a room full of folks and don't spot the asshole immediately, you'd better leave because you are probably it.

And now you know.

Anyway, Brian and I set out on our short sixty mile road trip from Troy to Auburn, with two ice cold cases of Dixie longnecks (exchanged for two rib-eye steaks with our liquor store friend) in a borrowed cooler that had mistakenly been stacked out of eyeshot beside the Rippy Mart. When we picked up the errant cooler we discovered it was trying to make a break for Auburn University also, so we both offered to give it a ride as long as he'd invite two bags of ice to ride along with him, and hold our beer for us. We'd even invited Dan the Man to come along with us, but Suzy the Floozy had plans for ole Dan that weekend. We usually borrowed (without their knowledge of course) a frat-rat shirt from one of the brothers to loan to a friend of our choosing, usually not a frat brother of ours, mind you, but someone that was on their way to being broke like us. It was usually someone we liked and wanted to hang out with, needing fraternal liquid refreshment and lots of it. The spare jersey was to aid the non-frat friend's access when we visited other college towns having Pi Kapp chapters there. Sometimes it wound up being the local toothless drunk when invited to party with another fraternity in a town other than Troy. We'd usually tell the hosts we'd seen an inebriated pledge stumbling about town wearing the letters. We were surprised and impressed that they would pledge such a "diverse" individual, introducing those less fortunate to the Greek system. It usually meant they'd dispatch a few brothers to see what we might be talking about. It gave Brian and me the opportunity to scout out where the beer and the chow was stored, for future reference sake, meaning when they'd all passed out. We utilized the Boy Scout motto, "Be Prepared," which for us meant know where the beer and the food were located and to have an escape route handy in case of incursions from unfriendlies, both within and without. It was a simple set of rules Brian and I lived by and was usually complicated by numbers higher than the two of us. Two meant we watched out for each other, three meant a possible babysitting job if the third was not like minded. Two was a good number and we stuck to it.

Brian and I also had a very important rule we never, ever broke and it was this; we never visited a town to party with another fraternity and allowed ourselves to get separated from one another. Why? This was Alabama, the state that touched Florida, Mississippi, Georgia, Tennessee and, for God's sake, Louisiana. Ok, Ok… I know Alabama doesn't touch Louisiana. It touches a state that touches the Coon-Ass state, meaning anyone from there could jump a train or hitch-hike to Alabama in few days, so that counted as far as I was concerned. I had been to Southern Louisiana and knew up close the type of folks manufactured therein. That fact alone made for caution when faced with unfamiliar surroundings and the people populating the places Brian and I visited. I had either played ball with or against dudes from all of the states previously mentioned and I will confess to you the ones from Louisiana, and some parts of lower Alabama, needed to be watched closely at all times. I filled Brian with all the knowledge I possessed concerning trusting those originating from the two regions I mentioned earlier. Brian soaked up my warning like a seasoned pro. Brain was a sharp dude and I had taught him well.

When we finally reached Auburn University it was about 5:00 pm and the parties were in full swing. It seemed like every human soul had decided to attend Auburn that particular long weekend. It took us a good two hours to find the Pi Kappa Phi house in Auburn and when we arrived we found the house empty save for one lone pledge. He told us where the festivities were being held that day, even drawing us a map of sorts to guide us on our way. I distracted the neophyte while Brian worked at procuring us some chow, requisitioned out of necessity "Rippy Mart" style, from our host home. It was indeed a big football weekend and what I thought might be homecoming, seeing the enormous amount of food and alcoholic type beverages in stock at the home of the host frat. Brian made short work of procuring us two roast beef sandwiches loaded up with what I estimated to be a good pound of sliced thin rare roast beef each, melted provolone, mayo and mustard, warmed to perfection jammed between two fresh hoagie rolls. I remember the sandwich so well because Brian practically needed a wheelbarrow to carry them both. He managed, somehow, exiting out a side door, away from the guarded stares of the lone pledge. We ate the awesome free sandwiches while we slowly navigated to the off campus party location the pledge accurately mapped out for us.

When we arrived at the festivities, I was quite amazed at the sheer number of people in attendance at the combination beer party and outdoor concert. The long lines filled with people paying a cover charge to get in, an ink stamp as proof of payment, and two beer tokens as a reward for entry. *Animal House* was still a popular movie and "Otis Day and the Knights," the juke joint band from the movie, was the headliner at the outdoor venue. Brian and I could recite the entire dialogue from the movie, knew all the songs, so we were stoked about being there. We were both in full Pi Kapp regalia. We proudly displayed our Greek affiliation across our chests, same as the Auburn boys belonging to the same fraternity/different college working the gate and security. The biggest difference between us being we wore our letters primarily as a means of gaining free entry and not as a show of unity. Brian and I parked then walked up to the gate, expecting the same red carpet treatment they had received when visiting our biggest party and fundraiser, all free of charge. The fellows enjoyed everything we had to offer, from our finest swill to our best morally declined women. We even put them up for the night and made sure they did not leave our house intoxicated and driving.

I am saddened to report to you that Brian and I were not extended the same courtesies by the assholes we visited via invite that weekend and we were not happy about it at all. I will admit it was somewhat chaotic with hundreds trying to gain entry to the show, but that did not matter to us and should not have mattered to them. It was just good manners to extend visiting *and invited* guests free passes to your festivities. Brian got really pissed and requested a meeting with the Archon, Pi Kapp speak for the President of the fraternity, the dude saddled with the responsibility of leading a bunch of other dudes successfully through his one year tenure. Truth be told, being Archon amounted to one undeniable fact, it was a job trying to lead the unleadable. The guy in charge of the front gate radioed the lead dog and he answered, very irritated, obviously tending to the numerous problems he faced whenever a gathering of this magnitude was planned and held. I'm sure he was overwhelmed that day, but it went with the president job he had politicked and lobbied for. The fool obviously wanting the job to appear on his resume to later be used as proof of leadership or stupidity. He showed up in a golf cart with a SECURITY sticker appearing on the side of the buggy in bright, fluorescent orange lettering and practically power slid the vehicle up to us, slinging gravel as he stopped. He was not happy and neither were we, but for two diametrically opposing reasons.

"What in the Hell is the damn problem?" he practically shouted at us and the fellows sporting the same colored armbands testifying to their status as frat rat party police.

I started to take somewhat of a diplomatic approach and was cut off mid-thought by Brian, very much pissed off over the way we were being treated. The president and head of security wasn't able to get a word in edgewise with Brian. I was not about to stop him, as Brian was on-a-roll, ripping these boys a brand new ass big enough to drive his golf cart through. Brian explained to El Presidente the standard etiquette rules as he saw them, meant when inviting someone to your home, extending more than the same courtesies extended them when they visited. Brian pointed out that it was downright anti-American of them to treat us like this. Of course, I am sweetening the speech up a considerable bit, as decorum limits his actual speech to the niceties I used earlier. His oration was intended to make the Auburn Pi Kapps feel ashamed of how we had been treated by them that day. It unfortunately had just the opposite effect on the overwhelmed leader of this three ring circle-jerk of a party, with him being the designated pivot man. He looked at the other brothers, ignoring Brian and his cries of poor brotherly treatment. He paused briefly, then looked past Brian and issued a two word response…"Charge 'em both" and then sped off to attend to another pressing issue blaring across his radio. The task he sped off to was obviously more important than two dudes from another smaller school. The gate keepers stood looking at us like we were criminals caught trying to steal their precious gate money. And that, my friends, would amount to a huge mistake for the frat boys we stood in front of that day. Brian told them all to shove their heads up their collective asses and jump, and promised that they'd see us again later that evening. Brian instructed me to get in the car so I did, knowing he was either cooking up a revenge plot or planning a homicide, neither of which I could not talk him out of right then. I'd bide my time and see how this unfolded. It was about to get interesting.

When diplomacy fails, war ensues and we were now officially at war with the Auburn Pi Kapps, meaning all normal rules of engagement were off. I think they had as much as 160 brothers plus another 40-50 pledges and there were just two of us. Conventional warfare would take years and cost thousands of lives we didn't have, so we planned on using guerilla tactics to achieve our victory. Brian said we were going to make a return visit to their frat house, guarded by the one lone pledge. Their house was foolishly left unlocked and awaiting the party planned later by the brothers currently working the festivities we had been so rudely turned away from.

When we left the parking lot Brian made sure we passed the gate and the tables manned by the thugs we had engaged earlier. He made his exit turn, slinging gravel and dust all over the gate workers and all over the folks attempting to gain entry to the outdoor festival sponsored by the gents we had just declared war upon, Smokey and the Bandit style. It was so crowded the mob could not retaliate and I am certain minutes after we left they had forgotten about us completely, focusing their attentions on the swarm of humanity facing them that cool fall evening. The ignorant frat-rats had no idea concerning the magnitude of the mistake they had made that day with my buddy Brian. We peeled out of the gravel parking lot, heading back towards the fraternity house. The two giant sandwiches we had enjoyed earlier was the extent of the courtesy we'd receive and one we'd gotten without the permission of the gents we'd briefly engaged at the festival. We were traveling a good ninety miles per hour and headed towards whatever revenge Brian had quickly planned out that day. His eyes practically glowed in the dark from anger. I was quietly thinking to myself on whether or not I could stop him if he tried to burn their house down out of retaliation. I outweighed Brian by a good sixty-five pounds but I had seen him mad enough to fight a time or two, and I tell ya the dude was as strong as a twenty mule team when his adrenalin was pumping. It was a spooky kind of pissed off I had seen on occasion in our short friendship, the vein supplying his brain with blood on full display on his forehead keeping count with his heartbeat, meaning someone was about to get a rock solid ass-whuppin'. It also meant that something was going to transpire that would need either medical or reconstructive attention in order for it to be restored to its original configuration. I reminded him that the cops, both local and campus, were out in full force that weekend and if he were to accomplish his goals that day, getting stopped by the police might hinder his travels and possibly land us in jail. I said way back at the first of this exposition and I say it now, Brian was the closest dude I had ever met who was totally fearless. I am sidetracking here, but I recall a time when he and I were driving back from Troy's campus and got pulled over by the campus police in Brian's birth control Dodge Swinger. Brian was in a bad mood due to a test grade he had received that made up 35% of his final grade and one he had come out on the short end of. We were right in the middle of Troy University on the southern end of the quad. We traveled it daily and were not speeding, nor were we in the opposing lane so it was any man's guess as to why the campus cop decided to blue light us. Brian slammed on his brakes seconds after the cop lighted us, causing him to swerve to miss rear-ending us and leaving him and his campus cop mobile in the middle of the street blocking both lanes of traffic. Once again all I could think of was *Oh Shit!* And before I could remind Brian of diplomacy and its practical uses when facing an opponent you could not easily defeat (like the cops). Brian jettisoned himself out the door like a test pilot from a crashing plane. He leapt out and all I heard was,

"I want to know what in the Hell you pulled me over for, damn it!"

Double-Decker sweet mother of Jesus, Brian! You have stepped in it now!! The cop was just as stunned as I was and a crowd gathered quicker than the promise of free beer might at a local pub. Next thing I hear are shouts from the crowd. "G-D cops!" "Assholes!" and as the shouts got louder and the bloodthirsty crowd grew, the cop backed down and just dismissed Brian with a warning. The ticket had nothing written on it but "warning" with no infraction noted anywhere on the fake campus cop ticket. When he got back in the car, I was about to pass out from gut laughing, amazed at the size of his gonads on full display that day. I observed all of what I am writing here sitting down. Meaning, I never even had time to get out of the car. I tell you, Brian was fearless and a force to be reckoned with if you screwed up and really pissed him off.

When we returned to the Auburn campus and fraternity row, Brian calmly pulled up to the house and was met by the young pledge we had engaged earlier that day when had first arrived. He asked me to distract the young-blood neophyte and I obliged him. I was hoping I was not about to hear an explosion followed by quickly made plans on where to bury the young pledges body, knowing he was the only eye witness we engaged in conversation at the house. I told him the party was going great but Brian had lost his wallet and he needed to check to see if he had dropped it when he had taken a dump in the frat house earlier. It was but a facade for the revenge Brian had planned. I was sitting with the pledge when Brian reappeared, walking up the front steps and through the front door, our original point of entry meaning he had ventured through the house and exited out the back, telling me the plan of revenge was afoot and in motion. I wished the pledge well and Brian completed his cover by showing his wallet to the young guard and thanked him for not finding it and emptying its meager contents. Brian was usually broke so I knew then he was creating a simple but brilliant diversion with his wallet. The game was on and he was as purpose driven as Dale Earnhardt's black Monte Carlo at the Daytona 500. I jumped in the Swinger and just sat quietly, grinning and staring at Brian, waiting for the secret information regarding the plan of attack we were to implement as a form of revenge.

As we sat there in the car, Brian looked at me and said, "Let's get the hell out of here" like there was a time bomb counting down inside the frat house we had just visited or a unattended gas stove awaiting an innocently lit cigarette to make the job complete. I point blank asked him, "Alright dude, what have you done?" and I continued asking him repeatedly to tell me what mischief he had created in defense of us both. All he said was, "You'll like it," with a mischievous grin, and I believed him. He could deliver when it counted, like a seasoned clutch hitter in the bottom of the ninth or a confident field goal kicker called on with time running out to win the big game. He assured me that no one would die and the young man we left back at the house would live to be an old man. I was satisfied our revenge was going to be along the lines of what the mansion owning, anal retentive jerk-off whose daughter Brian had briefly dated received. Brian had not been gone long enough to take a high tanker dump/upper deck crap in all of the toilets in the huge fraternity house the rude dudes occupied. I figured it took longer than two hours to process a pound of roast beef anyhow, so I knew from the tone of his voice he had a good one planned and I was ready for the plan to be hatched.

The game was afoot.

Chapter · XXXI

WE RODE through town, stopping a few times for Brian to gather information, taking a chaotic circuitous route. We were looking for someone, something, or someplace and only Brian knew who, what and where for certain. Now, at the time I was not familiar with the layout of the town of Auburn, Alabama. I had eaten a half and half at the Flush, thrown a roll of toilet paper over the trees at Toomer's Drug Store, post Tiger victory and had met Bo Jackson, the second greatest running back to ever play the college game behind Hershel Walker. I was as familiar with Auburn as I needed to be, seeing as I didn't live nor matriculate there. Brian was on a search and he didn't let me in on the secret until we reached our destination. Brian had been asking store owners where the government housing projects were located and he drove us there, pulling into the hive like he had free cash to hand out like some benevolent lottery winner or a man that had just signed a huge pro football contract and wanted to "give back." He looked at me and said plainly,

"Get out and follow my lead."

"Hmm," I thought. I was close to graduation and what the hell were we about to do? I had determined we were closer to the Opelika side of Auburn, a rougher part of town economically as told by the numerous liquor stores, gun stores, pawn shops, and malt liquor advertisements displayed on nearly every billboard. I got out and, as I suspected, we garnered the kind of attention one might get if you were a pair of white guys in a black part of town, particularly the projects.

It took only a few minutes for the crowd to form. Just as I thought Brian had lost his mind he opened the trunk to his Dodge Swinger and, lo and behold, there were two large boxes of brand spanking new, bright yellow Pi Kappa Phi jerseys emblazoned with the symbols we so proudly wore. Each Jersey had bright red letters, outlined in white and included each member of the Auburn fraternity's name (or nickname) spelled proudly on the backs of each numbered shirt. Some sported girl names which they had purchased for their little sisters, meaning girls each frat picked to be affiliated with the frat of origin. These were what I thought to be very nice and expensive custom ordered jerseys of extremely high quality, destined to be worn at the Florida State University vs. Auburn Tiger football game as a sign of Fraternal solidarity. That particular game was to be played the Saturday after the outdoor concert we had been so rudely rejected from an hour earlier. It all made sense to me then. It only took us about twenty minutes to hand out the free jerseys at the housing project that evening, allowing each person to take only one accompanied with a promise to wear it proudly the next day when the game was played. I assumed the new jerseys and the proud new owners of said jerseys made their way to Jordan-Hare stadium (pronounced Jerrdan-Hare just so you'll know I know what I'm talking about) on game day that following Saturday. It had been my experience that the entire town showed up at home games and this one was a biggie. We handed out a new jersey to 150-plus individuals that evening and they were each glad to get a new free article of clothing, thanking us like modern day Robin Hoods.

When we made our way back to the party grounds, we walked back up to the desk sporting the remaining two jerseys big enough to fit us both. New batches of dudes were sitting at the table when we returned from our mission of benevolence. The new boys let us in for free when we told them we were alumni, back for a visit to the fraternity we had pledged ourselves to so many years ago. Brian was laying it on thick, so I elbowed him as a means of getting him to shut up before any of the previous party police showed up again and recognized us. We walked down a 150 foot path into the area where the festivities were being held, a large opening surrounded by woods, and "Otis Day and the Knights" were walking on stage when we sauntered up to the platform victorious, knowing the type of revenge we had delivered as yet unknown to our poor hosts. The new gate keepers gave us the magic symbol written on our hands indicating alumni status, meaning free beer for the duration of the show and entry to the after party planned back at the frat house. I'm sure the after party was just an excuse to drink, eat and hand out the custom ordered jerseys that now hung on the backs of those less fortunate, but considerably more grateful wearers than these dudes. One thing I knew was this, Brian and I were indeed going to enjoy the show, but we were definitely not going to the party back at the house afterwards. I felt like these guys were a bunch of rich boy jack-offs, but they could add two plus two.

We began consuming whatever ice cold draft beer they had on tap and it was an enjoyable evening up until we were recognized by one of the Hitler youth who so boldly turned us away earlier that evening. I warned Brian of impending doom as the boys gathered a few troops to confront us concerning our current status and method by which we had gained entry to the big show. These boys had been drinking also, meaning they all sported big mouths and steel balls. It was a trait that drinking way too much free liquid courage provided. That gave us the upper hand over the six of them. It only took a few minutes for the thugs to reach us and I warned Brian to watch his six, as approaching danger was on the menu, so we prepared ourselves for a fight. I was not a trouble maker at all. I liked mischief, but I never went out looking to pick a fight. Football had taken the desire to physically confront another human out of me; at least as far as being on the aggressor side of the equation was concerned. I will confess I could fight, and fight dirty, when called on to defend a friend or a belief system I held if necessary. The primary difference between them and us was that Brian and I were on our own and these boys mistakenly thought overwhelming numbers might make us to back down or run like scared little girls. That was a huge mistake and one at least five of them would regret in a big way.

I sized them up from biggest smallest as they walked towards us. I was confident Brian had remembered our talks on taking out the biggest threat first causing the cling-ons to either run or hesitate, both of which presented itself as advantageous to us both. It was clear the boys intended to talk briefly then throw us out of the party we had weaseled our way into. I will admit they were technically correct in wanting to toss us out, due to our false alumni status, but very wrong to treat invited fraternal guests so rudely. I guess the bigger dude figured I was the cooler head of the two of us so he looked at me and asked "what in the hell do you two think you are doing here?" As soon as the word "here" left his lips, Brian caught him with a perfectly thrown jaw shot that dropped him like a 250 pound bag of pecans falling off the back of a delivery truck. His eyes rolled back in his head and, as predicted, caused his six other small-nutted friends to hesitate ever so slightly, which gave me the chance to punch two of them so hard I thought I'd broken my hand. Of the remaining four, one got his lights knocked out by Brian, one escaped, and the remaining two bent over to check on the biggest dude dropped first by Brian. I grabbed one, bitch slapping him, giving Brian the perfect kick shot right to the head of the other causing his nose to explode like a party balloon filled with ketchup. The one I jacked up just stood there with his hands held up like he was being arrested. It took only a few seconds for a crowd to form, knowing any fist fight was better than singing when you were shit-faced drunk. Brian had dropped three dudes quickly and I had dropped two, with one escapee and one bitch-slapped, frozen scaredy cat. The dude that ran away did so to warn his frat brothers of the scene he had witnessed, calling for reinforcements to gather. By my count, we had taken out six of the dudes, leaving the lone pledge left at the house and the dude so scared I'm sure his pissed his pants, meaning Brian and I had only 153 other fights to sort out for the rest of that evening, not including the additional 40-50 pledges. I told Brian of the odds we faced, and he agreed that we should leave as quickly as possible.

We were wearing the two remaining Frat Jerseys, so we quickly removed them in an attempt to throw off the search party quickly gathering in our honor, but certainly not for our collective benefit. We made a low running escape behind the stage, circling around the outside of the compound seeing every exit manned by an opposing guard on full alert. Brian and I had parked the car close to the exit at the northern most corner of the parking lot, just in case we needed to make an escape. The boys had strung yellow ribbon to limit access onto the grounds, so we had preemptively aimed our car out on the only other drive over access road offered, as the rest of the frontage had a deep culvert strung between the two pipes covered by gravel. We carefully snuck up to our car and made a speedy, non-lighted exit out of the fairgrounds. We gave a last obscene shout and the middle finger fellowship to the guys near the front gate, and put them in the rearview mirror.

We set out to find some friendlier companionship for the evening, and luckily we met a group of girls from Troy. They were attending the different parties and staying with a bunch of friends living in Auburn, and planned to go to the football game the next day. One of the girls had VIP passes but didn't have enough for everyone so, just to be fair, she gave the only two extra passes she had to Brian and me. This helped her avoid pissing any of her friends off by exclusion. From our awesome seats we could tell where the asshole Pi Kapps were sitting by the patch of mismatched jerseys they wore in a sea of Greeks all sporting matching frat wear. We had a killer weekend, giving two girls rides back to Troy under the condition they paid for the gas and beer and food on the way back, to which they eagerly obliged. These were two full on hotties with fathers looking to get them hitched via the "MRS" degree mentioned earlier in this adventure, meaning it wasn't a stretch for either of them financially speaking. Brian and I? Well, we just enjoyed the stimulating conversation we had with the fine female hitch hikers needing a ride back to our home campus.

When we made it back to our home base and the safety of familiar surroundings, I asked Brian where in the world he had acquired all the Pi Kapp Jerseys we handed out to the less fortunate citizens of Auburn/Opelika.

"Simple" he said. "When I was busy making us the two gigantic roast beef sandwiches earlier I noticed two boxes marked "to be worn at the Auburn/FSU game" and made a mental note about where they were located, an escape route and ready accessibility if needed." He continued, "After the boys at the party rejected our bid for entry, I knew immediately what we could do as payback for their poor treatment of us two. I remembered the jerseys and how we had taken a spare jersey and gave it to the local drunk when we went to other towns, so I just expanded on that theme with our new friends at Auburn. When we went back to the frat house post rejection, I had you distract the young newbie and I grabbed both boxes of jerseys, threw them in the trunk along with a bottle of Jack Daniels for good measure. We found the neighborhood, distributed the jerseys, and the rest is history."

We made one last stop at the Rippy Mart and (surprise), Brian found a full six pack of dented Cokes in the can, a perfect mixer for the Jack Black Brian had helped himself to, compliments of the unfriendly "brothers" we'd met earlier in our visit.

I told you he was a force to be reckoned with, didn't I?

It was pitch dark where we were walking and the stars were putting on a brilliant light show. We continued walking towards Troy, but could see a glowing off to our right so we headed towards it…

Chapter · XXXII

BRIAN AND I spotted a glow off to the right of our location, so we headed towards it thinking it might be a small town with a gas station where we might wash-up or maybe catch a ride supplementing our long walk back to Troy. Troy, Alabama...I never imagined I'd think of the town quite so endearingly but the two words reminded me where our clean clothes, our own soap, our discount steak, cold Dixie beer, remaining gallon of graduation gift Crown Royal, Rippy Mart, beds and hot water showers were located. All things we would never take for granted again. We had not seen the business end of a fork for almost two days. I remembered the two rib-eye steaks I left sitting on the cook top in a skillet, destined to be our brunch that day, all those years ago since we began this trip. It seemed like years, but in reality it had been roughly twenty-seven hours since we jumped from the speeding bullet. Twenty-seven hours since we had left our food on the stove and jumped a train. Kinda sounds like the beginning of a "Twilight Zone" episode if you think about it.

I figured we could hide more easily in the dark and observe the lay of the land better. That fact would aid us in laying out our plan of attack against all things unfamiliar, meaning everything. Cullman, as far as this trip was concerned, was just a memory and Brian asked me why I thought we should stay clear of the small town. I shared this tidbit of information with him concerning the numerous times I had passed through Cullman with my football team for a lunch visit when we'd travel to places north of us. Stopping in Cullman generally meant our gridiron business was happening in another state.

Coach Bradshaw liked to exercise twice yearly what some of the brothers called "white control." They all spoke of it in hushed tones when I'd visit the ghetto, the southern end of the fourth floor of Alumni Hall, "B-wing" and known specifically as the football player's floor. Since that floor was football players only it was off limits to everyone not invited personally by a teammate. There was an "A-wing" and a "B-wing," with us occupying the "B- wing" and rarely did a fool mistakenly cross into the Ghetto without being first questioned and generally turned away by the brothers. Those were the rules, man, and they existed long before I showed up and probably still exist today. It was a smart move on the college's behalf, because we were the roughnecks and skull crushers on campus and generally always sported headaches from hitting drills. The echoes of coaches' constant screaming in our heads meant that peace, quiet, and privacy, were a must. No one needed to pass through our floor to get from or to anywhere, so it was best you not bother to stop in. Any former, and I mean former, athlete making a crude attempt of proving how much of a badass he might have been in high school, regardless of how many Varsity letters he gained while there was best proven elsewhere. One so inclined would be better suited to prove their prowess on the intramural or frat-rat football field and not with those of us that did it for a living. I had one of my good buddies who hailed from the Ghetto tell me about Bradshaw's "white control" move and how he exercised it every year at least once or twice if necessary. He personally called it the "White Power Play" by Bradshaw and always followed it with a complimentary,

"No offense, man."

"None taken dude, continue…"

I said before that Cullman was the seat of the Grand Wizard of the Ku Klux Klan back in the late seventies/ early eighties and that much was fact. I had not been exposed to the KKK other than seeing an occasional documentary on public television or news blurbs on TV. Hearing J.B. Stoner's (past gubernatorial candidate in Georgia) racist election commercials being run on the local Atlanta TV stations was generally as far as my exposure to extreme racism went. Mark Twain said: "Of all the creatures that were made, man is the most detestable" and I think that applies to the pettiness that seems to keep racial tension so prevalent everywhere. My wish is that it could somehow go ignored, but I fear that will stay my wish for a long time to come.

When our football schedule was concocted, Coach Bradshaw made sure we made at least two stops in Cullman to enjoy a meal at the Cullman "All-Steak" restaurant, located conveniently in beautiful downtown Cullman. Directions are as follows: go to Cullman, Alabama to the intersection right smack in the middle of town, travel just 250 feet off the intersection Northeast towards Chattanooga, look right, then prepare yourself to travel 55 years back in time as soon as you walk through the front doors, and you have arrived. Bradshaw usually scheduled our arrival right around lunch time or right before supper when the town was slowing down for the day's end, or just slowing down for lunch. Either way, our visit meant that the entire town *was in town* when we arrived.

I will say again, I am from Atlanta and what I witnessed made me "start" (a North Carolina saying)…that's a back-country phrase for getting surprised by a happening or event and the outcome that follows. Remember, I was a "back of the bus hooligan type," so I dismounted last 95% of the time I rode the chartered buses to our scheduled locations. I could see the brothers getting uptight as soon as someone mentioned the fact that we were only twenty miles or so from Cullman, and even the bigmouth citified brothers spoke in hushed tones as silent as a defendant, quietly praying, awaiting his verdict from a hostile jury. I wondered what was up, so I asked one of my friends of color what might be causing all the quiet commotion. He said, very deadpan,

"Bradshaw's annual way of showing us who is in charge," with "us" meaning the black ball players I called teammates and friends.

When we arrived at the restaurant, our bus pulling right up in front of the door, it only took a few minutes for what seemed like the entire town to gather to witness the perceived invasion that was taking place right in the heart of Dixie. I thought nothing of it, but was warned by numerous brothers to stay clear of them when they left the bus as a sort of protective measure aimed solely at me. I asked why, and as soon as we stepped off the bus I knew why. Seeing the hateful stares and pointing of fingers by the locals, all acting like a traveling side show had broken down on the town square, invading the privacy of its residents. My African-American friends, ones I had practiced with, enjoyed victories and endured defeats with, bled and suffered with, was afraid for their lives when they exited the bus. If you recall the Louisiana mob, these folks stood silently across the streets and up and down the sidewalks, stopping the old pickup trucks they drove, mentally locking and loading at the sight they beheld. The white players entered the restaurant first, minus me of course, followed by the black players who walked in a tight pack as a form of security, heads down or looking straight ahead not making eye contact with any of the townsfolk. I assumed these might be decent people straight out of *Mayberry RFD*, but their disapproving stares aimed at the men of color I called teammates told me differently. I never heard a sound out of anyone until I entered the *All-Steak* at the back of the line, me taking up the rear like I always did when we traveled, revealing to me intimately what the definition of hate might be around those parts.

When we started up the steps to the meeting rooms I am sure were occupied by the local Rotary Club or the Lions Club on various days during the week. The entire restaurant went as silent as if E. F. Hutton was talking (remember, when E. F. Hutton talks people listen?), about to share a surefire winner in the stock market making early retirement a reality for the bulk of the crowd that day. I would like to report that stock tips from the lips of Mr. E. F. Hutton himself were what caused the silence on those visits to Cullman's most famous restaurant, "but if I told it I'd be lying it," as Twain so aptly assigned to young Huckleberry Finn's take on Jim's escape chances succeeding in a part of the south, not unlike this. This was the "Jim Crow" south as I had always heard of it, in living color.

In the ten seconds that seemed to last an eternity, the silence was broken by a barrage of human beings whose color I share, shouting to no one in particular to "Get those damn niggers out of here!" repeated over and over by numerous individuals who appeared to be God loving Christian folks right out of a Norman Rockwell painting, if Mr. Rockwell would have ever painted a picture of hate filled racists eating at a diner. Most shouted, some threw their eating utensils down and stormed out of the diner, but most just stared, snarling.

What really caught my attention were the people in charge of taking orders, serving and cooking the meals to the suddenly resentful customers that day. The servers were all black, wearing black slacks and shiny black patent leather shoes, white shirts with thin black ties and cream colored sport coats. They seemed just as surprised as the customers were when we arrived with our contingency of muscled, well dressed and well mannered football players that day. They froze in their tracks, stopping to look at us as we passed, holding fresh cooked orders and pitchers of iced sweet tea so still you'd have thought they were posing for a turn of the century tin-type picture.

In my mind's eye I can still see the sad expressions on their faces, almost looking embarrassed by the outbursts of the patrons that day. Lastly, I remember being called a "nigger lover" by a well dressed older woman with hate-filled eyes and a snarl so big and sinister I could see every one of her teeth. I realized it was because of where I was situated in line and who I was associating with, my teammates. I tell you it was the first time I had witnessed firsthand racism as a way of life, taught like it was a secret book of the bible reserved for those so inclined in that particular part of the Bible Belt. It made me glad that I was not God on that day; as I would have sent them all to Hell which I'm sure would have been a huge surprise to each and every one of them.

> *"Enter through the narrow gate. For wide is the gate and broad is the road that leads to destruction, and many enter through it. But small is the gate and narrow the road that leads to life, and only a few find it."*
>
> *Matthew 7:13-14; NIV.*

I remember the meal we had upstairs that day. It is burned into my memory banks as clearly as it happened yesterday. I also remember the sounds of forks and knives scraping against each other as we ate in silence, ice tinkling in tea glasses and no one uttering a single word throughout the entire meal, other than to say thank you to the kind servers that smiled at us as they went about their menial tasks. I remember trying to make words to apologize to my friends for what they had endured that day, but the words just wouldn't come. Any words would not have been sufficient. I was fire cracker mad at our head coach for this crap, intimidating players by fear and superiority as a means of driving home who was in charge that day or any other for that matter. This exact scenario played over twice a year every year while I played there and I disliked the practice and what it came to represent to both white and black players. I am certain it was thoroughly disliked by all in attendance, with my position coach daring to voice his dislike for the practice only to have his livelihood jeopardized for speaking up in defense of abolishing it completely.

In my later years I realized it was just insecurity on behalf of our older head coach and I pitied him for it only because of what he must have witnessed in his youth, convincing himself that this kind of intimidation was necessary and acceptable. It was also the first time in my young life I was ashamed of my affiliation with Troy and I was reminded of it twice a year. I could dislike the practice and even voice my own opinion on the subject but I could not stop being white and somehow feeling responsible for it all by my silence on the subject. I can say truthfully, my last year in West End I was the last white kid in my class before we moved to the suburbs so I knew what it's like to be singled out and hated for your color. Saying I'm sorry to my old friends and teammates is not enough, but sorry is all I have. The experience changed me. For the first time, I knew what "Injustice anywhere is a threat to justice everywhere" really meant, written in 1963 by a young pastor sitting in a Birmingham city jail. That fellow was named Martin Luther King. Jr.

As Brian and I moved slowly, ever closer to the lights, we started to hear the sounds of vehicles running and could see a string of headlights moving slowly and steadily towards whatever festivities were taking place at the point we both were headed in. When we got close enough to see what might be going on, I recognized torches, and lots of them, all attached to guys looking like transplants from the Southeastern Louisiana football game I described in detail earlier in this writing. We crawled up to the rim on the northern most side of the remote festival grounds, not wanting to get noticed by anyone before we figured out what might be happening that warm and humid late spring night. It was about eleven-thirty in the evening and this party was just getting started. By the looks of things we figured we had walked up on a huge hunting party. These boys were making ready to drink some beer and smoke some fresh killed game, cleaned and prepared for smoking or grilling earlier that same day.

I told Brian we should just wait and let things sort themselves out before we showed ourselves in an attempt to mingle and fill our empty bellies with beverages and chow from area red-necks sporting rifles and pistols. Oh, and loaded rifles and pistols too. These country boys repeatedly took aim at the heavens, firing off round after round at the stars, or maybe at the angels hovering over them, busy writing their names down to relay back to God himself the evil they witnessed and those participating. The fellows must have seen something they wanted killed, based on the direction their hastily shot rounds traveled. Just when I thought we'd just quietly mingle with the crowd, I noticed a bonfire of sorts being started up at the opposite end of the football sized grounds that lay before us. From our location, it was like we were announcers at the festivities and from our elevated vantage point we could see everything, but we had no idea what we might be announcing.

Then it happened, a huge barrage of gunshots fired off almost simultaneously and a huge cross lit up like a roman candle where the bonfire had started, like it had been doused with gasoline to get it going quickly. I looked over at Brian and his eyes were as big as mine then I worried we might both get spotted as the entire area lit up like stadium lighting did when the sun set at a football game and the pole mounted banks of sodium filled lights flipped on. We both instinctively ducked our heads down as low as we could, leaving just enough showing to watch whatever in the Hell might be going on that evening, but a much smaller target if spotted. I remember vividly that it was warm and very humid. I also remember the cold chills that rushed over me, like I had been deposited in the Antarctic, wearing only a pair of blue jeans (that honestly looked like a swarm of termites might have dined on them), and a filthy creosote soaked tee-shirt serving as the only means of keeping myself warm. We both knew what we were witnessing: a full-blown meeting of the local or maybe regional chapters of the Ku Klux Klan. We knew this by the white robes the fellows adorned shortly after the fiery cross lit up and the pointy hats they wore as a head dress (dunce caps) to complete the KKK ensemble. I became aware of how we both looked and if caught, might be misconstrued as an act of defiance against this boozed-up and well armed bunch.

It was quite a sight to behold, seeing so many hate filled human beings clinging to the twisted heritage they thought to be in jeopardy. They marched around in geometric patterns in an effort to make it all look important to whoever was looking down from above, confident their hate filled meeting was being met with approval from on high. Brian and I were frozen in both amazement and a little fear, thinking if we were caught by these boys we might have just as hard a time explaining ourselves, if you know what I mean. We watched for another ten minutes then gave each other knowing looks to say, "…let's haul ass before we get caught." We crabbed away a good fifty yards backwards, stopping only for cramps in our legs, making excellent time for two hungry white boys in full blackface.

We gave the well lit KKK meeting a very wide berth after we had backed out on our all fours. We headed west and south, making our way back towards the train tracks that eventually led to our safety. We decided we'd just stick to the trail and not stray again as we had dodged two bullets already, missing Cullman and the KKK party, and I didn't want to chance it again. I guess if you wanted to get really technical, it may have been the seventh bullet we dodged that day, if you added up all of the events that occurred spanning the short time we were gone up until then. Watching the KKK rally was the second time in my life, other than the Cullman All-Steak visits, I was almost embarrassed to admit it: these were people whose race I shared.

Brian and I made it back to the tracks, tired and dirty, but determined to make the rest of our walkabout as uneventful as humanly possible.

That was the plan…

Chapter · XXXIII

BRIAN AND I made it back to the tracks vowing not to stray from them again. The tracks were good, the tracks led back to our provisions, the tracks led back to everything we thought spelled normal. They lay out in front of us like twin shiny ribbons, reflecting the moonlight off the tops of its structure, like silver breadcrumbs left by Hansel and Gretel. Of course I was Hansel and Brian was Gretel, just so you'll know. I don't want to get all philosophical on you here, but Brian and I was hungry and tired, a little discouraged and still a very long assed ways from home. As I recall, we didn't even see Birmingham when we were riding the train so I was certain we'd not see it in the slow motion return "ride" we were currently engaged in. After the KKK meeting and the Cullman bypass, we realized we might not see civilization for another 10-12 hours if my calculations were remotely correct, and that was with a four hour margin of error.

Anyway you sliced it, we were not likely to see any proof of human beings, other than a passing train and maybe a fly over by a jumbo jet. That fact alone made for a little concerned speculation pertaining to our long-term survival. Reaching our ultimate goal, home, depended on how healthy we could stay during our remaining time walking in the wilderness and that fact was not lost in me. One thing this experience drove home to me was how easy a person could get lost and never be seen again. If not for the train tracks that lay out before us, we might just walk around in circles until our shoes or our resolve wore out. It reminded me of a true Bradshaw incident and I shared it with Brian.

I want to clarify something before I begin. I might portray my collegiate head coach as somewhat of a total lunatic and that would not be a fair assessment. He was a father and a husband and for that I must give him tremendous leeway. He was passionate about discipline, his built by the United States Marine Corps, and he had a way of enforcing his rules and getting his point across in the most unique of ways. He usually delivered the consequences of violating those rules in a way the violator never forgot. Bradshaw was saddled with the unfortunate job of molding and coaching young men into a unit that could and would produce wins and not losses. Any team could lose, but only a select few can win regularly and proficiently. His was a game of numbers. More wins, and asses in the seats because of those wins, meant he maintained job security. Plain and simple, if you're winning you're staying, as in keeping his job.

I spoke in the very beginning of this writing concerning my greatest influences and my college coach was one of them, whether I liked it or not. I denied his impact on my life with great prejudice over the first ten years I was out from underneath his umbrella of influence. My finding great satisfaction in the fact that my last year in college football was also his last sometimes makes me ashamed. I guess the years of being a Marine Corps drill instructor and psychology major backfired on him like most antiquated systems and methods tend to do. His methods utilized today would be like using COBOL and FORTRAN (the original computer language) versus a Windows based program in the computer world; it just wouldn't hold up. I will admit that more discipline among players is greatly needed these days. Winning has become far more important than molding the character of the young men used like farm tools to get those coveted wins. Today's coaches have press agents and spin doctors hired to cover every misstep and players are taught the art of the pre and post game interview. These same players are not taught how to cope in the real world when the glory of football fades, nurtured along by the remote prospect of going pro. Those kinds of coaches did not exist back in the late seventies and early eighties when I was involved in the college game. Football was a raw, yet scripted, sport and if you didn't like it, you should just stick to playing tiddlywinks, croquet or some other game that didn't involve physical contact, or wearing helmets...or keeping score.

I was going to include badminton but that would have been a mistake.

I'm going to stop here and relay a message to anyone considering taking badminton as a physical education class needing a one hour credit in college. Please, oh please do it, and take good note of the sarcasm in my writing of this, if possible.

I was entering my last quarter of school, the same quarter as the one that ended with this train ride odyssey. I was cruising along, not concerned about having too large of a class load, satisfied my last quarter would be a great one, with only twelve credit hours to take, then I'm out of college permanently. Things were not as computerized back then as they are now, with only large banks and colleges' utilizing the advantages of the very expensive tool a computer system was back then, so some things fell through the cracks academically. I'll cut to the chase and tell you I received a message from my guidance counselor via homing pigeon (if you catch my drift) meaning it was three weeks after my final quarter had started. The message read as follows and I quote:

"Mr. Hall, graduation is ten weeks away and I have discovered you are one credit hour short of graduation. If you do not correct this shortfall you will not graduate this year."

"Oh Shit!" was all I could muster. "OH SHIT!"

I felt my cods drop into my shoes as I read the warning I held in my hand, face turning pale and palms sweaty, head swimming thinking I might just pass out or crap my britches, both of which would ruin my reputation as a smart ass and a former tough guy. I bee-lined it to my counselors office, insisting I needed to see him immediately to the point of being rude. The thought of having to return to Troy to take a one hour class in the following fall quarter, then having to wait until December to embrace the graduation ceremony I so desperately needed, made me homicidal.

If I wanted to get the accolade I desired and earned, I'd have to take a damned one hour PE class. I'd get the full-Monty cap and gown treatment ending with the flinging of my mortar board to the tune of "Pomp and Circumstance," but the hopes of it happening quickly became complicated. A mortar board is that funny hat one wears when he or she graduates from either high school or college just so you'll stop wondering and can fully grasp the rest of this story. Now, if you are from Southeastern Louisiana, don't worry about what it is and just let whoever is reading to you keep on reading and showing you pictures, okay?

I was short one son-of-a-bitchin' PE credit! I had played football every day for four years and one quarter and I was short one PE credit, damn it! The college gave one PE credit to each football player for each quarter you were involved in the sport, that is until someone decided that was just too much of a giveaway program in credits, and decided to revoke the policy my last quarter playing the game. That change meant I was exactly one PE credit hour short of graduating. I guess I was getting a karma-styled payback for covertly joining a fraternity and keeping it a secret from my teammates. Maybe it was, in the grand scheme of things, arranged by God himself, a means of making me have to work hard one last time to get out of college. All I knew was that my lack of proper credit hours was knowledge not shared with anyone I knew (meaning me) and I was not a happy camper.

When I found this out I was pissed off and for this reason, all physical education teachers hated the "football for PE giveaway credit hour system" to which I was a previous benefactor. This meant I would have to go and talk to at least one, if not all of them, to get a shot at joining a class late, which was a stretch. I wound up talking to every single PE teacher that day and finally got the oldest, crustiest fellow teaching badminton to allow me to join his class, albeit reluctantly. This guy was so old he looked dead but was just too damned stubborn to fall over and make it official. The cartilage in his knees was so shot you could have struck a sulfur match on either of them, the big fireplace kind with the white tips, and this old boy would not even flinch. Even if you had to take two or three swipes at it to get it lit he'd wait you out.

It was three hours a week of full court punishment and what equated to full contact badminton Hell. If he'd had it his way, he'd have handed out guns and knives before class to make it more interesting. The old dude was determined to get at least one or two participants killed, or mortally wounded, as personal entertainment before the quarter ended. The final exam was just short of an all out brawl, operating under the order that the loser failed the class and the winner got an "A," ending with two fistfights and a good girl scrap before the conclusion of the exam. I received an "A" because I was obviously just a few months removed from living in the athletic jungle and survival of the fittest was right up my alley. I was what amounted to a Rhino with the rashy ass playing a full contact sport with a bunch of piccolo players. Mr. P.E. gave me a good degree of shit every day knowing he had power over my graduation in the form of a one hour class. I could cut his proverbial mustard and he knew it, so he rode all the other participants a whole lot harder. He'd use me as an example of how to adapt and overcome, citing Badminton as a sort of ballet played by those considerably more refined than the likes of me. I survived his class and took my "A," never to take the game of badminton for granted again. I have seen Badminton played a time or two on some high numbered ESPN station, at two in the morning, but it was indeed not played like we played it under the tutelage of Coach No-Knees "Il Duce" Mussolini and probably involved a wine and cheese party afterward with a poetry reading and bongo drum music tossed in.

    I must swing this story back around to where it was originally going, which was the way Coach Bradshaw handled insubordination when we traveled a long distance to play an opponent using a chartered bus as our modus travelus (author's Latin). It was always rumored that Coach Bradshaw would actually put a player off the bus, as a random act of discipline, once a year. This disciplinary act meant leaving the recipient in the absolute middle of nowhere, kinda like our current situation with cold calculation thrown in for good measure, leaving the "offender" to make their individual way back to Troy. It was another really sad and dangerous way of displaying his authority over us, except it was a cold hard reality for some poor dude. If you were dumb enough to get caught out after curfew or missed class too often, you made the list of potential candidates. It also included infractions like low grades or smiling at practice (I kid you not) or any other litany of violations Bradshaw might incorporate into his repertoire of doom and domination. We would usually be riding down some out-of-the-way back road, not utilizing the interstate system, as dropping a human being off on an interstate was against the law in any state in the union. He generally made sure we had accomplished our mid-way meal so the prize winning offender was, at least, sporting a full belly before being ejected from the safe haven of the bus. Coach always waited about thirty minutes after the meal, when everybody was dozing off, before he instructed the bus driver to pull over to the side of the road in the middle of nowhere.

    I recall my roommate my senior year playing ball, Bubba Mueller, getting "the toss" on one of the long trips to God only remembers where late in the football season, maybe game eight or nine. The greatest part of the whole "Bubba got tossed" incident was how it all went down and the events afterward landing Coach Bradshaw in major hot water with the NCAA.

Bubba (he was one of four Bubbas that particular year, keeping the multiple Bubba tradition going) was a dude that could play some football but just wasn't cut out to be a college student. He knew it, I knew it, and probably our coaches knew it. Bubba tended to get a lot of free passes, extremely rare back in the day, because of his uncanny ability to play football. Bubba could play the game with extreme prejudice but physically looked like he might not survive warm-up drills. He was about six feet tall, maybe two hundred and thirty pounds, and a serious Florida redneck (he admitted it). He had a pot belly on him that would make a lifetime beer drinking truck driver jealous. Bubba looked like he had literally swallowed a fully grown watermelon but his belly was as hard as a rock and so was he. He hated running, a daily requirement if you played at Troy, and he complained about the practice every chance he got. At game time the dude always got this great big old smile on his face and said with great excitement, "Today we are the kings of the world boys and folks are paying to see us kill somebody, so let's give 'em their money's worth!" He was right, in a sick and demented way, but right just the same.

I really didn't care for Bubba when I first met him (maybe it was his not giving a shit attitude about all of it), but I really started to like him when I found out he and I had similar goals. Bubba and I practiced the wholesale rejection of authority by trying to piss off Coach Bradshaw, making us kindred spirits. Our joint saving grace was having the ability to produce tackles, making us both indispensible to the results-oriented, win-producing-as-its-only-means-of-existence program Coach Bradshaw had formulated. Bubba was always on the cusp of being in some sort of trouble for missing class, serial tardiness and low grades. Throw in missing curfew, sneaking out after curfew (then getting caught) and many other numerous infractions that violated team policy and it spelled a long walk home for my friend Bubba Mueller.

Back then, I kept a cottage industry going from filling out tardy and missed class forms, then forging professors and teachers signatures on those forms that the coach distributed twice a quarter in football season. I made ten bucks for each forged signature and fifteen each if the instructor had a doctorate degree, i.e. "Dr. Green" or "Dr. Smith." I justified the 50% higher fee by stating the risk I was taking by forging a doctor's signature, a crime only a step below forging a fake prescription. It was all BS, but it worked, and I prospered because of the positive cash flow generated from my forgeries.

My offerings were spot-on and never questioned by any of the coaching staff or administrators charged with reviewing and approving such documents. I did have a competitor on another floor do some cheap knock-off signatures, but he sustained injuries after his low-rent forgeries were found out by the school's administration. He got worked over by two members of the track team that year for his transgressions and came to know personally that you shouldn't make a discus thrower and a shot putter, on steroids, look stupid, dishonest or both. Getting those boys in trouble due to cheap, low quality forgeries might get your legs broken. I generally only provided the service to the football team, the baseball team occupying the fourth floor "A-wing" opposite us, and most of the golf team. The golf boys always had money and got a five dollar surcharge, just because I heard one time golf was a thinking man's sport and I thought they ought to pay more. The attendance/tardy program, implemented by Bradshaw, was an outward attempt to keep all football eligibility intact, at least on the surface. It was an effective deterrent, but it was also the only way a candidate for the "get off my bus" club was chosen. It happened once and sometimes twice a year, so somebody was walking home. On this particular outing, Bubba was getting his walking papers, and that fact led to a confrontation between him and Coach Bradshaw neither I nor my teammates would soon forget.

I knew in my heart Bubba was not going to last much longer in the football program Bradshaw stood watch over. Bubba was the type of guy that just went along with any deal until it pissed him off, he'd say "screw it" then move on to the next thing, regardless of what it might be. He was a sophomore my senior year and we had racked up only a few wins, unusual for any team Bradshaw coached. We were going to play an opponent that we could beat handily meaning the stage was set for the "put off" we had all grimly anticipated. Bradshaw always put his victim off on the trip *going* to play our opponent rather than the trip back, making sure the offender had pre-game strength to walk back to Troy as a sign of mercy. I assumed Bradshaw thought this move "upped" his stock on the mind games he played. When the bus's momentum began to slow, I knew immediately something was up and the "put-off" was afoot.

As for me, I never slept when we were traveling. Sleeping made me tired and sluggish and I just didn't like to sleep before a game, so I'd pass the time reading. The night was made for sleeping in my opinion, and sometimes it was for staying up all-night, but not sleeping in the day. It was a rule I rarely broke and this day was no exception. I was in the very back of the bus and Bubba (the subject Bubba, not any of the three others) was in the seat in front of me, snoring like he was in a competition to see who could sleep the longest and loudest. As the bus slowed I nudged him awake telling him to be prepared as the axe was about to fall on someone. I didn't know for sure who would get their walking papers but I knew it wasn't me. I never violated any rules, overtly at least, and my attendance was perfect in every class, at least as far as the coaching staff knew and my perfect forged documents conveyed.

When the bus driver made his full stop ending with the whooshing sound of air exiting the brake system, Coach Bradshaw waited for a good thirty seconds before he left his seat. He'd then rise up from his front seat throne, slowly, then eyeball every player up and down the aisles before he made his calculated power play. He'd have the driver turn up the interior lights so every player could see him and anxiously wait for the verdict to be read. There had not been one single player who hadn't violated his rules in some form or fashion, as they were too numerous to avoid. Any player, regardless of their goody two-shoes status, could unintentionally violate one of Bradshaw's rules at least four to five times a day. It was like being blindfolded and being required to successfully walk in a mine field for your daily bread. It was any man's guess as to who might get the privilege to walk back to Troy that day, but I just knew Bubba was the guy. Bradshaw gave his standard "this is considerably more painful to me than it could be for you" speech, choking up like a seasoned actor reaching a perfectly timed and much rehearsed scene. He then followed the charade with a few seconds silence before he nailed the coffin shut. The time had arrived...

"Bubba Mueller" Coach Bradshaw said in an elevated and irritated tone, like he'd just revealed the results in a voted upon contest.

"Right here dude." Bubba replied from the back of the bus Jeff Spicoli style, reminding me of when the pizza guy showed up in Mr. Hand's class in *Fast Times at Ridgemont High* to deliver the surfer dude his pie. Bubba's reply and style of delivery did not sit well with Coach Bradshaw and he challenged him to use a more refined tone when addressing him.

"Use respect when you address me son," he said, utilizing his much used and rightly timed drill instructor voice. Bubba just sat there and didn't say a word, never breaking eye contact with the man that held his short term traveling plans in his hands.

"Son, you need to exit the bus for missing curfew numerous times and multiple other team violations you have accrued over the past eight weeks." Bradshaw said with General Patton like confidence.

Silence.

"Did you hear me Bubba?"

More silence. Bradshaw walked quickly halfway towards the back of the bus as a way of showing Bubba he really, really meant what he said (a vital part of the charade). His aggressive style was akin to challenging Bubba to a physical contest and one our coach might surely come out on the losing end of.

"Bubba Mueller, get your ass up out of your seat and exit this bus!"

"Or what, you're gonna throw me off, you worn out old son-of-a-bitch?" Bubba shouted as he sprang out of his seat and headed for Bradshaw like he was going to turn him inside out. Instantly, the assistant coaches all jumped up from their seats and bolted towards the back like movie extras coached to hit a well timed mark. We all sat hoping Bubba might bury his fist in Bradshaw's face.

"Bubba Mueller I know you are upset but rules are rules and…"

Bubba cut him off mid sentence. "Take your rules and stick them right up your ass, you fucking bastard!"

I was speechless and wide-eyed along with the rest of the riders on the bus.

"Move your dried up ass back and let me pass." he said, not moving until Bradshaw exited the pathway, giving Bubba a clear passage to disembark.

Those of us who had money handed Bubba cash as he exited as a means of helping him make it back to Troy or wherever he planned to go that day. We all somberly watched him leave the bus, stuffing the bills into his pockets. Bubba stuck his bird finger right in the face of our head coach as he passed by, just to seal the deal.

"I guess Bubba didn't like getting woke up," one of my team mates whispered half joking, half ironic. I wanted to laugh my ass off and was duly impressed by the wit and timing of that well placed and unexpected morsel of comedy. I kept my amusement to myself, however, and was certain any peeps from the peanut gallery might quickly afford Bubba a walking partner. I liked the dude but I acknowledged that today this was his show, not mine.

I looked out at Bubba when the buses brakes whooshed and the diesel engine revved, sounding more like a stampede of horses from my back seat, the huge power plant situated directly beneath my seat. I waved at him through the slightly tinted windows and he returned my salutation with a "thumbs up." I found comfort in his reply for some strange reason. I felt like it was him giving us the "OK" to carry on. I watched Bubba walk in the opposite direction of our bus until he disappeared like an ant eclipsing the horizon. I looked around the bus at my team mates, some going back to sleep, some staring out the windows, feeling fortunate their name had not been called and wondering what in the hell they were doing on this team.

We kicked the butt of our opponent that weekend, but not before Bradshaw accused me of being a poor influence on Bubba. Bradshaw stating that he (Bubba) would not have confronted any authority in such an egregious manner if I'd taken him under my wing like a good senior would have. What he didn't know was Bubba was a loosely contained forest fire and any illusion of control by any authority figure was just that, an illusion. I agreed with Coach Bradshaw concerning all the counts he accused me of that day concerning Bubba, just to be patronizing. He even threatened to make me walk home just because I agreed with him and I decided that was also fine with me too. Hell, it all paid the same with this guy.

Bubba had single-handedly embarrassed our head coach in front of God and the entire team. That reality meant collateral damage would ensue in the form of more threats and reprisals if any additional violations of his numerous rules occurred, perceived or otherwise. I knew if he sent me packing, that meant his starting nose guard and his starting left tackle would be busy walking home and not playing the game our scholarships required of us both. The odds of a loss loomed considerably larger when two pieces of the defensive puzzle went missing due to some strange power play, enacted semi-annually as a way to show young men who's the boss. The black players had the "Cullman All-Steak" intimidation twice a year and the white players had the "get off my bus" intimidation once and sometimes twice a year.

Bubba had single handedly changed the rules when he stepped off the bus that day late in the season. Bubba didn't go back to Troy that weekend, he walked to a nearby gas station and called a friend to come pick him up, staying gone for nearly two weeks. The NCAA quietly came down on Coach Bradshaw like a ton of bricks for that stunt. TV news crews and newspaper reporters camped outside our field house awaiting some sort of verdict as to Bubba's whereabouts. Bubba eventually was heard from, purposely missing the last game and basically telling Coach Bradshaw to shove it up his ass in a way no one had done before. That incident and many, many others spelled the end of Bradshaw's tenure at Troy and no-one was saddened by the loss, but many sent letters saying they approved.

I saw Bubba one last time when he came by and picked up his stuff from the dorm room we shared. He filled me in on his trip and the circumstances surrounding it. He told me point blank he was going to flunk out that year. Bradshaw's power play was a perfect way of telling the empire Bradshaw had erected with wins, but maintained with fear and intimidation, to just "F-OFF," as he liked to put it. Bubba *said* he called his parents and told them both where he was and what he was doing. I don't know if he was telling the truth on that particular point, but it was his world and he was the king of it. He told me half-jokingly that if Bradshaw was going to stick it to him, he was going to return the favor in spades. Bubba said he hung out with a buddy of his who attended another college and stayed wasted, enjoying college for the first time since he signed up.

It was probably for the best, as I thought Coach Bradshaw had tired of the three ring circus he called a coaching job. Bradshaw did well after his Troy days with the help of his lifelong buddy and close friend Paul W. "Bear" Bryant. The Bear's political pull and formidable influence advanced coach Bradshaw's career far beyond his coaching days. Rumor number one was that Bryant arranged for him to be the general manager at the Dog racing track near beautiful Tuscaloosa, Alabama and home of the Alabama Crimson Tide. Rumor number two was Bear left a generous stake in Golden Flake Potato chips to Coach Bradshaw and he lived a privileged life for the rest of his days. I spoke to my old Coach via telephone twenty years later, when he was ultimately confined to a nursing home, late in years and grasping at life, lamenting to me about the numerous mistakes he made during his time there. He surprisingly acknowledged his regrets surrounding the ill timed *All-Steak* trips and the bus "put off" incidents, a few regrets I'll keep private out of respect for him and my other teammates involving his harsh disciplinary tactics.

His mind was still sharp in his last years. He rattled off my statistics, my home town, and my parent's names almost twenty years after I had played for him. He even asked me to forgive him concerning the way he treated me, and I, of course, did. I still maintain he is one of the five top influences in my life. I know now that I needed a man like Charlie Bradshaw to keep me "in the rows," as my Dad used to call it, referring to a stubborn mules desire to stray off the neatly laid out rows destined for crops to be planted in. I needed a Marine Corps drill instructor and a fully engaged psychology major to guide me and Bradshaw was that man. I'm thankful for that now.

"Damn" was all Brian said as we continued to walk…I could see the sun starting to show its first signs on the eastern horizon. We still had a ways to go.

"My turn" Brian said…

Chapter · XXXIV

IT HAD become painfully evident to us both that we needed to stay on the straight and narrow path leading us back to Troy and food. We were both beaten up, our clothes unfit for cleaning up burnt motor oil, much less wearing. Our feet hurt from walking on the uneven rock-laden path we had pledged ourselves to stay upon. That particular commitment had a central component; do not stray off the tracks for anything, save for food and a cold drink. Now, that was a thought to ponder: a cold drink, ice cold brewski, sweet tea or dog piss, anything relatively potable with ice in it and so cold that its drinker it might not care what was on tap that hot humid day. Wet, on ice, and lots of it was our only requirements for an adequate thirst quencher. There wasn't a lake, stream or even a cesspool Brian and I might take a much needed sip from. If we could indeed find ourselves any watering hole, we'd drink first then pray to God that whatever de-facto refreshment we might consume wouldn't kill us both before we could get back to civilization and medicine(s) designed to cure dung-water consumption.

This trip was getting more interesting by the hour based on recent events. From the way things were progressing we might see human sacrifice, Bigfoot, or the splitting of the atom before this adventure reached its conclusion. Our two year friendship might ultimately end in cannibalism, for one of us at least, if we didn't locate some chow pronto. I knew we needed to pass the time doing something besides listening to the sounds of our bellies growling.

As Brian and I continued on our walk, he recounted a time we ventured to New Orleans for Mardi-Gras, from Fat Tuesday until Ash Wednesday (that'd be one whole day) and the circumstances surrounding our shortened visit. We decided to travel to Louisiana despite my objections to the notion, factoring in the past experiences I had endured there. I gave it the old "what the hell" and went anyway, but only after a small degree of prodding by my good buddy, partner in crime and now walking buddy called me a few names directly challenging my manliness.

My agreement to return to the state of Louisiana was borne purely of resignation on my part (see aforementioned prodding) and it was a mistake. The word had gotten out that the New Orleans Police department was possibly going on strike again. A large dose of "Blue Flu" was rumored (for those of you who don't know, Police wear blue. When they want to collectively protest, they all call in sick-thus, the "blue flu"), similar to the fiasco that was Mardi Gras in 1979 and the lack of a police presence meant this year it was going to be the party extraordinaire. Call it the bash to bash 'em all, the "Coupe Dee Grass" as I heard a hillbilly so eloquently say once without so much as a hint of a French accent. He'd used the term in reference to a time when he described having to shoot a fella over moonshine (in Tennessee just in case you were wondering) and I called bullshit on him for that particular remark. Come to find out later he'd actually ventilated a dude for messing with the family moonshine still.

Note to self: don't mess with a man's moonshine still, even if you are stuck in the proverbial middle of nowhere and have nothing to drink.

Before we left, Brian and I stocked up for our trip in the usual fashion, making a stop to see our illegally blind Rippy-Mart buddy, Dan the Man. We paid our sight impared friend a visit the night before we headed out for the land of the lost boys. We decided snack foods and high protein items were our best bet, as we would probably not sleep much. We took into account the fact we didn't have a place to officially park our asses for the night, or nights, as the case might be and depending on luck either good or bad. We decided we'd just get to New Orleans and see which way the wind blew us after we arrived, our typical modus operandi and one that brought us repeated success. We always set the bar low, so low a fat man would think it was a broom handle laying on the ground rather than a bar which needed leaping over to measure success.

The directional wind I mentioned earlier would prove to blow exceptionally hard for us, gale force if you will, sending us into another biker shit storm and resulting escape from the Big Easy. After our trip concluded I considered the name "Big Easy" to be a bullshit name, the place was neither "Big" nor was it "Easy," for us two at least.

Whatever prejudice I might have had against the "Coon Ass" state during my football career, I had decided (at least temporarily) was borne of a scheduled good-versus-evil scenario. The scenario played itself out every other year when my football team invaded the space of the Louisiana opposition and our poor treatment there was a reminder of our foul trips. I noted, on the in-between years, the way they (the coon asses) were treated by the University when they visited Troy to engage us in the gridiron activities that purposed our annual meeting. Treat them like you'd like to be treated, the Golden Rule of inviting a guest to your town. Bradshaw insisted upon Southern hospitality before he laid an ass-whoopin' on you you'd lie to your grandkids about many years later. Truth was, you'd bury the revenge-style ass-whoopin' Bradshaw laid on you in the dark corners of your mind where most ass-whoopin's go to hide and just pretend like it never happened. I had done it and so had most of the dudes I had ever played ball with at one time or the other. Concealing a good ass-whoopin' was a fact of life and one every man must face. The feel of cold concrete on your back after you've had your ass kicked in was not an event a dude would go 'round braggin about afterward. A smart man knows that sometimes the cold concrete is metaphoric in nature, but it's there just the same. Any man that says he hasn't had his ass handed to him at least once in their life is a damn liar and probably a Vespa rider. Nothing against Vespa, mind you, but you gotta admit, a beautiful woman on a Vespa scooter is a hell of a lot more appealing that a dude on one. Hulk Hogan on a Vespa is like John Wayne on *Queer Eye for the Straight Guy*. It just wasn't meant to be. Now try to link ass-whoopin's and Vespa riding in a story.

Mardi Gras is as wild as the March wind as far as a party goes. The event is totally out of control and the police are present just to make sure no one gets purposely killed. Imagine an open voodoo ritual or Santeria styled ceremony, replete with sawed off chicken heads and candles burning, then throw in floats, beads, jazz music and lots of drunk people and you have Mardi-Gras. During the Mardi-Gras season and if you had enough money, you could catch the any of the previously described voodoo rituals six times a day in just about any back alley in New Orleans. Mardi-Gras is when the whole world just tells New Orleans, "OK, you can do just about anything you want except kill people in public and call it a party."

I will confess that on my one and only trip to New Orleans Mardi-Gras I saw it all and then some and Brian and I would be glad our trip would be short lived for number of reasons. As the saying goes, the way to a man's heart is through his stomach, so I guess if you are trying to cripple a guy, you can go through his stomach also, and Brian found that out the hard way. I'll share more on that detail one in a minute.

Brian and I had pre-planned this particular trip in that we both went to our professors and laid down a lie as thick as a concrete slab on an airport landing strip. Our excuses usually involved having to donate a kidney to a family member or something so far-fetched that the deed would not be easily verified by said professor. I think Brian donated seven kidneys and two livers my senior year, grand total, and maybe his heart twice. I was a senior anyway and I made good enough grades so I was golden, excuse or not. I'm not sure if Brian went through the same procedures I had when planning our Mardi-Gras adventure (as far as fabricating up a surgery story or an organ donation) but he was always game for a road trip.

We had stocked up on snacks and cheap beer, sold blood for a tank of gas (not really, but it sounded a hell of a lot better than the truth), made two sandwiches for the road consisting of two 18 ounce rib-eye steaks cooked to perfection and jammed between whatever two slices of fresh bread might be available at the time. They qualified as sandwiches simply because they were indeed cooked meat resting between two slices of bread. The actual truth was the bread was our small way of staying in step with good manners based on Southern traditions taught to us at a young age, plus the fact we didn't want to eat the steaks bare-handed. Not to say we wouldn't have (*and* have before), mind you, but there is no substitute for good manners and the bread represented the difference between having them and not having them. If you ate a steak with your bare hands you were a miscreant and a savage, but slap it between two slices of bread holding your pinky finger up while you ate, and you were practically a poet. Add in the fact that consuming a steak, on a plate, using a knife and fork, proved exceptionally difficult when driving or being a passenger (yes, we had tried it), and steak sandwiches won. The bread also served as a sponge for the juices that typically ran out of an excellently cooked, medium-well rib eye steak seared to perfection by yours truly. And last, but certainly not least the bread kept our shirts from being a bib, meaning we maintained our cultured poet status for one more day and our pinky's clean in case we needed to pick a booger.

Brian wondered out loud if the cow born with the rib eyes we were eating knew how much we enjoyed his (or her) sacrifice at the moment of our consumption. I'm sure the knowledge of our pleasure would have made whatever bovine death the cow might have experienced worth it. That is, if cows indeed have an afterlife, a sense of pride, or could be happy anywhere outside of India, where the term "Sacred Cow" was coined and still the only place the two names might show up in the same sentence or used as a colloquialism. Our bovine consumption conversation wasn't a deep one, involving the duality of man or the vastness of the universe, but it was deep enough so I played along. I still maintain if God did not intend for us two legged folk to eat cows, he would have put rib eyes and filet mignons in squirrels, making them harder to catch and much more exclusive. I, for one, am glad God put steak in cows and made them easy to catch. I've had squirrel, and let me tell you it's close to chicken but not even on the same continent as steak. Squirrels are a whole lot harder to keep in a corral, and God showed his mercy by placing something so delicious in cows. Plus, he made Cows slow, dumb and easy to catch so God worked it all out perfectly as far as I could tell.

Brian and I should have known this was going to be a trip for the record books, based on the simple fact that we got pulled over three separate times on our way to New Orleans. I guess the word got out that Brian and I were headed to the Louisiana's party capitol. We were stopped by the law, both local and state, and for the life of me I didn't know why. As hindsight is always 20-20, I'm certain that maybe God himself was trying to keep us from going to the Big Easy by sending as many messengers as he could to try and prevent it from actually happening. I will say I mentioned that fact to Brian a time or two, but we both just laughed it off as coincidence and pressed on. I guess anything short of a meteorite landing on our hood couldn't have stopped us, so we kept on plugging towards our goal. Initially, we were pulled over by the Troy cops one hundred feet from our driveway between our frat house and the Rippy Mart. He asked us where we were headed and we both said simultaneously, "Mardi Gras."

Three second pause. He then just shrugged and said, "Stay out of trouble men."

Same thing happened on cop number two, also a Troy cop, issuing us a warning ticket for a busted tail light or something along those lines, and for good measure. The third cop was an Alabama State Trooper that pulled us over at Tillman's Corner, on I-10 just before we crossed into Mississippi. He lighted and sirened us like we might be escaped convicts, and maybe that wasn't very far from the truth looking back on it. Brian suggested we jump out of his car and be waiting, spread eagle and IDs on the hood, for the trooper to do his thing which we did. The State Trooper laughed at us and asked us why we were in such a hurry.

"Mardi-Gras," was our two-word simultaneous answer, and one that was a two-time winner after we said it. He also let us go with a general purpose warning and wished us well, whatever that might mean. We climbed back into the sex mobile (aka birth control Swinger) and Brian stated, "I don't care if we get pulled over every twenty times; I'm gonna be drinking fresh Dixie's and making shrimp Creole turds before this night is over."

We both snickered at the prospect of eating spicy food so hot you'd have to duct tape an ice cube to your butthole just to cool it off. I wasn't big on spicy food back then but even the water had hot sauce in it during Mardi-Gras, so you girded your loins for the visit and kept the whining to a minimum. Unless you imported your own chow you were guaranteed to be eating hot and spicy food for breakfast, lunch and dinner for the duration of your stay. Even the chicory coffee had a twang to it so strong it would make a seasoned coffee drinker switch to Ovaltine, or maybe give up coffee drinking altogether. Most all of the local consumables in Louisiana took a whole lot of getting used to and I didn't plan on being there very long anyway, so it was all good as far as I saw it. I recall Brian and me stopping at a convenience store just inside the Louisiana border, on the Mississippi end. Most convenience stores in Georgia, Alabama and every other State that I considered "normal" had hot dogs spinning on the odd looking roaster machine with the buns warming underneath. The machines in question usually accompanied a small kiosk that included all the fixin's a hot dog might need. Mayo, mustard, pickle relish, onions, hot sauce, anything as long as it fit inside the little 1/3 ounce foil packets you had to use your teeth to tear open before application.

That was not the case in Louisiana, based on my observances, and one I still marvel at whenever I pass through the state on my way to somewhere else. There were indeed cylindrical shaped items spinning on the large machine resembling hot dogs. The odd colored meat filled casings dripped juices that sizzled from its ingredients reacting chemically to the metal surfaces they rested upon rather than the temperature of the actual item itself. I swear, one of the selections had a skull and cross bones warning label concerning its consumption. The florescent orange sign was posted on the machine, warning you not to get any of the drippings from the item in any open wounds or near your eyes. This same spinning object was a shade of red or pink I had never seen before or since, and one I'm sure must have been a byproduct of some abandoned NASA experiment because the color didn't show up in any ultraviolet spectrum in our known galaxy. I guess if you were going to offer a food item that might kill you, or make you wish you were dead post-consumption, then coloring it the alarmingly reddish-pinkish-ish hue these death dogs were colored might (maybe *should have* is more appropriate) serve as a warning of sorts. That is, if the skull and cross bones didn't work sufficiently, or you were deaf, blind, mute and void of nasal membranes or taste buds.

Typical of most stores in Louisiana, this one sold live bait and I noticed the crickets closest to the skull and crossbones red devil sausage were all dead. My curiosity got the best of me and I picked up one of the Red Devils (it was what they were called) with the rusty steel tongs closest to the machine and smelled it, just for the sake of smelling it, like a fool. Let me tell you my eyes watered for a good hour and fifteen minutes just from getting that sausage too close to my body. It was like snorting Chinese hot mustard then needing commercial grade Visine, to clear your eyes of the reddish glaze that late night activities without sleep usually brought. It should note here that I figured out why the bait crickets died closest to the hot dog machine. Someone either used the same tongs to grab the crickets for bait and the juice from the death sausage killed them, or, maybe the crickets just killed themselves as relief from having to smell the acrid stench the death sausages let off.

I dared Brian to eat one of the same cricket-killing-tong-rusting Red Devil sausages from hell and he foolishly agreed. He managed to get it in the bun and to the counter, holding it like it would bite him before he bit it, awaiting whatever fate might be dealt him for taking the challenge. I will say right now, although Brian bit it first, it would definitely bite his ass back later on that evening.

"You gonna eat that mister?" the rode-hard and put-up harder cash register jockey, named Carlene, asked Brian from behind the counter.

She was partially hidden in a haze of gray cigarette smoke, standing with one hand on her hip and one eye half closed from the dark colored, Cigarillo styled half cigarette/half cigar she filtered her breathing air through. The Cigarillo emanated smoke that seemed to flow towards the half-closed eye regardless of how she turned her head and it made her look pissed off when she addressed Brian or breathed. The Cigarillo she toked upon bobbed up and down as she spoke and the falling ashes kept time with her words, fluttering white specs on top of the counter like some snow globe scene gone way wrong.

"I had considered it, Carlene" Brian said with a confidence that was misguided at best and fueled by youthful pride and a self proclaimed cast iron stomach.

"Listen Sweetie, I'll make a deal with you. If you'll just throw that thing back on the rotisserie, or in the trash, we'll call it even and I won't charge you for it…trust me, you'll thank me later."

She said it with the confidence of someone who had witnessed the carnage that one of the frighteningly reddish-pinkish death dogs would surely bring to its unwitting consumer. Brian looked at me as if my words of approval were the only key to his needing permission to put the well done Red Devil Death Dog back where it came from, thus bypassing the experience altogether. I was going to give him that permission, and even had the words formed in my brain running to the downspout of my mouth. When I opened my cake hole, the only thing that came out was,

"You pussy."

Brian purchased the scary sausage thing, grabbing two packs of the tiny spicy mustards and a splash of Tabasco brand hot-sauce, along with our other items then made his way confidently towards the door.

"Honey" the cashier aimed at me, "I put one of those on the rotisserie every day and at the end of the day I throw it away…even the locals won't eat those damn things. One kid ate one on a bet and was hospitalized for burns to his exit chute when it finally clawed its way out."

She continued, "I wear rubber gloves when I take one frozen out of the box, in the cooler, so I won't get any of the juice on my skin. I also turn my head away when I walk it over to the cooker and shield it with my other hand just for good measure. It's February, and if he doesn't throw it back it'll be the second one I've sold this year, the first being to the kid I told you about earlier with the scorched plumbing." She finished by saying, matter of factly, "He'd be safer to just go to the bathroom, sit on the toilet, and just drop it straight into the bowl bypassing all the trouble his digestive system will give him for eating that God awful thing."

For a brief second, and it was brief, I thought I might go and warn Brian not to consume the Red Devil and we'd just call it even. I would even retract the "you pussy" statement that brought him to the inglorious state he would soon find himself in (he didn't know it yet but he would be in a most inglorious state, and soon).

"Nah, Carlene, Brian likes spicy food" was all I could muster, snickering as I turned and walked toward the door.

"Don't say you weren't warned," was all I heard as the heavy glass door closed behind me.

Chapter · XXXV

As I walked towards the car I noticed Brian taking a big ole honkin' bite of the death dog thing colored by the blood of the Devil himself.

"Oh…shit," was all I had.

I froze in my tracks when I saw Brian take a bite from the Express Elevator to Culinary Hell resting innocently on a semi-stale, top-split bun. Brian had judiciously coated the thing in spicy mustard and topped it with Tabasco just to cool it off, I assumed, or to make it somehow more palatable. When he bit into the thing it was like he had a hot ladle full of macaroni and cheese or a cup of molten lava poured into his mouth then spilling into his lap from the way he was twitching. I assumed it was not so much from the temperature of the sausage, but mostly from the combination of fiery ingredients contained inside the strangely colored sausage looking thing he was trying to consume. I fully expected the thing to grow legs and run off or sprout wings and fly away, like some ancient primeval beast awakened by tooth enamel piercing its outer shell. I noticed it took Brian a good minute to chew the first bite up (I assumed to fully kill it) and then swallow it. He looked completely winded after the first bite and he still had a lot more chewing to do before this dare was officially in the history books.

I have never before seen someone go from fully animated to nearly catatonic as fast as Brian did when he completed his first bite. His nose began to run so fast he needed a bucket to catch the fluid. His nasal membranes must have broken down in protest of what it had endured during Brian's consumption of the death sausage. His eyes began to water so badly I thought he might be crying, except he looked more shocked than upset. I can truly say I have never seen a person lose so much clear liquid from their nose and eyes as fast as Brian had done, and that was after only one bite. He attempted to speak but only squeaky sounds came out, sounding not so much human, but more like he had trapped a wharf rat in his throat and it desperately wanted out. I felt kinda sorry for him, albeit briefly, as the expression on his face was similar to what dudes meeting their end in quicksand might make. If the movie version of a quicksand death was what it might really look like, then Brian was headed for a Golden Globe Award at the least and an Oscar at best for his performance. Maybe, I reasoned, an actor faking a quicksand death was what someone eating a death sausage really looked like, learned in low budget "B-Movie" acting school. When I see a movie involving quicksand I think, *Wow, that's what Brian looked like when he ate the Devil's hot dog.*

I wasn't even sitting inside the Swinger yet and I could smell the fumes from the hastily chosen lunch snack Brian had only bitten once. I reached for the door handle, pulling the door open to be met by a wall of acrid spiciness so overpowering I cannot even begin to describe to you here using the King's English with a lot of cuss words thrown in. Brian quickly rolled his window down in what I assumed was the fastest way to dispose of the remaining six inches of anthrax in a bun. I think he was stunned or in shock, unable to move, when I hopped into the seat next to him. He seemed paralyzed by the full frontal assault on all of his senses, so I did what any friend would do in a similar situation: I asked him if he needed me to drive. It was the only thing I could come up with at the moment and proof that I was also under attack from the spicy odor radiating off the Red Devil he had held in his hand. He gazed at me with a pitiful look as if he needed me to read his mind.

"You need something to drink?" I asked him.

He gathered himself then slowly nodded his head, looking like a bobble-head doll might in the back window of the family Chevrolet, it purchased as evidence of some long-ago beach vacation. It was mean, I know, but I snickered at his calculated misfortune and inability to utilize the wisdom given by the convenience store clerk oracle and a well placed skull and cross bone warning.

We had not even circled the parking lot before I was back inside the store. I was seeking medical advice from a woman that looked like she might double as a rodeo clown from all the make-up she wore. Her bee-hive hairdo, sky blue eye shadow and thick white smoke made for a sight seen only when UFOs appeared in the night sky and a TV station needed an expert local commentary. When I re-entered the store, Carlene the clerk was straightening out the Velvet Elvises stacked lean-to style by the beer and chip aisle. She whirled around, staring at me like I was someone she had not spoken to in the previous ten minutes of her life and like I might have startled her with my quick re-entry.

"Help you…" she droned, sounding more like a statement than a question, with a hint of annoyance thrown in for good measure.

Carlene's hazel green blood-shot eyes locked on me like I might be at our hometown Rippy Mart and she was the new cashier, warned about two college boys with smart-ass attitudes looking for dented merchandise. I could only assume she didn't get a lot of company during the time between lunch and dinner so she probably took the time in between to clean up the joint. She stood quietly waiting for me to tell her why I had invaded her space, puffing on her stogie, her head barely visible through the thick white haze that circled her face like the rings around Saturn or a temporary picture frame made of smoke. The smoke provided so much coverage I was sure if James Bond himself would have been there he would have "got wood" and been jealous, seeing the fogbank she laid down and the camouflage cover it provided.

"Uhh, I think my friend might be about to explode" was all I could say, my nearly completed college education hiding itself from my vocabulary.

She hesitated for a split-second, then blurted out, "I told you and I told you but neither of you would listen…Milk, uhhh milk, yea, that's what he needs…and lots of it."

She nervously shuffled and mumbled like she might be having an LSD flashback or called as a material witness in a murder trial. She was nervously puffing on the stogie like her life depended on it and from inside the thick smoke haze that surrounded her, a finger pointed towards the stand up cooler and the beverages. I grabbed a quart of whole milk only to be interrupted by her reaching over my shoulder to grab a full gallon shoving it into my hand.

"You're gonna need at least a gallon…and here, take some Pepto-Bismol and Rolaids, layering the three as you go."

We stood there for a brief second, eyes locked, and she said "It's free of charge, honey, but you can't stay here."

She shoved me out the door with her hand on my back like I might be a long lost moocher-in-law on the way back to where I might have come from, post unexpected visit. Just when I cleared the door, I felt the slightest push right at the end of her finger tips when I exited toward Brian. I started to turn back in acknowledgement of the gesture, but I swear I heard the door lock behind me. It was obvious that we were no longer welcomed at Carlene's Louisiana convenience/bait store. I assumed she got on her CB radio and warned the rest of Louisiana we had made it into town.

As I walked back towards the car for the second time in fifteen minutes, Brian was sitting there, red faced like he might have painted his cheeks and forehead with war paint. He was wide-eyed and drawing very short breaths like he might be using Lamaze breathing and soon having a miracle baby. I noticed when I reentered the car that the sausage responsible for Brian's malady was nowhere in sight, not in the floor board of the car or under the seat. I got out, walked around to the driver's side and didn't see it on the ground nor did I see a dead animal within a fifty foot radius of the car. I figured that was as far as a critter would get if he ate the meat-fashioned angel of death Brian had attempted to consume. I was standing at the driver's door to the Swinger and calmly told Brian to get out of the car and I'd drive us to New Orleans. I had to help him maneuver the short trip around the car, him walking like he was an elderly man and me practically holding him up from his weakened state. He was lucid when I sat him in the passenger seat, communicating with grunts, points and squeaks rather than words. I instructed him to drink some milk, then layer the Pepto-Bismol and Rolaids, repeatedly, per Dr. Rodeo-Clown-Cigar-Smoker-Convenience-Store-Clerk's orders. He did as I instructed while we proceeded onward towards our destiny, him glassy-eyed and mumbling with a spice induced speech impediment or the language of some ancient tree-hugging druids.

I drove for about thirty minutes when it happened. Brian had finally made it to a point where he could talk audibly and all he said was,

"I gotta puke."

He sounded more like a talking volcano, warning villagers of its impending deadly molten payload. We were traveling a good seventy-five miles an hour when he hung his head and half of his body out the window and let her rip. I had to grab him by his belt as he hurled, thinking he might fall all the way out of the window while puking and grunting like a ruttin buck in heat.

My friend dropped some serious industrial puke down the side of the Swinger that day. The toxic contents of Brian's stomach decorated the side of his car like some late 1960's abstract Picasso or Salvador Dali painting gone very wrong. He hurled for a good thirty minutes and dry-heaved for another twenty and it all came to an end when he flopped back in the seat, looked at me and said one thing and one thing only,

"Smooooth."

I just looked at him, hesitated for a brief second then began to laugh so hard I almost wrecked. I had spent the last hour holding him by his belt loops and he made it all good in one word. I fully expected to see a hole in his chest like some alien seed had been planted then gestated exiting like the critter did in the *Alien* movies. We decided to leave the Picasso/Dali racing stripe down the side of the car, all pink with chunks of Rolaids and death sausage, looking like a decoupage nightmare or modern art masterpiece, depending on your perspective and love for the arts.

When we finally pulled into New Orleans, we went straight to Bourbon Street to look for some late night action in the Big Easy. It had taken us six hours to get to our destination, factoring in the time spent babysitting Brian's hot-dog affair, so we cut to the chase when we arrived not wanting to waste any more time than necessary. We walked into the first sleazy dive on the street and ordered some brewskis after grabbing a seat at the bar. It wasn't long until the place was populated with rowdy bikers and like the Atlanta trip, it became quickly obvious to me we were not welcomed based on our looks alone. One particular biker dude looked at Brian and flat out told him "haul ass city boy" followed by a quickly delivered "now!" his bellicose tone familiar to us both. The roughneck, asshole biker dudes we seemed to attract like flies to picnic potato salad had found us again. Not the Atlanta biker dudes we befriended, but the specific breed of asshole biker dude. I kept my mouth shut looking for the biggest dude in the group, just in case we had to make a run for it and kicking that specific dude in the balls might be in short order and key to our escape. When he stood up, Brian bowed up, a southern term for sticking out your chest and marking one's territory with bravado rather than urine (like the animals do), and the biker dudes followed suit. I quickly noticed that picking the biggest dude out of this bunch was like picking out which bullet to shoot if you were a lone good-guy and faced with a lot of bad-guys to kill, armed only with a single shot rifle. Once again the math was not in our favor so I implemented the diplomacy act when faced with such odds. I told the biker dudes we were just about to leave, making living for one more day a reality I hoped Brian could latch onto in his weakened state.

When we made it to the door, I noticed that numerous bikers were perched on Brian's car and that just didn't seem to sit well with him that day. We had four-wheeled in it, roof surfed on it, jumped stuff in it, slept in it, got Auburn revenge in it and even double dated in it when necessary. The difference was Brian had extended his permission to do those things. These guys were obviously friends with the other biker dudes who had just run us out of a bar we had bought a beer in, and they were sitting their big asses on Brian's car. We knew this because their biker costumes matched, as Brian put it. Brian casually walked over to one of the big hogs and calmly slung his leg over the big leather seat, plopping his ass down on the Harley-Davidson motorcycle parked closest to his Swinger. I noticed the abstract pink racing stripe painted down the passenger side of Brian's car contrasted nicely with the sea of black leather presently on full alert and staring at my friend. It only took a second for the owner to identify himself by quickly removing himself from Brian's hood and marching over to where Brian sat making "Vroom-Vroom" noises while spinning the throttle. "Whaaaaaaa, wa-whaaaaaaa, wha-whaaaaaaa, wha-whaaaaaaaaaaa" was the sound Brian was making as the biker dude walked over to his motorcycle. Brian was imitating the sound of a bike in full haul ass mode shifting through the gears, and doing a very respectable job of it I might add.

The biker dude said and I quote "You must have a death wish sitting on my god-damned motorcycle, boy."

Brian just smiled and kept on making the same sounds and flipping his wrist between "whaa's" making the biker dude madder and madder by the second. Brian abruptly stopped and said with a blank look on his face I might add,

"You dick heads don't seem to mind sitting your fat asses on my car, do you?" followed by a perfectly timed pause, "I thought I'd just extend the same courtesy back to you, you degenerate, anti-American, smelly, shit-sucking excuse for humanity. And by the way, do you kiss your momma with that mouth?"

About the time the word "humanity" faded to silence two New Orleans cops rounded the corner and walked straight over to our location. "Any trouble here this evening, gentleman?" the two officers Fife asked with a verbal dryness that conveyed "please, give me and excuse to use my night stick today…"

"Naw," both Brian and the biker dude said simultaneously, knowing the local cops were fresh and Mardi-Gras had not gotten started yet, so the jails were empty.

"Keep it that way," was the last thing the law men said before exiting making eye contact with both parties.

I knew any dumb moves by either one of them would land them both in a freshly hosed out cell for the duration of the five day party. As soon as the cops crossed the street, the biker dude grabbed Brian by his tee-shirt and told him to get his G-D M-Fing no good Son-of-a-Bitching ass off his bike right then or face death.

Brian grinned and replied, "OK, but you'll have to tell your boyfriends to get their fat asses off my car first and only after you chew on a breath mint, or two."

Oh Shit! Was all I could manage. *Here we go again.*

From where I was standing, I could see the dude balling up his fist ready to punch Brian when he least expected it, but not during Brian's dismount in fear of knocking over the other bikes. His buddies were also removing themselves from Brian's car in anticipation of showing Brian how much they objected to being called girls. As soon as the bikers hopped off Brian's car, a string of "black cat" fireworks went off, startling everyone within a one hundred foot radius of our location and sounding like small arms fire. The dude holding Brian drew back to punch him while everyone else was busy being distracted. Before he could connect with Brian's skull, I drilled him squarely in his temple, him toppling over the motorcycle he owned and causing a domino effect with the other bikes parked next to his. He was out cold, not moving a muscle and that gave Brian and I the cover we needed to get to the car, dive in and haul ass.

Brian quickly cranked the slant six and blasted the horns causing the crowd that had formed to part like the Red Sea for the Egypt-fleeing chosen ones. The other biker dudes were attending to their cold-cocked friend, pulling him off the toppled bikes and onto the curb. I assumed the knocked silly dude told them what had happened based on all the pointing and cussing he did. I locked the doors just before one of the biker dudes grabbed the door handle in an attempt to snatch me out. Brian floor-boarded the trusty Dodge, driving straight over the upended motorcycles like they were part of Bourbon Street's cobblestone pavement. The bending and scraping sounds emanating from the belly of the Swinger must have sounded exactly like Brian's stomach sounded when he attempted to digest the death dog now painted down the passenger side of our escape vehicle. The leathered up tattooed biker dudes stood in stunned silence, watching the whole event unfold like some nightmare out of a biker dude Twilight Zone episode. We made the first right available off Bourbon Street, just about the time I saw the cops run over to where we had initially made our hasty exit. The last thing I remember seeing, as I looked over my shoulder down Bourbon Street, was a biker pointing at the back of our car as we sped away.

We drove through six parishes that night with our headlights off before we found I-10, escaping sure death or a jail visit. We both enjoyed a good laugh out of it and talked all the way to Dauphin Island where we'd hide out until the whole thing blew over or our provisions ran out. We went to the vacation house of the young lady Brian briefly dated in Troy, the daughter of the anal retentive hi-tank dump dude who had been so rude to him when my future best friend and I first made acquaintances. Brian knew where the key was hidden so we stayed there for the four remaining days of Mardi-Gras and had a great time. We both attended Mardi-Gras that year, from Fat Tuesday until Ash Wednesday, approximately four hours tops, escaping with our lives yet again and living to tell about it. We ended up having a terrific time at Dauphin Island in our free digs supplied by none other than Mr. Anal Retentive high-tanker dump guy, only he did not know it. I did check the crapper tanks before we left the beach house for evidence of our visit, but none was to be found.

I laughed at Brian's telling of that story like I was hearing it for the first time but knowing I was indeed there. I could hear what sounded like the highway, so we ran towards the noise and, lo and behold, we were back in touch with civilization! All we needed was to figure out exactly what interstate we were on.

Troy, here we come!

Chapter · XXXVI

"I have found out that there ain't no surer way to find out whether you like people or hate them than to travel with them."
– Mark Twain

WE WERE finally on a major highway in Alabama and we were both positive about one thing: We had absolutely no idea which highway we were looking at. It might have been 231 above Montgomery or maybe below, or it could have been I-85 towards Atlanta or I-65 towards Birmingham. All I knew was, I was happy to see some sort of proof of civilization. Planes, trains and automobiles were a welcomed site to us both. Come to think of it, just planes and automobiles; we'd done the trains thing and look where it landed us. We both grabbed a seat on the hill overlooking the roadway, contemplating what might be next. I think we were both happy to see the dual black ribbons decorated with yellow and white lines made to tell drivers what side of the road they needed to stay on. Order in the midst of chaos. Symmetry in the midst of the abstract. Paved roads in the midst of wilderness and a black asphalted yellow brick road leading us back to the great Oz. It was a sight these eyes welcomed like a dirty man might embrace a hot shower. I was so thankful for taxation and representation and the Eisenhower Interstate System I could have cried at that moment. Brian and I had been walking, running, hiding, pursued, chased, nearly eaten by a pack of wild dogs and witnessed a Ku Klux Klan meeting, all inside a thirty-six hour time span.

We still had to figure out where exactly we were geographically but I could tell we were indeed headed south. Which way south I didn't know for sure but I felt certain we'd have to run into a sign eventually. Most states had signs telling folk traveling much faster than us where they might be headed. Then I remembered we were in Alabama. We were headed south and that would have to do.

I calculated we had been walking and running, after our dismount, for at least thirty-two hours based on the approximate time we had left Troy. I calculated we had jumped the return train around 11:30 a.m., and ridden for a good three and a half hours at speeds averaging 50 miles per hour. That calculation was based on timing between mile markers and length of travel. I figured we'd traveled a good 175–185 miles north of our starting point. I was unsure of how we navigated ourselves through the backwoods of Alabama winding up near Cullman, fifty miles north of Birmingham as the crow flies. I knew it was fifty-one miles from Troy to Montgomery, straight up 231, and it was ninety-one miles from Montgomery to Birmingham up I-65. I guess we didn't see any towns and highways as we rode due to the train's backwoods navigation coupled with the initial excitement of the adventure. We had our backs to the wind sitting at the front of the train car seeing everything as we passed it instead of seeing it before we got to it. We talked and laughed and lamented about the short two years we had become such good friends and all the situations we innocently found ourselves embroiled in by no fault of our own. We both sat silently, looking down on the road that would eventually take us back to Troy.

We both knew the black pavement spelled the eventual end of my time at Troy and our friendship would be a memory we'd both have work at to keep strong. I knew who my wife was going to be, the lovely Miss Becky Jackson, and she was waiting for me at the end of this trip. There were still a few days before my graduation and the thought of a life with her excited me. She and I had already had a very serious talk about marriage, and she'd caught my eye so many years before we met again. I had dated some real beauties in my life, but none captivated my innermost being like her. For me, she was perfect, in every way a man could adore a woman. It was magnified by the long walk, lack of sleep and eats, but as true as scripture for me. I had relayed that information to Brian and it was met with joyous approval.

Brian knew he was going back to Mobile, his hometown, and he'd eventually meet the love of his life too. A beautiful girl named Dana he'd meet and later marry.

We sat and talked for a good thirty minutes, resting briefly and getting our story straight, but mostly drinking in the moment. The color of the sky, how many shades of green the Alabama wilderness produced with the help of God and rain. The silent understanding we shared as friends closer than brothers. Brothers fought but we never passed a single cross word between us and I was going to miss my friend after this adventure drew to a close. The smell of asphalt was a welcomed scent and provided us with an even walking surface. It was like an old friend, the highway, and I had not walked on the street in a good lot of years.

I silently prayed we did not wind up between Troy and Montgomery, my needing to prolong this journey knowing full blown adulthood awaited me just days from then. I was not sad about the events to come; it was a chapter in my life that would go unnoticed and remembered only by the two of us. Our memories and the strength of our bond might fade in the years to come depending on our ability to maintain our friendship between Atlanta and Mobile, the towns of our origins and where we'd plant and grow our futures. New and different lives meant priorities revolving around family and I thought maybe we could grow old and fat together, our wives and kids annoyed by the endless tales we could spin. Oh, the stories we could tell if we both had the guts to tell them all truthfully. I could think of a lot worse things that might be able to happen to me than to have Brian as my friend as we both grew old and our kids grew up.

I sat silently and pondered my future.

"Hey, you fag," Brian broke the silence with his usual direct style, "We got a hell of a lot of walking to do, so let's get on with it."

So we did. We slid down the steep embankment to the concrete drainage easement and casually walked up to the highway. We stood right at the edge of the bright white concrete contrasted by the fresh black pavement. The bright yellow line was like the proverbial "yellow brick road" described earlier. We stepped over the line and headed south towards LA and left UCLA to our backs. UCLA is the "Upper Corner of Lower Alabama" and LA is "Lower Alabama," for you dill weeds that like to read the very end of a story first. There is an earlier chapter explaining the nomenclature, so stop here and get to it if so inclined. There was not a car in sight in either direction and from our vantage point we could see two miles in either direction, telling me we either entered the *Outer Limits* or we somehow made it onto a section of the interstate that was not opened for traveling yet and we had somehow navigated ourselves to it. We walked a good twenty minutes right down the middle of the road before a semi truck blew its horn warning us of it arrival. We did not look back but stepped to the median and before I could think of sticking out my thumb the giant tractor trailer passed us going a good eighty miles per hour. He blew his horns so loud I thought I might go deaf from the noise and Brian, in his typical style, shot him a bird as he passed. I hoped the dude would stop out of protest and I could use my much appreciated diplomacy to score us a ride. We would not get that lucky for another four hours.

We still had not seen any sort of signs telling us where we were going. I didn't care anymore and just mentally shrugged my shoulders and pressed on. I bet we didn't see sixty cars while we walked and just a handful of semi trucks, unusual for an interstate. Every mountain we walked down, then up, led to another mountain and valley. Sometimes I thought the next curve might bring us to a truck stop or an exit where humans with a little empathy might give us a ride. That particular curve never came. At the beginning of our sixth hour of walking we struck gold, in the form of an elderly gentleman riding in his old pickup truck. He pulled just past us and, with what little strength we had, we ran to his door. I asked him where he was headed and he had a single word answer,

"South."

I told him we were headed south also and could we ride along with him for awhile.

"Can't see why not" he said his words sounding like Christmas music to these tired ears. "You colored boys should not be walking out here in the middle of nowhere."

Brian and I walked around to the passenger door and the old fellow said, "You both are way too dirty to ride up front here, climb in the back and take a load off."

Had I just heard him right? The old Coot thought Brian and I were black men? Sweet mother of Jesus, we must have been coated with creosote so badly he couldn't tell us from our heritage. Maybe he was just illegally blind, like Dan the Man of Rippy Mart lore, difference was he wasn't wearing glasses. His old dog barked at us, and maybe that was his (Coot's and his dog) identifier. Coot's dog apparently barked at black folks and strangers and he (the dog) thought we were both. Hmmm, that was interesting. I climbed into the truck's bed and parked my back against the cab of the truck and Brian did the same. The low humming of the truck's engine, my horizontal configuration, and the total lack of sleep spelled a short twenty second recognition of the truck trip. I was out like a light and so was Brian.

I don't think I dreamed at all when I fell into the thick black darkness of the wonderful sleep I enjoyed in the bed of "Old Coot's" truck. I was laying on farm tools, shovels and a pitchfork, and maybe something else but it mattered not to this old tired bag of bones. I eventually heard a voice calling out to me and felt a prodding in my side.

"Hey…son!" I heard twice when I was coming to, "It's the end of the road for you two."

I snapped awake, thinking he might have taken us back to the KKK regional gathering we had accidentally strolled up on earlier. I was lucid enough to recall him thinking Brian and I were two black men at the beginning of our journey, so if he hauled us back to the White Sheet shindig we'd all get a huge surprise before it was over. He started to poke me again and I grabbed the cane he held out of instinct.

"Take it easy there sonny, I'm a friend."

His words sounded like a grandfather comforting his grandson's tears for the first time, and it made me feel comfortable if even for a moment. Brian was standing alongside the old fellow outside of the truck when I came back from dreamland, so we at least weren't about to be the main course at some backwoods carnivorous feast. I had seen *Texas Chainsaw Massacre* and knew I'd never get those two hours back as long as I lived, but gleaned a little info from the experience so it wasn't all bad. I sat up and immediately recognized we were off the side of the road.

The old fellow told us, "This is as south as I get, I'm headed east then north to home. I went to Birmingham to visit my Daughter and her family and I am headed to Tallassee."

I knew from numerous trips back and forth from Atlanta to Troy that Tallassee was between Montgomery and Auburn on I-85 so he had covered some serious ground for us while we slept.

The old guy told Brian that he had picked us up on I-65 sixty miles above Montgomery. He had taken us through Montgomery and deposited us on US Highway 231, 49 miles from Troy. I was so overwhelmed with appreciation I would have hugged the old fellow if I thought he might not crown me with that cane he toted. It took him a few minutes, but he figured out we were both white guys and he asked Brian what in the hell were we doing that far from Troy. Brian half-explained the scenario to the sensible old guy, but hesitated, thinking the wise man might make us climb back into his truck and take us back up the road to walk a little further as punishment just for being so stupid. I was wrong about my assessment and the sweet old man. He told us that after World War II and his stint with the navy, he hitch-hiked across the USA a time or two just to *sort things out* after the experiences he had. I recognized the faraway stare when he talked, almost in code, about having trouble reconciling war and its purposes. I had seen the same stare in Kenny's brother Gordon, and my Uncle Sheridan's eyes as he was a Vietnam veteran and had been "in country," military lingo for actually being in the shit (for those of you who do not know). I started to ask Old Coot more about his experiences but decided to let it pass. He said he'd admired us for taking the chance train trip and reminded us how the best parts of it might never leave us, giving us comfort in harder times that would surely come.

I saw a slight tear in his eye when he extended his hand towards mine to shake. I guessed he'd been alone and he was glad for the company, even if Brian and I never said a word to him. If not for the brief conversation, we might not have known anything about the gentleman that so kindly given us a ride. When I latched onto the old man's hand I noticed a strong grip, I assumed from years of hard labor on a farm, and a tattoo on his forearm. The way we shook and the area the tattoo was located made the inscription easy to read. It said:

"U.S.S. INDIANAPOLIS"

I was standing with a member of the "Greatest Generation," as Tom Brokaw so accurately identified them, and a true hero. I looked him straight in the eye and told him,

"Thank you, Sir, for your service to our country." my voice quivering, knowing what that phrase truly meant for the first time in my young life.

I knew the story behind the USS Indianapolis, and to be standing with one of its survivors rendered me speechless. When the ship was torpedoed, 1,196 men were on board, 300 went down with the ship. Four days later, 316 men were found by accident, the rest perished in shark infested waters in the sea around the Philippines. I had read the story numerous times and studied it in history books. The USS Indianapolis was the same ship described by Captain Quint in "Jaws," when he and Richard Dreyfuss' character are matching bites and scars. The Indianapolis had carried the Bomb. It was top secret and there was no record of her sailing, carrying her world-changing cargo named "Little Boy" that would eventually level Hiroshima and spell the beginning of the end for Japan.

Old Coot had helped deliver the bomb, floated and survived in shark infested waters for four days with no sleep, all while listening to his friends get eaten alive wondering if he was next. His Captain was incorrectly held responsible for the deaths of the men who perished that fateful day. Old Coot told us he hitchhiked across the USA a few times to "sort some things out." My God, this great man had seen more bad things in those four days than Brian and I might see in a lifetime combined. What an honor to have stood in his presence if even for just a few minutes. Meeting him made all the hardships we endured by our own hand seem small in comparison. I've thought about Old Coot a lot through the years and prayed he had found peace in some form or fashion. I hoped he was in heaven because I knew he'd seen and been through enough hell right here on earth.

The ride he gave us put us ever closer to Troy and I was rejuvenated. We both thanked Old Coot one last time then aimed ourselves towards Troy. If we averaged three miles per hour we'd be there in fifteen short hours!

Chapter · XXXVII

ONLY FIFTEEN hours to go. It didn't seem so long anymore and at least we were on a road more populated by cars and semis, increasing our chances of scoring a ride back to Troy. One very positive thing about being on this road was this: *any ride* was a move closer towards the frat house and Highway 231 South went straight through Troy. North Three Notch Street was in downtown Troy and we'd have to hoof it another four miles off 231 when and if we were lucky enough to hitch a ride the rest of the way there. I didn't care though, the ride from Old Coot knocked a good fifteen to twenty hours of walking time off our trip and I counted it a blessing just to have met the guy. Of all the impromptu trips Brian and I had taken, this was the best one I could recall. That'd be in retrospect, considered years later, but it was a good trip just the same. Old Coot was right; it was a trip I'd remember for the rest of my days. I have laughed about it over the years, calling on the best parts of our friendship in the rough times that indeed came for us both. The journey served as a marker of sorts for us, all set in motion by a desire to ride a train across town and back. The "across town" part was not such a huge issue. The "ride back" part was what landed us 187 plus miles from home. I don't care how intense or serious a human you might be, that's some funny crap right there.

We walked and talked about a lot of little things we'd experienced in our lives, lamenting about the girls we'd been dumped by and those we'd dumped. Small slice of life things we'd dismissed initially but recalled as time allowed us the luxury of reliving them during our long hike back home. Time to lament over these things would be a rare commodity after I graduated. I took advantage of the time, recognizing it for what it was. This was the last bridge before adulthood. No more hiding in the frat house and no more classes to take, no more conferences with counselors and no more changing of majors. It was here and that was that. I was about to be considered a real man and I'd be itemizing my deductions in just twelve short months. No more "EZ" forms and full refunds of tax withholdings at the end of the year for me. The time had come and I was ready. I hoped Brian would go on to finish his degree and prosper back in Mobile. I pledged to call him once a week after graduation to give him pep talks concerning the matter. Maybe the best thing for him was to get away from me and moving home might serve as a catalyst in his quest for all things academic. I loved the guy and I wanted the best for my friend. He'd make it. Somehow I knew he'd make it. Maybe he'd take something good away from our friendship. I knew I would. We were finishing off our story-telling so we'd have recollection of them for the years to come. We still had a few stories left so Brian took his turn at telling this one.

One of our brothers, I'll call Casanova, insisted he'd somehow score with every co-ed at Troy University before he either died or got killed by a boyfriend, STD or a father. He was not so particular about where he'd plant his evening seed, but the time of night determined how attractive the subject of his injection was. This dude was such a horn-dog he would go after the crack of dawn if he didn't score the night before. Brian and I made it our business to knock him out of the saddle as often as we could. He hit on my date at a frat formal once and he'd done the same to Brian. I truthfully didn't care, seeing the 7.9:1 girl to guy ratio, but it didn't sit well with Brian. I guess the brotherhood thing could be only stretched so far. Trying to score one of your frat brother's dates was a real no-no and Casanova had crossed that line. Brian was my very good friend and if he needed me for solidarity purposes concerning Casanova's infractions, I was at his beck and call for revenge.

Brian and I called Casanova by that name because, well, he looked like the character of the same name. He thought he was "sway vee and de-boner (suave and debonair)," and could convince any and all women, both young and old, to fall under his spell. He was a true legend in his own mind. I will say he subscribed to the "if you keep slinging shit against the wall, some of it's gotta stick" theory and I had to salute his consistency and non-stop efforts to get laid. But holy crap man, give it rest when it comes to your friends and frat brothers. He'd bring a steady stream of girls to our parties and he'd usually have the formal room, generally reserved for parents on the designated days they'd get invited and of course, brothers trying to score with chicks. He was a busy dude and he kept the room tied up on a regular basis. We'd also secondarily nicknamed Casanova "Bird-dog" or "Bird" for short, because he must have had an erection 23 hours a day including sleeping. We never knew when the one hour "off" might have been, but I assumed it must have deflated every now and again. He scored a very good looking date at one particular party and he was putting the full court press on her every chance he got. In between "Gatoring" songs and numerous *Animal House* selections, we spotted Casanova making the final maneuvers on his date just before touching down in the family formal living room. That's where we'd hatch our plan and seek our much deserved revenge. Knockin' a dude out of some was a crime in all 50 states, but Bird deserved it and we were just the guys to deliver.

We had the standard Oobeedo purple punch, cheap and effective, and lots of it. Casanova and his date had made the rounds to some of the local pubs so she was slightly hammered before she arrived at our festivities. Brian had warned the entire pledge class my senior year of school concerning his plan and he hatched it as a payback for Casanova trying to score his date. It was a simple plan and it was this: when he maneuvered his way to the Formal Room we'd be waiting for him. There were eleven of us waiting for Casanova and his date when we heard him rattling the door handle in an attempt to gain entry. When he did, we gave him revenge flavored companionship only his brothers could deliver, served ice cold.

It was pitch dark when he finally got the large heavy door opened. He fumbled for the light switch briefly; his date giggled from what I assumed might be his advances and the Oobeedo punch kicking in. He managed to get the door opened, aiming his date towards one of the six plush leather sofas that lined the large formal room, normally reserved for dates and family. She landed between Brian and I in the middle seat not knowing we were in the room until the light switch was found. Casanova finally found the switch then engaged it, filling the room with the beautiful light filtered through the hundreds of crystals hanging from the antebellum chandelier. The transition from total darkness to bright caused everyone in the room to squint.

When Casanova's date finally adjusted to the bright lights, she hesitated for about five seconds before she screamed like a banshee, practically knocking him down as she swiftly exited the room in shock. Casanova's back was to us when she exited and when he spun around and adjusted his eyes, he was met with what I'm sure was a shock to his dates delicate constitution. She had lost her hard earned buzz in just a few seconds and Casanova received ample payback for being such a whore-dog. There were eleven buck naked dudes sitting bare-assed in the formal living room. We all held individual gallon jugs of Oobeedo, sipping on them like a Southern Belle might sip a glass of iced tea or a mint julep in summertime. Bird stood there motionless and Brian said,

"Hey Dude, what's up?" in his typical smartasses style I recognized so well.

"What in the Hell are you assholes doing?" Bird asked knowing he'd been knocked out of a chance at getting laid.

"Sitting here in the dark, buck ass naked, drinking Oobeedo and talking to our pledges. Why do you ask?" Brian said sarcastically.

Casanova started to protest, but we all busted out laughing before he could flap his trap. He stormed off in search of another victim (and I assumed another location) in which to ply his amorous trade. He was relentless, reload and retry was Casanova's motto, and one I'm sure made him a millionaire after he graduated (if he did). Neither of us ever heard from Bird again, post graduation. I guess he carried a grudge too.

Brian and I had finally come across a sign saying "Troy - 35 miles." We had walked fourteen miles and it took only four and a half hours. Maybe we'd be home by dark if all went well and neither one of us broke a leg or had a piece of Skylab (the original space station) fall on us. We made decent time to be so tired and "raggily', a term one of the brothers used when he was worn out from practice, and one I placed in my vocabulary for use in proper context, or when called on to interpret "jive"… my second language.

There was not a single item of clothing I deemed salvageable hanging on either of our backs. We truly looked like we had been stranded in a coal mine or drafted into a paint battle with black tar as our only weapons. I would not have given us a ride either if I had spotted us while driving. I might even have called the proper authorities if I had been a respectable-type and two black faced hoodlums were near my property.

It brought to mind a time when Brian and I helped a pledge feel at home in one of our frat house neighbor's front yard. Our poor pledge roommate, named Shannon, chose to room with us his pledge semester and it was one he'd never forget. That poor dude, nicknamed "Shodden," a name we called him after he'd consumed massive quantities of the purple party punch we made in fifty gallon batches before our massive social gatherings. It was close to time for Shannon to be initiated into the frat and we had green lighted him to get shit-faced at the very last party before hell week and indoctrination began. He got fully toasted, needing our help to get his small carcass to our room and into his bed. He was so totaled he didn't even know how to pronounce his own name. "Shodden," was all he could say when quizzed the next day by the neighbor that found him sleeping in his front yard in his own bed.

Shannon was diminutive gent from Eufaula, Alabama, a beautiful town full of southern tradition and mansions lining the streets. Standing in beautiful Eufaula, it looked like you had been suddenly whisked back in time, waiting to hear news of the civil war. Shannon was one of Eufaula's finest sons and his family had raised ten generations there. It was evident he was from a proud family with a long standing "Tradition of Existence." His grandmother visited with his parents on family day and I met the sweet southern belle during a family weekend. She sat on one of the sofas her grandson had been parked buck naked upon weeks earlier as a part of "Bird's Revenge" as we'd call it afterward.

I introduced myself to his parents and when she introduced herself, she said "I'm Movell E. Thomas, of the Eufaula Thomas's and Shannon is my grandson. We have a long proud heritage in Eufaula and Shannon is our baby."

"Shannon is our finest pledge and we're honored to have him as a future Pi Kappa Phi," I told her with all the regality and respect I felt like she deserved. She was the obvious matriarch in the family, doing 90% of the talking, all the bragging and she held the key to Shannon staying at Troy. Knowing that secret, I laid on the southern charm as thick as I could. She seemed to be pleased with her visit and Shannon looked well fed, so he was safe for now. I really liked Shannon; the dude was a little guy but scrappy as hell and I liked that. Maybe five feet, six inches and 135 five pounds soaking wet. I always told him I took dumps bigger than him every morning but he took everything Brian and I threw at him and came back for more. He looked forward to the green-light party and the chance to get a buzz for the first time that semester. Brian and I ran full herd on him for the duration of his pledge-ship. I can truthfully say we wanted him to complete the pledge task at hand and become a brother.

To say he tied one on at the green-light party was like saying frat boys liked nekkid women. I will tell you now the remainder of why Shannon was nicknamed "Shodden" by Brian and me, lest I forget. When he passed out after the party, Brian and I took every last stick of his furniture, his carpet, his dresser, his hanging rack and clothes, all his shoes, toiletries, everything and carefully moved them five houses up the street. We then set his bedroom up exactly like it was in our giant room in the upstairs of the fraternity house. The three of us shared the room but Shannon was relegated to the floor, with Brian and I having beds constructed ten feet off the floor opposing each other, with a ladder in the middle for easy vertical access. Lastly, we carefully moved his bed, with him passed out in it, to the front yard of the house up the road from us on the main drag into downtown Troy. It was sight to behold, I must say, and one Brian and I were proud to have accomplished under the cover of darkness. When the sun came up and the people living in the house arose, they discovered they had a new bedroom in their front yard. That's where the best part of this story transpired.

We heard a gentle knock at our front door. Brian and I had not gone to sleep that night/morning and immediately made our way downstairs towards the large leaded glass entryway and the massive front porch. I opened the door and there was poor Shodden, blankets around his shoulders, hair matted up from slobber and smelling like he had eaten a grape flavored distillery. The kind old man that lived in the house up the street told us he was surprised to see Shannon sleeping so restfully and marveled at how neatly the room was set up. We invited him in and we sat and chit-chatted about the prank. The old man was good natured about the whole thing but asked for us to please remove the furniture before the day got going good and his bride lost her sense of humor. We woke all the pledges, chiding them for not properly looking out for their pledge brother and made them go retrieve the furniture immediately. I told you why we'd nicknamed Shannon "Shodden"; when the old man woke Shannon up he asked him his name. Shannon, in his drunken, half asleep stupor could only say, "Shodden." When the kindly old man delivered Shannon back to us he said, "I asked the boy his name and he said 'Shodden,' over and over again."

The name stuck. Shodden slept with one eye opened for the rest of the semester and stayed a little upset with us both for a few weeks. He got over it after we threatened to black ball him from the frat in the eleventh hour due to his "attitude problem." We both were not at all serious about it but it worked, his attitude improved, so what the hell. In a few weeks he became a brother and all was well in Pi Kapp land. It was his turn to be the master of his first pledges and he kept the tradition up, started by Brian and me, in a mighty way. Shodden was five feet, six inches of hell on wheels. That dude was a veritable Superman after Brian and I got through with him. He was one of us.

We rounded a corner and saw a sight for sore eyes, legs, and every other part of our anatomy. It read, "Troy, 27 Miles." We walked on and talked on…

Chapter · XXXVIII

"Not all those who wander are lost."
– J.R.R. Tolkien

IT WAS getting later in the day, I guessed it was about seven o'clock and we had been walking for approximately seven hours since Old Coot dropped us off on Highway 231. It seemed like the road grew longer and longer as each hour passed. I was amazed to view, in relatively slow motion, all of the sights I had passed a few hundred or so times in the five years I spent traveling back and forth between Douglasville, Ga. and Troy, Alabama. They had all served as minute markers in my mind's eye telling me I had one hour to go, thirty minutes to go, ten minutes to go until I reached Montgomery. I'd then take I-85 north towards beautiful Georgia and my hometown. I never utilized those same markers when I was on my way back to Troy from home, simply because I never wanted to get too accustomed to being there. I have called it home a time or two during this story, but let me make one thing clear: I'm a Georgia boy to the core. When I get a cut, red clay is the color of my blood. It's the dust from which I was formed and the dust to which I'll return, at God's appointed time. Alabama was a temporary stop, home to millions, but only a place for this ole boy to get an education playing a kid's game. My home is in Georgia, where I'll live out my life until I'm done.

There were not many things I would miss after I left Alabama and the list grew shorter every day. I didn't hate Alabama; after all it was the state responsible for Georgia never having to be next to Mississippi. College football had served its purpose for me and I was happier than a jackass in briar patch to be leaving. I heard that particular saying once, the jackass in a briar patch saying I mean, when visiting the home of one of my teammates, Gary McGilvary. His mom said it about us two while he and I were consuming a homemade mountain of spectacularly fried catfish she had prepared for our visit. Her's was the best I had ever enjoyed and it was so good, you'd get upset from being full, unable to eat any more. The thought of that catfish made me hungry and reminded me of a story concerning Gary, my one-time roommate, and one of the best interior linemen I ever played with or against. I was glad I never had to line up across from him in a game, fortunate he was on my team.

We still had a considerable amount of walking to do, so I shared this story with Brian as our trudge continued, concerning Gary and his then girlfriend. I carefully unfolded the tale as we walked, with Brian grinning with anticipation as I talked.

Gary was a walk-on I met when I was a freshmen signee at Troy. He sat by me in the dining hall when I first arrived at Troy, considered a breach of etiquette back then, when two-a-days were taking place. It was an unspoken rule that all scholarship athletes sat together, quietly ostracizing the walk-ons or those without scholarships, and the first of many rules I broke after I arrived. The walk-on dudes generally got the short end of the stick, playing and practicing wise, as the attrition rate was above 90%. I would not have put up with the crap these dudes had to endure just to say I had played the college game. They were called the "shit squad" because they did all the shit duties, like hold blocking dummies and get the tar beat out of them daily.

Gary was a good dude, tougher than a 20 ounce round steak cooked well-done, and I liked him instantly. I called him Irish because he was red-headed and pale skinned, freckled and eyes as green as grass. The dude was six feet one inch and probably fifty pounds overweight, but willing. You can coach a lot of things but willing is one thing you must be born with. If you are not willing, then nothing else matters on the field. I had the opportunity to go up against Gary a time or two in scrimmages and let me tell you the dude was as solid as a rock and technically perfect. He dropped twenty five pounds in his freshman year playing in the grueling heat and it did him good. He survived two-a-days, rare for most freshmen players, and he established himself as eager to learn the system. He played the entire first year as a shit squad man, paying his dues in ways most scholarship recipients never would have endured.

I told my position coach to watch Gary and his abilities, in hopes my defensive coach might relay that info to the offensive line coach thus helping Gary get noticed. He came back in spring training after winter drills ready to compete for a scholarship and was rewarded with a partial ride, telling him he was in, at least partially. The next fall Gary came back ready and was rewarded with a full ride after the two-a-day drills, a dream come true for him I'm sure. I was proud for him and he had earned it the hard way. He came from a small private school in the Middle-of-Nowhere, Alabama, where nary a college recruiter dared venture when searching for a player. When the season got started good, maybe the seventh game, Gary got in a pile up and broke his leg in the worst possible place a man could; four inches above his ankle. We were practicing full speed and a blocking back fell on his leg, snapping it clean but through the skin. I was close to Gary when it happened, and I heard the sickening snap. He looked at me and calmly said,

"Jimbo, I think my leg is broken."

It was broken alright, and the sound of Gary's pain as we carefully dismantled the pile up made me sick at my stomach. When the smoke cleared, Gary's leg was at a perfect ninety degree angle below the knee, his large shin bone exposed through his skin and as white as the center of an Oreo cookie.

I thought Gary's football career was over, but I grossly under-estimated his ability to overcome adversity. He rehabilitated himself, losing an additional thirty pounds over the winter break and doing our grueling winter drills with a leg cast. He got the cast removed and carefully rebuilt the strength in his leg, coming back to be an All-Conference lineman candidate his junior year and a true bad-ass in my book. He served as inspiration for our team; with coaches on both sides of the ball using his iron will as a coaching tool and something to which one might aspire. Of course, Gary was a quiet humble guy who hated the attention and just wanted to play ball. My buddy Mr. Twain said,

"Few things are harder to put up with than the annoyance of a good example."

Twain's quote applied to Gary in spades. Attention was something Gary would have just soon skipped and he was just glad to be playing ball again. We became roommates my junior year and we got along marvelously. He was a great friend and a guy that had earned everything he got. Most of the prima-donnas I played with thought everything they received were somehow owed to them. Those guys proved to have a short life under the hellacious circumstances that came with being on our team and Coach Bradshaw could find them faster than a fat guy could eat a Twinkie. It was one thing my coach and I agreed on and that was we both hated prima-donnas. After Gary achieved his full scholarship status he was just one of the boys and no one dared to screw with him.

In our junior year we had a freshman player, named Theory, sign on with our program. Gary and I were assigned to him by the coaching staff to be mentors as such, a wolf guarding the henhouse job. Our unofficial job was to keep a South Georgia farm boy introduced to the big city (Troy was big city to him) out of trouble. It wasn't long until Theory was getting caught out past curfew, drinking and smoking dope, and generally pissing the coaching staff off on a weekly basis. Gary and I got pulled aside by our position coaches after practice one day and reminded to watch over Theory in an attempt to keep his playing status active. Gary and I invited the big dumbass to our room to have a "come to Jesus" meeting with him in an effort to get him straight. When he appeared at our door, he was stoned out of his gourd and unable to keep a straight face.

Theory was a big dude, and I mean big. He weighed a good 350 pounds and at five foot eleven inches he was as round as a basketball. He was quick and knew the college game, but he was going down a deep well and taking every offer to get wasted while he attended Troy. During our meeting, Theory became sleepy and wanted to lie down on our sofa. He tripped and landed on our coffee table, smashing it to toothpicks and stayed right there until we got enough guys together to pick him up and transport him to his own bed. He made it one year inside Bradshaw's barbed wire fence program and went home. Theory eventually made it to Georgia Southern and played under the late legendary Erk Russell, alongside my future brother-in-law, Ronnie, a hero of the Gulf War, awesome helicopter pilot, and true friend.

I've given you some background on Gary here for two reasons, one, to tell you how tough he was, and two, to share this one particular bit of information. I got punched the hardest I had ever been punched, by a man or a woman, in Gary's presence. He dated a good looking girl who happened to be an eccentric drama student and one that didn't take rejection well. She was a fire breathing dragon, one of the rare beautiful red heads with green eyes and brown skin so tanned you'd think it was painted on…and she loved Gary. Her downside was she was possessive to a fault and Gary couldn't handle the third degree every time he wanted to go get a brew with the boys. He asked me to come along with him in an attempt to break it off with her, kinda like a witness in case gunfire erupted and someone got killed. She was driving Gary's pickup truck (for the life of me I didn't know why, maybe Gary's way of keeping both her hands occupied) with Gary sitting in the front seat in the middle and me occupying the shotgun position, passenger side. Again, I wasn't sure why he asked me to come along, but I did anyway seeing he was my friend and all. I guess he pissed her off by saying something a dude might say, like I don't want to go out with you anymore, and she locked down the brakes with tires squealing. She power slid the truck into a parking lot near the golf course on the backside of campus like a seasoned stunt driver. She immediately started to cuss Gary, and then jumped out of the truck with Gary exiting behind her like they were connected by a short rope.

As soon as he exited, he ran right into a jarring left hook from the redhead and I saw his knees buckle a little. I jumped out to get a better look at the activities, because every dude likes to watch a good scrap. It was, after all, a fight with a girl in it and dude law stated it must be watched. I went running around the front of the truck just as she took another swing at him. He pulled away, her missing his jaw by a whisker. He retreated to my position, in front of the truck and I backed away as best as I could but was stopped by the ditch on the passenger side of the vehicle. He was in full defense mode, blocking shots thrown like she might be related to George Forman, ending with Gary grabbing both of her wrists in an attempt to stop her pugilistic advances. When she realized she was pinned, she started to cry, telling Gary he was hurting her. Being from the south, Gary fell for the trick and loosened his grip, receiving a perfect shot to the nose in return for the trust he extended to her. She was, after all, an actress. I felt like I needed to step in, in an attempt to bring some sense of calm to the situation, and therein lay my folly.

When I walked up behind Gary he ducked and I caught the full force of her might, right in the mouth. It knocked me silly and pissed me off at the same time. I guess she realized what she had done and backed off. I'm sure I gave her the look of death and I could see that she was upset. All Gary could say was,

"How in the hell could we stay together when you punch out my friends and can't control your anger?"

She busted out crying, ran off over the golf course, and I never saw her again. Gary and I jumped in his truck and went and got a beer. He was happy with the outcome and I, well I just laughed it off. I thought I might punch her back if I ever saw her again. I wouldn't have, but I considered it for the first time in my life. I drank my beer through a straw that day fat-lipped from the fray and Gary looked no worse for the wear.

Brian liked that particular goody and he had a good return story.

We saw the next road sign telling us we were within 19 miles of Troy. Time was getting short! Just as soon as Brian started to talk he was interrupted by the sound of a decelerating truck. Victory was ours in the form of a flatbed truck driven by an elderly black man inquiring if we needed a ride. He asked where we were headed and we both said simultaneously,

"TROY!"

We jumped up on the flatbed, assuming he wouldn't let us ride up front either, based solely on our appearance. Brian and I ensured ourselves a shorter ride by bolting up on to the trucks flat bed knowing that even if we rode just one mile it was one mile less we'd have to engage otherwise.

"I'm headed that way boys, you're in luck," was all I heard before he shoved the old work truck into gear revving the engine like he might be in a drag race.

The truck surged and Brian and I looked at each other knowing we'd soon be back in the land of high quality discount meat and ice cold cheap beer. We rode quietly, enjoying the man-made breeze that blew, not talking, and thinking we'd finally made it home free. He was headed to Brundidge, just twenty miles below Troy and back to whatever business was painted on the side of his truck. All I saw was Brundidge Supply and didn't know of another Brundidge anywhere close. He made good time, knocking out the remaining 19 miles in less than 14 minutes, shortening our walk by a good three to four hours, maybe more. He blew past our stopping point, the turn off that would leave us with four miles to make it back to our frat house. He was kind enough to take us into the city of Troy, the back way, depositing us within one hundred feet of where we'd jumped the return train, back towards the fraternity house. If you started here, added one hundred and eighty miles and the adventure that was now almost officially in the history books, you'd have been us over the last three plus days. It was an irony that wasn't lost on either of us at that moment.

We thanked the kind fellow for doubling back for us and when we thanked him he said, "Damn!! You are two white boys! What in the name of all things holy happened to you?"

We looked at each other and calmly said, "It's a long story," pausing to see if he might be up for the condensed version, similar to the one we shared with Old Coot.

"Gotta get myself back to Brundidge, it must be a good story though!" he said as he revved the truck engine and grinded the truck's transmission into first gear.

His words faded as he disappeared around the corner leading him towards his destination.

Brian and I had made it. One more mile straight through beautiful, downtown Troy and we were back at the frat house. We stood on South Three Notch Street facing north. North Three Notch Street was the name this street became as soon as we crossed the square in Troy and the same road our fraternity house was situated upon. It was the final leg of our journey before we reached the frat house and a retracing of our steps of sorts. As we turned towards the town square and our walk back, a train slowly made its way into town, like a siren calling us to our doom. It was headed back towards the fraternity house on the same tracks where this journey began.

It was also the last leg of the Pledge Course we had run completely nude a year or so earlier. I was certain of one thing; I didn't care how sharp any eye was that *might* have spotted us the night of that legendary run, regardless of how close we might have come to them. When we ran through town in the buff, as naked as the day we were born plus running shoes, we didn't look like we did just then. We had most recently been mistaken for two black dudes, by both a white man and a black man, so I figured we were good to go. The identities of the two naked running frat boys would remain a secret for another day.

We looked at the tracks one more time, looked at each other, smiled and started walking.

Chapter · XXXIX

"The journey not the arrival matters."
– T. S. Eliot

AS BRIAN and I walked slowly towards the square, I noticed people staring at us like we might be aliens invading their small college town. I had seen our reflection in the plate glass windows fronting the numerous building that lined the streets of Troy. All of the small businesses occupying the other sides of the glass windows all had one thing in common. Every single window had human beings in them who stopped their tasks to watch us as we passed by. If you've ever seen a movie where a UFO suddenly appears and the camera pans to the faces of those watching you get an idea of what Brian and I saw looking back at us. I thought I might be annoyed at first but the more I beheld our image the more I felt their pain. It was obvious that we were the UFO. It was educational for me, knowing what it was like to be different, and a lesson I had learned before I moved from the West End in Atlanta.

Brian and I had faced a lot of adversity on our trip and these people had no idea what we'd been through. I wasn't sure how to take the stares so I did what came natural, I smiled and waved. *Hi! Hello! How ya doing…assholes!* I think Brian also became aware of the spectacle we must have been to the W.A.S.P. crowd, staring at us with horrified faces practically pressed against the inside of the windows as we walked past. I was sure I saw a shotgun or two getting quickly loaded and a few folks hastily calling the local police for protection. I took the bull by the proverbial horns and suggested to my good friend that we take a little time and browse the selections of those so bold as not to look away when we met eye to eye. I felt like maybe we'd get to know some of them better and after all, they had air conditioning, and we were hot, filthy, and starving.

When we entered the first establishment, we were met with a nervous, "Uh, hello, uh, is there, uh, anything I can, uh, do for you?"

Brian answered in the best countrified voice he could muster;

"Yep, how much for everything in the store, right now, cash on the barrel head, how much for me to buy you out right now?" Brian said with an excited voice.

"Well, uh, I'm not sure, uhh, I'll have to answer that one in just a minute" the shop owner said.

Brian continued, "While you're doing your *gozinta's* and *multipliers*, I might take a minute to use your facilities, you got plenty of toilet paper, now don't cha?"

Oh the look on the face of that poor shop keeper.

"Uh, sure we do, right over there" he said pointing nervously towards the back of the store.

Brian excused himself and inside of three minutes he returned saying "Allrighty then, how much for all of it?"

I just stood there with a stoic look on my face playing along with the charade.

"You mean you can't tell me right now, with five minutes to think it over, how much you'd take for every item you have for sale in here?" as more of a statement than a question, expressing the perceived stupidity of the shopkeeper. Brian then looked my way and said, "James, let us leave this establishment, never to return."

I answered with my best Morocco Mole impression, "Yeeess, Master. Let's leeeave this place."

Brian then looked at the shopkeeper, and said, "This is no way to conduct business, my good man, and, uh, you probably need a plumber. I think I plugged the crapper up…to much guv-ment cheese in my diet and I just had a breakthrough. Good day to you, Sir!"

When we had just about cleared the plate glass window I saw the shop keeper running towards the bathroom Brian had visited just a few minutes earlier.

"I just took a piss" was all Brian said.

We slowly walked through the square, cars slowing down to gaze at us, couples suddenly ceasing conversations as we approached. Women pushing strollers crossed the street as we drew near thinking we might grab the babies they pushed in an attempt to consume them for our supper. It was a sight to see I must say, all the finger pointing and dental work Brian and I got to inspect due to the dropped jaws of our gawkers. One boy, holding onto his mothers arm as she exited one of the local shops said,

"Mommy, look at the Negros."

I guess we had hit the tri-fecta that day what with one little boy and a white and black man mistaking us for African Americans.

"Hat trick!" Brian excitedly exclaimed.

That woman nearly yanked the little boys arm out of the socket when she nervously said to us, "He's just a little boy, please pardon him, won't you?"

"We get that a lot," Brian quickly said to her back as she scurried away, in fear that we might require a human sacrifice for the young boy's indiscretion. Brian and I made it a point to stop at every window and peruse the items displayed there. We pointed and made out like we might be interested in purchasing some of the proudly displayed antiques. Brian would make gestures like he was decorating some false wall somewhere, pointing and measuring, with enough animation to make a seasoned mime consider another profession. We also noted the fear on the faces of the customers and the owners of each store, their faces in full view of us as we acted out our farce. All we wanted to do was to make them sweat a little and it worked.

We circled the square twice just for the fun of it, noting that two of the business conveniently closed when we made the second pass by their door, the "CLOSED" sign still swinging from its occupants swift turn. Brian made sure to rap loudly on the windows of the suddenly closed shops. I'm sure the owners were hiding in abject fear, thinking we might enter and attempt to buy something or maybe plug up their plumbing systems too. He beat on some of the windows so hard he loosened the panes from their caulking just for good measure. It took only two passes around the square to bring commerce to a complete standstill in the picturesque, small town. The only thing missing right then was tumbleweeds and wolves howling off in the distance.

That's when the police showed up. Two marked cars with two cops each, positioning themselves at each end of the street placing us strategically in the middle. When the cops parked their cars, two of the boys in blue faced us and two (one from each car) walked parallel to each other and locked us in, to prevent us from running I assumed. They closed in on us as Brian and I sat down on a bench on the North Three Notch Street end of the Square. We were within sight of the frat house and now the cops were going to hassle us. Neither of us had identification and even if we had, we didn't look like the photos anyhow. I guess our last three days in Troy would be spent in the county slammer if we couldn't talk our way out of this one. Three days of jailhouse chow and a story to tell my folks about how I landed in the joint before graduation was something I'd just soon pass on.

The policemen approached us and before they could speak I preemptively said, using the whitest voice I could, "Fine day for a stroll isn't it, officers?"

As the officers got closer I could hear the other two officers behind us approaching from the radios clipped on each of their belts. "Names please," the closest officer said, his voice as dry as a dirt sandwich, sporting a cop-issued muted stare he surely must have practiced at home when shaving.

Brian looked at me, the diplomat, and I said "Jim Hall and Brian Horst, officers," making sure each one felt the respect in a plural manner as opposed to singular.

"What are you two doing in our town…" he said, but was interrupted by a voice behind us.

"Well, I'll be a son-of-a-bitch," we heard as we turned to see our accuser. "You two look like you've been eaten and shit out of an elephant's ass."

"Llama Salama, you dirty rat bastard, the only ass we've been close to lately is your mother's!" Brian said. The lead cop had his hand on his pistol as Brian spoke. We were standing face to face with a Pi Kappa Phi alumni that had graduated with a criminal justice degree a year earlier and had begun his career in law enforcement shortly thereafter. Mike, our cop friend, served as our pledge warden when we pledged the frat his senior year and last quarter before he graduated.

"What in the Hell have you two been doing and why do you look like two upright logs of shit?" he added. "These two are good fellas, they're with me, although I might have to beat them with my night stick for general purposes just to get truthful answers out of them." Our friend dismissed the three other cops, and as soon as he did he said, "Spill the beans boys, what in the shit have you two done to look like such aborigines?"

I said, "Llama, my good man, you want the long version of the short version?"

"Gimme the condensed version and I'll give you a ride to the house" he said knowing he was still at work and the house was just a few minutes away.

"Only if you cuff us and throw us in the back of the car first, asshole," Brian said meaning every word.

So, Llama cuffed us and placed us in the back seat of the squad car, patrons and business owners emerging from their shops in collective relief. Our personal Andy Taylor had saved the day and boy if the city folk knew the real truth. Officer Llama Salama circled the square for good measure and, in typical style; Brian and I gave them all snarled looks as we passed just to complete the show. I recall one woman hiding the face of her baby as we passed by. I'm sure she silently vowed to never let her small child grow up like the two hoodlums that had fallen off the straight and narrow path decent Christian folk never strayed from. We might even get mentioned in prayers that week at some of the local churches based on the nature of gossip in small towns. It was perfect. We gave Llama the condensed version and he just laughed saying,

"Shit-fire boys, I told you two to be originals but I'll be damned if I meant it that way!"

We made it to the house in few short minutes and asked Llama to at least hit the lights and drive us through the Rippy Mart parking lot so Dan the Man could see us. He came to the door as we passed and we both waved at him only to be met with confused stares and puzzled looks. We'd get to him later, we vowed. We still had liquor to drink and needed mixers.

We did the last half mile back to the frat house in the back of a black and white chauffeur driven limousine, compliments of the Troy Police Department. Llama pulled into the driveway of the antebellum mansion and removed us from his cruiser. He uncuffed us and we both gave him the double-tap man hug before we made our way back inside the house and modern conveniences.

"Hey assholes," Llama said with a degree of admiration and a little bit of inquisitiveness, "Did you two run the pledge course naked last year?"

"Damn right Llama, it was us," we said to our frat brother and pledge warden, we owed him the truth. He looked at us and gave us the thumbs up as he left us standing in the front yard of our house. He sped off to his next call laughing as he exited, pumping his fist in excitement. Brian and I walked up to the front door and as I reached for the doorknob Brian said,

"If you tell anyone about this for twenty five years I'll swear you're a liar and a homosexual."

"Deal."

Chapter · XL

Sojourner—A temporary stay; a brief period of residence.

IT WAS Wednesday afternoon, three days before my graduation ceremony was to take place and my immediate family including my future wife, were to be in town early Saturday morning for the festivities planned concluding my long stay in Troy. Brian and I had cleared the front door after being dropped off by our cop buddy and pledge warden, absorbing the air conditioned comfort like a sponge, the words of the twenty-five year challenge of silence surrounding our train ride still hanging in the air. Our first step was to go to the large cooler in the kitchen, pull out a case of cold Dixies and drink them until we were no longer thirsty. When we entered the room, we were met with the smell of two partially cooked steaks in a frying pan, just as we'd left them a few days earlier. I grabbed the pan by the handle and walked out to the back porch of our frat house and heave-hoed the entire assembly as far as I could chuck it. The frying pan sailed considerably farther than its bovine-derived contents, but the lift and trajectory I utilized made sure we'd not catch a whiff of the undercooked abandoned rib-eyes ever again. We had wasted two of the most beautifully marbled steaks I had laid eyes on the day we jumped that train. The trip, now that it was over, was worth the sacrifice and we even gave a bit of respect to the loss of the steaks with a moment of silence after they landed in our back yard. I opened the refrigerator and, yes, there were indeed twenty more rib eyes awaiting our consumption, only now we didn't have to ration them out between now and graduation time.

We had a decision to shower up and then drink more brews and eat steak, or, eat steak and consume more beer then shower the nasty tar-based creosote off our bodies. We decided to eat a steak, drink more beer, then shower and then eat another steak after the shower and drink more cold beer and maybe do the entire process over again if we had the energy. My steak cooking consisted of three main ingredients, butter, Worcestershire sauce and salt, with a little garlic thrown in for good measure and bad breath. I whipped us up two eighteen-ouncers, perfectly medium, and we ate like ravenous wolves. We both ate the two huge steaks in less than five minutes including sawing and chewing. Upon completion, Brian looked at me and we both said "let's have another," mine as a question and his as a statement and that's what we did. He and I ate three perfectly cooked steaks a piece and consumed a twelve pack each of the ice cold Dixie long neck beers, and all in less than fifty minutes. I looked at Brian and he had steak juice all over his face, his neon blue eyes staring at me through the blackface paint he wore, a shit eating grin and white teeth on display.

"Best steaks I have ever eaten in my life, Jimbo" he said burping as he spoke, retrieving the last bits of meat stuck between his teeth with the butcher knife he used to cut the steak just minutes earlier. Three days of starvation and nothing to drink would have meant a dead dog freshly run over by a school bus would have tasted good spiced up properly and cooked medium well that day. I am bullshitting of course; rare would have done just fine. The rib-eyes I had quickly cooked tasted like I had never tasted steak before in my life. A tribe of lifelong non-carnivores could have been converted by those six steaks I cooked that afternoon.

We finished our meals and exited for the showers. There were six showers in the frat house and the frat president had the very best, most hot-water-producing shower in the house. Brian told me to take the big dog shower as a gift for cooking such good meat. I considered it a graduation gift of sorts.

It took me two hours and four Brillo pads to scrub off the creosote from my arms, face, neck and hands. I took a dining room chair into the walk-in shower so I could sit, from being so damned tired from the previous few days' festivities. I walked to my room, put on a fresh pair of shorts, skivvies and a tee shirt and waited for Brian to show himself. I heard the shower running and thought Brian was finishing up. I waited for a good thirty minutes before going to the door and shouting his name only to be met with silence. I cracked the door and there was Brian, fast asleep in the tub, snoring like he was in a contest, bubbles up to his neck from the Mr. Bubble bottle he used as the only soap available to him, I guessed. I reached over and cut the water to full cold, a crappy thing to do but he'd have done it to me, and he did not budge an inch from the icy cold bath he now was taking. I hollered his name a few times and when he came to, he was surprised to find himself in a bubble bath, asking me if I had somehow made the bubbles he sat in. He was worn slap out and I knew he was talking out of his head, so I just instructed him to get out and dry himself off, throw his clothes away and get into the bed. He complied, but was destined to take a few more showers before the black tar evidence of our trip would be eliminated from his carcass. He climbed into the bed closest to the floor and was out like a light before his head hit the pillow. I walked back down stairs, retrieved a six of cold Buds (the fancy stuff) hiding in the back of the well stocked cooler, pulled a recliner out onto the massive upper porch outside of our second story room and planted myself in the comfortable chair. I planned to contemplate life, drink a few cold Budweiser's in the goose neck bottle, and listen to the silence. I took one drink of the cold brew, reached down for the shifter and reclined the overstuffed chair to full back and noticed a satellite passing overhead hundreds of miles up in the night sky. It was the last thing I remembered before falling asleep. It was eight thirty in the evening on Wednesday.

I woke up to water falling on my face and realized I was not the subject of a prank. It was raining and I was on the upper porch, fast asleep in the recliner I had dragged out there the night before. I quickly jumped up and dragged the huge chair back inside when the bottom fell out of the sky dropping enough rain to make Noah consider taking up boat building again. I looked over at Brian and noticed he had not moved a muscle from when he mounted the low lying bed the night before. I figured he was as tired as I was, and sleep was all we had to fix the problem that plagued us both. I looked at the clock on the wall and it said 7:15. I had slept from 8:30 pm until 7:15 am, a record of sorts for me as I never operated on much sleep.

I flipped on the TV to check current events and to my surprise, the evening news was on. I was immediately disoriented, thinking the station had screwed up somehow; it looked like 7:15 am, but in reality I had slept almost twenty four straight hours at one sitting! It had been overcast and I was under the large overhang that protected southern belles from the harmful sunshine, meant only for field hands and poor people back in the Old South. The rain was the only alarm clock I needed, and I might have slept for another twenty four hours had it not blown in on my restfully reclined body. My body was getting re-acquainted with the process of processing meals and when the need called, I took that huge dump and I am sure it outweighed most kindergarteners, and some grown up gymnasts. I had to save it for Brian to see, a combination DQ with a Loch Ness Monster, rare when judging a crap for content and style. When he roused himself up (with a lot of prodding from me), he immediately went to crap and when he shut the door, I heard the lid to the toilet clank on the tank.

After a few seconds of silence, I heard, "Sweet mother of God... that's a nine point nine-nine, or quite possibly a ten!" A brief moment of silence passed and he slightly opened the door, stuck his head out and said "Excellent work, my good man!" accompanied with a thumbs up. Sorry ladies, all dudes do it (judging how big a turd is) at some point. I got past it after I graduated college, needing to better assimilate into society outside of hanging with a bunch of heathen men. Your sons do it, my son did it, your dad and granddad did it. It's a dude ritual that I didn't start and certainly can't stop. It is and that is that. It's genetic and all dudes inherited it from Adam, as in Adam and Eve, Adam, and second only to farts.

We stayed up for the majority of that night, ate more steaks and drank beer until the wee hours of the morning. The next day we took one last ride around the city of Troy in the trusty Dodge Swinger, drinking Crown Royal and Royal Crown in the bottle, pointing to all the places we had created mischief, laughing at the shit we had survived. We were headed back to the frat house, taking the much heralded pledge course route, three miles covered for the last time before Saturday and the graduation ceremony that awaited me there. I can only think God himself might have given us one last test before we parted and it came in the form of a kid riding a bike. A part of the dreaded pledge course was an exceptionally steep hill, and as we drove I looked over at the side walk and there was a boy of approximately eleven years old looking like he was preparing himself for something big.

He was seated on a Schwinn bike, the cool kind with the slick on the back and chrome forks on the front, five speed shifter to change gears and a high chrome "sissy bar" as they were called when I was a kid, his metal flake seat bolted to it. I didn't think much of him until I glanced over a few seconds later and saw another boy, a ramp and ten other boys and girls all being lined up like cigars, and all laying in the path of the ramp.

"LOCK 'EM DOWN BRIAN!" was all I could blurt out, but fast enough to see what was about to take place. It was like seeing the birth of a con-man or a politician, unsure if it was the bike rider or the kid instructing the kids to lie down so the biker could jump, but one or both was about to be hatched just the same. I realized I had a decision to make right then and there. Would I get out of the car and stop the rider, telling him of the impending pain that might be dealt to both him and his participants if he didn't achieve his lofty, Evel Knievel goal? Or, would I impress on the promoter of the event, the kid whose selling ability I admired even if misguided, the one convincing the kids to allow the bike rider to jump over them.

I guess Brian recognized my conundrum, and when I reached for the door handle to use my newly attained and self professed college wisdom on the rider and the promoter, Brian grabbed my arm and said "Would you have stopped you if you were approached by you back when you were their age?"

I understood what he meant and just decided to let it go.

I saw the young promoter look up at his friend, perched on his trusty steed made of chrome and orange metal flake painted steel. It had all come full circle. Anaconda Jim was on the bicycle, and the narrator (the promoter) backed off to his safe position to see if Jim would indeed clear the pit of snakes laid out before him just beyond the hastily constructed ramp. He gave the rider a "thumbs up" and when I quickly glanced at the rider, he returned the thumbs up like a seasoned pro. The promoter then ran like a stick of dynamite was lit, by him, with a short fuse. He quickly stopped and, from mine and Brian's vantage point, we could see the events unfolding. I still had time to run and cut off the rider, possibly avoiding destruction and dismemberment for the poor kids lying on their backs, innocently awaiting their unknown fate.

By the time I could make my brain tell my hand to reach for the door knob, the young rider appeared in my peripheral, really digging in to get up adequate speed. He hit the hastily constructed ramp and that thing disintegrated like it was made of wet cardboard or Balsa wood. He wiped out, tumbling over the other kids, the bike all tangled up in his legs after the failed jump ramp crumbled. It was an epic wipe out, and Brian and I had witnessed it. In an instant, kids were crying and parents were running out of houses and par for the course, the promoter kid did what Brian and I had done numerous times when faced with such looming consequences. He ran. The college graduate in me wanted to shout to the parents that it was his idea, but we would then have been exposed as witnesses to the entire set up and disastrous outcome.

That would not be good.

The kid on the bike got his ass worn out by his mother right there on the spot as the kids that got landed on told their tale of woe. I felt sorry for the rider, but also realized he's been suckered by the promoter kid that ran and hid after the calamity had hit. Brian and I looked at each other, shrugged, and drove away. Adulthood, for me at least, would have to start after I got my diploma. And that was one day from right then.

Standing there on the podium, right hand extended toward Dr. Ralph W. Adams, personal friend and college roommate of the honorable George Wallace, Governor of the State of Alabama, I realized it was official. I heard my name called, "James Thomas Hall, Marketing and Finance." I had only five more steps to take before my diploma was in my hand. Nothing but sudden death or a well placed missile strike was going to keep graduation from becoming a reality five years in the making.

I took two steps, and from the very top row of the massive basketball arena our graduation ceremony was being held in, I heard war whoops and shouts of adulation from my dear friend Brian. The master of ceremonies had asked for family members to refrain from shouting and clapping until the entire graduating class had been announced and applause should be reserved until then. Those rules did not apply to Brian, we were not blood kin but we were brothers. He was free, white and over eighteen, so he could do as he damn well pleased. When the shouting began, I received somewhat of a dirty look from the president of the college as I approached, and I thought he might make me go shut the offender up before he'd hand over the sheepskin with my full "you are in trouble now young man" name emblazoned across it. Like when you were little and got in trouble with your parents…they always call you by your full name.

When I made it to his predetermined spot, I grabbed his hand and shook it judiciously, quietly commenting on the riff-raff that somehow always side-stepped the rules and found their way into the hallowed ceremonies we were engaged in. He looked at me, managed a slight grin, and ever so gently held tight to the diploma I was to receive that beautiful day. His gesture was one borne of experience, him thinking maybe he should not send a guy like me out into the world owning a diploma with *Troy University* stamped so prominently across the top. I wonder if it had suddenly occurred to him, based on my "file," that I assumed all governmental bodies kept on folks like me, that maybe I was not worthy of the diploma he held in his hand. This I knew, he was old and I could take him, even if it meant wrenching the proof of my degree out of his hand, whacking him with my mortar board then running off stage. Then I realized, he held on a split second longer so a photographer could seal the moment for eternity, available in numerous overpriced combo packages that would be mailed to our homes in just a few short weeks. There was no grand conspiracy taking place, he was just trying to squeeze a little more money out of me by trying to sell me graduation photos.

I guess I had a lot to account for before I could rest and whatever guilt that lingered passed in the seconds I held my breath, waiting for some official to tell me, "Sorry, you are short one P.E. credit for graduation," or "Anyone shouting and dancing like a fool when your name is called nullifies your diploma." Both of those phrases scrolled across the movie screen of my mind at that moment. It seemed like an eternity, so I took control.

I literally snatched the diploma from his hand, post flash bulb, and made my way off the stage. As I exited, I caught a glimpse of my future bride, my parents, my brother and sister all smiling at me. My awesome dad was fighting his emotions and my mom just held onto her husband, a sign they had somehow done something right as far as their kids went...mainly me. I was the first on both sides of their extended families to obtain a college degree and they were as happy as I was.

I made my way down the stage steps and joined my fellow graduates, all seated and waiting for the last name to be called before the community celebration was allowed. A ceremonial speech from a nationally recognized multi-millionaire would come next, extolling his brand of wisdom upon the unhearing ears of the fresh college graduates prepared to break new ground in the world that lay ahead of them. I drank in the moment, the sounds, the day, all of it, knowing that this was the turning point for me. I sat back down, reminded of the way our trip on the train had begun and ended, all approximately in the same spot. Kinda like the short trip I had just taken to receive my much deserved diploma.

The days leading up to my graduation ceremony passed through my mind, like one last reminder of where I had come from to get to the seat I occupied at that moment. The event, I was certain might not take place (for me at least), was taking place and I was indeed a qualified participant. All I had to do was listen to some stranger make a poignant speech, throw my funny hat in the air after I had moved my tassel, and it was done. I had a good thirty to forty-five minutes to contemplate my final hours in Troy and my friendship with Brian as it pertained to our common home. I sat there in my cap and gown and looked up at where Brian was seated. When I found him, he waved at me giving the thumbs up, dancing around like he might be auditioning for a Broadway musical, or just happy that his friend had made it to the other side.

I was brought back to reality by the applause for the entire graduating class, all the witnesses standing and shouting, thumbs up and high fives exchanged between graduates. The applause went on for a good ten minutes and was much deserved by those receiving the attention. I had been through much to get here. I was guessing that not one single person wearing a gown and a hat in that crowd had been chased by a pack of wild dogs intent on eating them earlier that same week. No train riders, no long walkers, no KKK party watchers, no story tellers, starvation, nothing like the road I had traveled with my good friend that week. I had no tangible proof that I had endured much to be there, no fancy ribbon draped around my neck like those with straight A's or honor societies reserved for a different kind of ass-kisser than the ones I had been accustomed to playing football with. Nope, I was a face in a sea of students that day, but I had a unique story to tell about my trip there unlike any other in that room, save for one. I guess a ribbon for not getting eaten by wild dogs and successfully jumping from a speeding train were ribbons I'd wear proudly in my mind. The best thing was I had a friend as a witness and it was a testament to true friendship, so rare anymore.

Brian and I were but sojourners, and our brief stay had come to an end. I was happy for the life to come and sad for the life that was to end. I was right in the transition place, the evening of this part of my life, the gloaming. I was to become fully accountable to the world and all those that had prayed and hoped that I would make it to this point, and disappointing those who hoped and was certain I wouldn't. The responsibility of that truth was like stepping under a barbell with the world on both ends, and my job was to squat that weight for the rest of my life.

I was ready.

Chapter · XLI

"Once you have traveled, the voyage never ends, but is played out over and over again in the quietest chambers. The mind can never break off from the journey."
– Pat Conroy

THE CEREMONY had ended and it was official, I was now a fully accountable, taxpaying citizen officially hunting a job and looking forward to getting married to my girlfriend and soul mate. My parents and siblings were all present and accounted for and I was looking forward to leaving Troy for the last time, never to return. It would be many years before I would even consider passing near the small college town on many trips to the beach, our children finally old enough to ask where daddy had gone to "Collich," the word our middle daughter, Jessica, had pronounced so sweetly.

Becky had finally convinced me to pass through the small town and drive through the campus, passing Alumni Hall and the field house situated next to the practice fields and stadium where I had toiled so many years ago. The two structures were still as far apart as I had remembered them being. It was like every corner I'd turn I would expect to see someone I knew, but as time whittles away, people and places change and some things just fade to obscurity. I drove the pledge course, showing Becky the antebellum houses that lined the path, her not knowing why I grinned the whole way through.

I did stop at the frat house and it was still occupied by the Pi Kappa Phi's. I talked to a few brothers there and asked them about the pledge course and if the pot for best time still existed. I also asked if the time had been eclipsed by anyone running it. I questioned them about the myth of the two naked brothers that had indeed run the pledge course in record time. They speculated on whether or not it had actually happened at all, and I assured them it had indeed happened while I was a brother there. I'm not sure if they believed me, but they humored me like a couple of seasoned politicians, bullshitting a visiting parent. Some things never changed. I asked them if I could walk upstairs and out onto the balcony, the place where I had slept for almost twenty four straight hours, and now where I stood and contemplated the life I now lived in earnest, the place where the vow of silence concerning our train ride had been made and kept by me.

I had not whispered a word of that trip to anyone, including my lovely bride, and I had been removed from Troy for a good eight to nine years by then. I felt like it was a bond between me and my friend and sacred to us both, so I honored our pact. I had not ever mentioning it, even to strangers, when stories might come up concerning one's mischievous youthful days. I didn't want to give my son Jimmy Jr. any ideas either, so keeping mum had a two-fold purpose. I'd have put him in lock down if he attempted to pull any of the stunts Brian and I had lived through. Add in the fact that Becky didn't care to know too much more about me from those days anyhow, so keeping quiet became easier and easier as the years passed by. I stood there, on the upper porch, breeze blowing similar to the one that blew the morning of my graduation, the very last day I would have to be in Troy for a purpose other than reminiscing about days gone by.

I remembered back to that time, when Brian and I woke up early, cleaned up the place as best as two dudes that never intended to darken the doors of the house we called home again could, and talked about the future. Brian said he'd be downstairs making breakfast, so I packed my all bags in five minutes or less, prepared to go home or circumnavigate the globe. I could have accomplished either of those tasks with what I had in those bags. I proceeded to the kitchen for the last rib eye steaks Brian and I would share as fraternity brothers, and when I walked into the kitchen, Brian was sweating over the hot stove steaks and eggs sizzling in two separate pans. He had us two OJ and Crown Royals poured (it was twelve o'clock somewhere) and we ate and talked like we had weeks left before we parted company.

It was a joyous time for me, and I could tell Brian was anticipating getting back to Mobile and on with the rest of his life, a new beginning for him too. We finished the last of the steak, drank all of the Crown Royal and the last of the available mixers, took our plates to the back deck and ceremoniously threw them into the woods. We were ending all things Troy and Pi Kappa Phi, and it was a happy and sad moment I have never forgotten. We stood there, looking into the woods behind our house, remembering all the parties and shenanigans we had jointly engaged in while time was not an enemy to us both. I heard cars pulling up in front of the house and I knew my family had arrived. We walked toward the front door, through the massive party room where Brian always won the picture with the fattest date contests, through the formal living room where we had instructed the entire pledge class to strip and hoodwink Casanova's efforts to get laid, through the formal dining room where Dan the Man and Suzy the Floozy had met and secured their futures forever. I was thinking about all of that when the door opens and the first thing I saw was my lovely future bride, suntanned and lovely, her green eyes sparkling like emeralds. My Dad and Mom, brother and sister trailing behind, more entertained by the size of the mansion I lived in at that moment rather than seeing me.

I hugged my sweetheart long and hard, squeezing the air out of her like I had not seen her for years. Brian cut in on my efforts and he hugged her too, them being friends from the few trips we took together to Atlanta, double dating with Becky's friends from back home. I introduced my parents to Brian for the first time and Brian immediately became the southern gentleman he was raised to be, away from my influence. His "Yes Ma'ams" and "No Sirs" delivered with perfection, covering up the person I knew him to be. I had forgotten what a magnificent bullshitter Brian was and I knew he was going to be fine in the years to come. It was ordained to be so, as this was the beginning of the procession, the dance towards the grand procession I had eagerly anticipated and commented on numerous times during our long trip.

I had worried I might not make it to right then, right there and Brian knew it was important to me. His impeccable manners and perfectly smooth delivery of the lies he had to tell in order to cover up the circumstances of the five days prior, left all questions concerning how we'd really spent those days unanswered. We showed the folks around the house, my mom and dad marveling at the intricate woodwork and moldings on the twelve foot high ceilings, the handrails and the intricate stained glass windows held together by tooth paste and bubble gum, damaged and repaired after the rambunctious parties we had hosted there. When the grand tour was completed, my sister reminded me that the ceremonies were to take place at high noon and it was 10:30 a.m. and we needed to secure a parking spot close to the arena and they needed to get seats secured also.

My brother grabbed my lone large zip up suit/duffle bag containing every possession I owned, and placed it in the trunk of Becky's car, knowing I wanted to ride back with her. Brian had to do some packing himself so he shook my dad's hand, my brother's, said his goodbyes to my sister and mother, then gave Becky one more big hug turning to me last. I asked my parents and Becky to give us a minute, and on cue they loaded into the separate cars they had driven and waited.

Brian stuck his hand out for me to shake, and I shook it, unable to make eye contact with him. He then hugged me so hard my back popped and we held it for a good minute, longer than I have hugged a dude before. I didn't care, this was the end, man, and it was damn sad.

He looked at me and said, "I'll be hollering for you at your graduation and then I am hauling ass home. Look for me in the very top row and I'll do the dance we invented during our pledge quarter."

I laughed at the prospect, and Brian and I parted company. I climbed into my future bride's car and headed toward my new life. I didn't look back over my shoulder at Brian but stuck my hand out the window giving the thumbs up, tears in my eyes and a lump in my throat. Becky could feel the gravity of the moment and she sweetly slid her hand over to mine and just held it.

When we arrived at the arena, my brother said, "You and Brian must been best friends Jim."

I told him "He's the most loyal friend I have ever had, George. I hope someday I might have one more like him."

I slipped my robe over my head, the crowd gathering outside the arena, future graduates filing towards the side double doors, some already wearing the black mortar board hats reserved for graduating seniors that special day. I made my way inside and took my place alongside my fellow graduates feeling a sense of accomplishment I had never felt before. I would have that feeling again when I married the girl of my dreams, the lovely Miss Becky Jackson, my family and all our friends there to watch our nuptials and the beginning of the greatest life I could ever have hoped and prayed for. She was a sophomore when I was a senior in high school and I remember the first time I ever saw her, I was hooked to her from that moment forward. I know God has a great plan when I look back on the insecure young man I was then, keeping me separated from her, aiding me in my maturity walk saving our union for when I was prepared to fully love her and make her my lifelong friend and partner. When I had asked to sign her annual my senior year, all the guts I could muster as I could not make words when I was near her. I signed her annual on page 82, my football number at the time, and I inscribed it with a simple request. When I was positive we were going to spend our lives together, I informally asked her to marry me by asking her to retrieve her annual I had signed all those many years ago when we were still in high school together.

I asked her to please turn to page 82 and answer the question I had written there. She looked at me puzzled and when she turned to the appointed page, seeing my long ago wedding proposal, she looked at me and said, "Yes! I will!"

I remember looking at her signing my annual, her chestnut brown hair smelling like flowers and her skin as smooth as a baby's, and I knew then I loved her. I signed her annual, thanked her and slammed it shut. I smiled at her and walked away, hoping someday we'd meet again under better circumstances. I knew we had no future at that time and all I could hope and pray was she'd not get snatched up by a millionaire or someone better looking than I.

Page 82 in her annual said, "Remember this page. I love you and marry me.-Jim Hall."

It was more of a hope and a prayer then, and I knew she was way out of my league. We crossed paths again the night before Thanksgiving Day five years later, and when I saw her I immediately asked her out on a date, knowing this was possibly my one and only chance. We married on December 29th, 1984 in a ceremony held in a small church, just the way she wanted it, and Brian was my lead groomsman with my dad as my best man.

I returned the favor to Brian when he married Dana, the love of his life, when Becky was pregnant with our third child, Jenna Kate, due 30 days after Brian's nuptials. I was his lead groomsman and when we went on his bachelor party, all of his friends said,

"You are the dude from all the stories Brian has told us over the years…did that stuff really happen or is he just making it all up?"

He and I told all the stories from our Troy days to a crowd of men who sat silently, rarely blinking, mesmerized by the tales and probably wondering why their lives had been so boring. He'd talk and I'd pick up the story line, then he'd fill in the blanks I'd miss confirming the truthfulness of the much doubted tales he told to an unknowing batch of friends he'd made since he moved back to Mobile. Brian stuck it out and graduated from the University of South Alabama, and I was there, war whooping up in the very top row of the arena, dancing the same dance we had learned many, many years earlier. I had surprised him by showing up at his graduation ceremony unbeknownst to him before it began. When his name was called, the same protocol was requested, please refrain from applause until all graduates received their diplomas and hold your excitement until the end. I was as free as any guy I knew who was married, two kids on the hoof and one more to come later, way over twenty-one and itemizing deductions every year so I could do as I damn well pleased. Brian and I weren't blood kin but we were brothers just the same. Time had not erased the bond forged between us, even after kids, wives, houses, cars, braces, elementary school and all the domesticated things that tend to drown out the memories of a past life. It felt good to scream and holler in the silent arena for my good friend, he had made it to the other side and I was happy for him.

When he stepped on stage, I hollered "HORST!!!" as loud as I could and he instinctively looked up in my general direction, unsure of what might be transpiring right then. He completed his business, did the split second hesitation for the snapshot, and walked down the steps toward the rest of his life.

When he made it back to his chair, I hollered "Brian Horst!!" and stood up and did the dance. It took him a second to figure me out and he then stood up, pointed at me and he started doing the pledge dance too. He knew it was me and I could see his white teeth and blue eyes shining, knowing that I had kept my promise to him to be at his graduation ceremony. He was telling his fellow graduates sitting around him who I was and they all looked up in my direction, waved and gave thumbs up. I did as he did so many years ago at my graduation. I didn't hang around to see him afterward, but jumped in my car and drove straight back home, eight hours there and eight hours back in one day. My mission was not forgotten, and accomplished years later.

We stayed close friends for all the years after we had graduated, talking sometimes once a week and sometimes once every two weeks. We'd miss sometimes but we'd make up for it by calling twice sometimes three times a week to make up for lost time. We agreed we'd not even say hello, but tell a joke before we'd begin our conversations, a standing rule between us. If I couldn't get him on the phone or him me, if you know what I mean, we'd always leave ominous messages, cryptic in nature, and generally from the IRS or the CIA. My code name was Dick Johnson and his was John Dixon, making me laugh out loud all twenty-five of the years later when he and I were both making a career for ourselves. We shared joys and heartaches, birth announcements and accolades, thousands of jokes told and hundreds of messages from governmental bodies whose acronyms spelled trouble for the receiver, at least as far as the secretary taking the message knew.

Becky and I vacationed with our children on Dauphin Island every summer, spending a week at the secluded beach, and always shared time with Brian and his family, our children played together, his Gabby and my Jenna Kate, like we had hoped for all those many years ago on the train ride we had taken years earlier. We were full grown men now, and we had not told the train ride story to anyone, even our wives had still not heard the story. We had told parts of it, like walking up on a KKK meeting, or getting chased by a pack of wild dogs, but never shared the circumstances by which we had done those particular things, and how they were glued together. The smaller stories were a part of the bigger story and the train ride was the frame work by which all those stories were made possible.

Of course, he and I would retell the story between ourselves when we'd cookout at his house and far from earshot of our wives. I wasn't sure why after all those years, mind you, but the twenty-five years statute of limitations was swiftly approaching and that story was going to be told by us both. We had to decide when we'd tell it, confessing to our wives about the self imposed sanction two younger men had agreed upon at the front door of the fraternity house after the trip made its conclusion. It might just sound to them like another bullshit story told by the two of us, but it was true and the only other person that knew the truth was my friend Brian.

It was the twenty fifth year after the train ride when the call came.

Chapter · XLII

"The Holy Passion of Friendship is of so sweet and enduring a nature that it will last through a whole lifetime."
– Mark Twain

IT WAS May 18th, 2008 and I had called and left Brian a few messages without a call back, unusual for him. I thought nothing of it until a few days later when I received a call and subsequent message from his brother, Mike. I assumed it was for something related to Brian's phone being out after I left a few messages for Brian at his real estate office. It was a rare occasion that Brian had not called me back within a day or so, but he had two young kids and a life too, so I thought nothing of it.

I was at home in Douglasville, my wife and two daughters at a wedding of a long time friend and former baby sitter, and I was enjoying a little time to work on my 1970 GTO convertible. It was a way for me to unwind and there was a good chance I might not ride in it for a number of years, but I didn't care. I had my son in college and my middle daughter about to get married so a few minutes alone with my hot rod and my tools seemed like a good way to spend the day. I was under the car when my cell phone rang and I was fully engaged in a four speed shifter install requiring both of my hands, leaving the call for later. I had the cell phone positioned where I could see the incoming number and recognized the prefix as L-A. My phone beeped telling me that Brian had left me a message, and I was glad he'd either (a) purchased a new phone after he'd lost his, or (b) he was calling from a land line and I could call him back there.

I figured he was fully aware that the statute of limitations was quickly approaching concerning the telling of our train ride odyssey, and he wanted us to get together during our annual visit to tell the whole story to our wives. It was silly when I think of it, waiting all that time to tell, but we had made a blood oath to not tell and it became somewhat of a contest to see which one of us might first spill the beans. As our hair grew grayer and our financial condition improved, we made a wager as to which one of us might tell the story before the twenty-five year time limit expired. The wager was a case of ice cold Dixie beers in the long neck bottle and two rib-eye steaks. The loser would have to drive to the winner's hometown and convey the spoils of victory, humbling himself, forever shamed by the inability to keep an oath. I would lose that bet, telling the story of our train ride to almost five hundred people all at once, Brian in attendance, when the bet was lost by me.

I picked up my phone, dialed my voicemail number and to my surprise, Mike, Brian's older brother, began to speak. His message still burned in my memory banks like it was just a few minutes ago. It was:

"Jim, this is Mike, I have terrible news to give you…Brian was power washing the gables on his house when he slipped and fell twenty-five feet to the ground. He laid there for four hours before the neighbor's son found him and called 911. I'm sorry we didn't call you sooner to let you know. Unfortunately, Brian passed away this morning from internal injuries he received from the fall. There was nothing the doctors could do, they tried everything to save him but to no avail. I'll let you know when the funeral is to be held. I'm so sorry Jim, I knew you and Brian were so close"

I laid there on the concrete floor of my garage thinking Brian had engaged his older brother to pull the prank of all prank calls on me as a way of weaseling out of our bet. I would call him back and threaten to kick him in the butt for such a low rent maneuver and thinking of it before I did. I hit the "star" button on my phone to call back the sender of the message and the phone did not ring one full ring before Mike answered the phone.

"Hey Mike, this is Jim. What kinda crap has Brian sucked you into?" I said.

After a few seconds of silence Mike said, "It's real Jim. We lost Brian."

I could hear Brian's dear momma crying in the background and I knew this was no joke.

"Oh Shit…" was all I could say. "Oh Shit…."

Mike continued, "I went to Brian's car and saw where you had called him a number of times, he had CALL JIM written on the top of his message pad…" he trailed off, obviously emotional from the loss of his brother and my best friend.

I promised him I would call him back when he had a better chance to talk. I knew he was going to have to be the strong one, his mother and father would be devastated by Brian's passing.

"You say when and I'll be there, Mike, to help in any capacity I can" were my final words to Mike.

"Thanks Jim. Brian loved you like a brother," he trailed off, sniffing back tears and doing his best to be the rock he needed to be right then.

I laid there on the floor of my garage, in shock, and mourned the loss of my friend. I cried like I had not since I was a child. I wept at the birth of my children, graduations, and the few funerals I had attended for acquaintances and elderly church members when they passed. This one, however, was too close to home and a loss I could not fully accept. Brian and I had plans, the train ride's twenty-five year limit was about to expire, we had a lot more living to do and both of our youngest daughters would get to play with each other every summer we visited.

I was devastated.

I spoke to Mrs. Horst the next day, listening to a mother who had lost her beloved son, and her telling me how much Brian always spoke of his friend, our friendship kept strong by the bonds forged over two years of college and twenty-five years of communication. I just listened to her talk, agreed with her about his life and commented about his beloved children and his wife, who had also lost a father and a friend. I realized I needed to be a rock also, for his mother and father. They had always treated me like a son and I needed to man up for them right then. Mrs. Horst told me the date of Brian's funeral, May 23rd, 2008 at the First United Methodist Church of Daphne, Alabama, at noon. The viewing was to be held the evening of the 22nd, and could I please come.

"Absolutely, Mrs. Horst, I wouldn't miss it for the world" my promise challenged by a new job and no days off. I asked my new boss if I could please attend the funeral of my closest friend and to my surprise, he said, "Absolutely."

I agreed to work the day of the 22nd, leaving at noon, giving Becky and I enough time to make it to the viewing if there was no adverse traffic to deal with. If I broke the speed limit by five miles per hour and no stops, I could barely make it. The seven hour trip that usually took eight-plus hours to complete required a land speed record breaking effort by me and a challenge I was mentally ready for.

We arrived at the church where Brian laid in state, and thankfully the casket was closed. I wanted to remember my friend smiling, his slight wandering cobalt blue eyes shining like it was his wedding day. Mr. and Mrs. Horst greeted me like the son they had not seen in months and I was glad to see Brian's entire family in attendance. There were hundreds of cars in the large parking lot, all friends of Brian and Dana, and the entire Horst family. We had arrived late in the day, 7:45 pm when the viewing was at its tail end. Mr. and Mrs. Horst asked me to say a few words at Brian's funeral, maybe tell a story about how long we had been friends. I, of course, agreed and that would be the stage where I would tell the train ride story to every friend and family member he had. There were four men scheduled to say a few words, a father that had met Brian through his son's baseball team, a brother-in-law who told of how much Brian loved his wife and children and one long time realtor friend that relayed about how ethical a man Brian was.

And then it was my turn, someone most of the dudes in attendance had only heard of, the guy from all the stories Brian had told over the years. I took the stage in front of approximately five hundred people and this is the story I told them:

I am "that dude" most of you have heard Brian talk about: his fraternity brother and friend of twenty-seven years. He and I made a bet twenty-four years, eleven months and two weeks ago that I am about to lose right now, but it bears telling and I'll risk it.

When I was a senior in college, after my college football days had ended at Troy University, my residence was at the Pi Kappa Phi fraternity house in the City of Troy, Alabama where Brian and I met while pledging. Our frat house was a mansion on North Three Notch Street, three stories tall and you could see for miles. One Friday toward the end of school, Brian and I were on the very top of the frat house, in the observation tower, where folks used to watch for trespassers and rapscallions back in Civil War times.

I knew my time was short at Troy as graduation was but a week away, we were drinking unpasteurized Dixie Beer from Louisiana- this particular vintage had a skull and cross bones on it warning you not to drink its contents if it ever got above 72 degrees. We were both poor, but the bargain basement suds purchased for $2.99 a case would do nicely and we were pondering ideas to pass the time. Brian and I were bored and about that same time a train was coming by about 1/4 mile away, on the tracks across a very large parking lot that ran behind the old Piggly Wiggly and through Troy. I had always wanted to ride a train across town and jump off just to say I'd done it. A "bucket list" item, if you will, and one I was itching to give a try. About the time I had it on my mind making its way to my vocal chords, my friend Brian said, 'Ever want to just jump on a train and ride it ten, maybe fifteen miles across town, and hitchhike back?'

I just laughed. We agreed that the next train to come we'd race across the parking lot and jump on. Twenty trains later and a whole lot of running amounted to no train rides for us and a worn out constitution. Sunday, two days later and final exams complete, Brian and I were the only two dudes left at the house awaiting my graduation ceremony the next Saturday, meaning we had a whole week to do absolutely nothing. We got settled and what did you know, a train came poking by doing two miles an hour. We both hauled butt and made the train, jumped on a flat car, and off we were to the other side of town. We jumped off the slow moving beast only to be met by another train, headed back up the tracks to our original location, moving slowly, so we jumped back on thinking we'd ride back, jump off, bucket list item successfully checked off.

Or so we thought. By the time "the other side of town" came, the train was doing 75 miles an hour. By the time the train had slowed down to the point that we had the guts to jump off, it was going maybe 35 miles an hour and was approximately 190 miles from Troy, north above Birmingham, Alabama outside of Cullman.

If you know the way train tracks are laid out, you know that they usually take the straightest possible route, and mostly through the back country.

Yes, my friends, we were 190 miles from home in the middle of nowhere. Why did we jump then? Because the next stop was in Somewhere, Alabama, maybe Canada, many more miles from Troy than he or I planned to walk back from that day. We made the decision and jumped. First we quickly debated on whether to dive off (break an arm in the middle of nowhere) or jump (break a leg in the middle of nowhere). Jump and roll was the plan. Next was to get a running start or not to get a running start, and running start won. Next choice was run toward the back of the train to slow down our momentum but have to land basically backwards, whack your head and eat dust OR run towards the front of the train: Better launch, forward landing, more momentum to clear the giant rocks (called rip rap) with the downside of having more acceleration to deal with at landing. We decided that a forward running jump, not dive, with roll if possible was the best plan. Understand that we debated this for about three miles (about 9 minutes at speed).

One, Two, Three…Jump!

When Brian and I basically "came to", we had no bones broken but beaten like a cheap throw rug hanging on a clothes line, but not dead or mortally wounded. It took a few minutes to be able to stand up. And when we did, it looked like a bomb had been shoved down both of our pairs of blue jeans. The butt was blown completely out of mine, legs torn, shirt ripped and both of us covered in creosote (the black tarry material that covers Rail Road Cross ties). Brian's clothes were also blown up, but he ripped the butt out of his blue jeans and boxer shorts so bad that he had to take them off (the boxers) and put them on backwards so the full butt crack was not showing. Neither one of us had our wallets, no money, nothing.

We shared numerous stories on the twenty-nine straight hours it took us to walk/run back to Troy. We had endured much on that trip, way too much to share here with the time allotted. We had gotten two rides, one from an old WW II veteran, sixty miles above Montgomery on Highway 65 South, who made us ride in the back we were so filthy, and one from an elderly black man that picked us up 13 miles outside of Troy. I would like to add that both men thought Brian and I were black men based on the thick creosote make-up we both wore. He dropped us off one hundred feet from our original starting point and we made the final one mile trek through town, women crossing streets and children pointing at us like we were boogiemen. Some businesses closed as we passed through the square in fear of the bad element we represented. When we finally made it home and as were walking up the front steps of the frat house, Brian turned to me and said, "If you tell anybody about this for twenty five years, I'll swear you are a liar and a homosexual."

We agreed right then and there not to tell that story for twenty-five years. Two weeks from this day would have been twenty five years and it looks I lose the bet."

My wife and his wife have heard them all. Only he and I knew this story and we'd laugh about it every time we got together over the twenty-five years of summers at the beach, and the phone calls to each other every two weeks or so to the point that our wives would get pissed at us for laughing every time we'd see a train or hear some story about something stupid that had been done by someone. We had made a blood oath not to tell. Both of our wives, his family, and all his friends heard this story for the first time on Wednesday, the 28th of May, 2008, when I told it at his funeral. The place was rolling with laughter. All five hundred or so people were giggling and snickering at first then the attendees began to laugh uncontrollably. His entire family and friends were laughing so uncontrollably you'd have thought they were in a comedy club rather than attending a funeral.

I realized then that Brian and I were to save this story for the time when it was needed the most.

I miss you Brian.

THE END

Never shall I forget the days I spent with you.
Continue to be my friend,
as you will always find me yours.
~ Ludwig van Beethoven

Jim Hall

The author, Jim Hall, is as southern as a "runt over possum" being born on Peachtree Street in Atlanta, Georgia spending his young life in the West End near Fort McPherson where he learned to be sneaky and mischievous. A love of sports led him to play football at a young age, playing the game from seven years until graduation from college in Troy, Alabama where the story "The Train Ride" originates and ultimately ends. Jim met his bride of twenty-sixyears, Becky, in his senior year and has three grown children and two grandchildren.

As the whale spit Jonah out on the biblical shores of Ninevah, so Jim was spit out by the banking industry on the shores of an unknown future. A post graduate life in the banking business ended with the downturn in the world economy led Jim to write about the numerous stories told at family gatherings, to friends, men's groups, all revolving around the time "The Train Ride" was actually happening. A natural story teller, Jim was encouraged to write down the story of his friendship with Brian, his lifelong friend. The result is "The Train Ride," the author's first effort in book writing, is a true account of his last two years of college, football, fraternity life, and a life-long friendship that involved a 25 year promise broken two weeks shy of the self imposed "statute of limitations."

"The Train Ride" is a Twain style story replete with modern day (early eighties) Huck and Tom, a long ride on a locomotive with a death defying dismount at speed. The stories told on the ride and subsequent walk back by the author and his best friend Brian, along with the next twenty five years of friendship and a bet made at the conclusion of the train ride make up the impetus for "The Train Ride." It's a humorous look at life and friendship, and the unexpected turn just ahead.